# State of Subversion

This volume looks at the interface between ideology, religion and culture in Punjab in the 20th century, spanning from colonial to postcolonial times. Through a re-reading of the history of Punjab and of Punjabi migrant networks the world over, it interrogates the term 'radicalism' and its relationship with terms such as 'militancy', 'terrorism' and 'extremism' in the context of Punjab and elsewhere during the period; explores the relationship between Left and religious radicalism — such as the Ghadar movement and the Akalis — and the continuing role of radical movements from British Punjab to the independent states of India and Pakistan.

Expanding the dimensions on the study of Punjab and its historical impact in the South Asian region, this book will interest scholars and students of modern Indian history, politics and sociology.

**Virinder S. Kalra** is Senior Lecturer in Sociology at the University of Manchester, UK. He is the author of *Sacred and Secular Musics: A Postcolonial Approach* (2014). Widely published, his areas of research include Punjabi popular culture, British racism and themes in creative resistance.

**Shalini Sharma** is Lecturer in Colonial and Postcolonial History at Keele University, UK. She has written on radical politics in Punjab and is currently working on Indian intellectuals and the USA.

# South Asian History and Culture

Series Editors: **David Washbrook**, University of Cambridge, UK
**Boria Majumdar**, University of Central Lancashire, UK
**Sharmistha Gooptu**, South Asia Research Foundation, India
**Nalin Mehta**, Institute of South Asian Studies, National University of
Singapore

This series brings together research on South Asia in the humanities and social sciences, and provides scholars with a platform covering, but not restricted to, their particular fields of interest and specialization.

A significant concern for the series is to focus across the whole of the region known as South Asia, and not simply on India, as is often the case. There will be a conscious attempt to publish regional studies and bring together scholarship on and from Pakistan, Bangladesh, Sri Lanka, Nepal and other parts of South Asia.

This series will consciously initiate synergy between research from within academia and that from outside the formal academy. A focus will be to bring into the mainstream more recently developed disciplines in South Asian studies which have to date remained in the nature of specialized fields: for instance, research on film, media, photography, sport, medicine, environment, to mention a few. The series will address this gap and generate more comprehensive knowledge fields.

**Also in this series**

# State of Subversion

*Radical politics in Punjab*
*in the 20th century*

**Edited by**

Virinder S. Kalra and
Shalini Sharma

Routledge
Taylor & Francis Group

LONDON AND NEW YORK

First published 2013 as a special issue of *South Asian History and Culture*

First published 2016 by Routledge

2 Park Square, Milton Park, Abingdon, Oxfordshire OX14 4RN
711 Third Avenue, New York, NY 10017

*Routledge is an imprint of the Taylor & Francis Group, an informa business*

First issued in paperback 2017

*British Library Cataloguing-in-Publication Data*
A catalogue record for this book is available from the British Library

*Library of Congress Cataloging-in-Publication Data*
A catalog record has been requested for this book

This edition is for sale in India, Pakistan, Nepal, Bhutan, Bangladesh and Sri Lanka only.

ISBN: 978-1-138-95642-1 (hbk)
ISBN: 978-0-8153-9310-8 (pbk)

Typeset in Sabon 10/12pt
by Glyph Graphics Private Limited Delhi 110 096

# Contents

# Contributors

**Kamran Asdar Ali** is Associate Professor of Anthropology, Middle East Studies and Asian Studies and the Director of the South Asia Institute at the University of Texas, Austin. He is the author of *Communism in Pakistan: Politics and Class Activism*, 1947–1972.

**Waqas Butt** is an independent researcher, former Lecturer in Anthropology at Qaid-e-Azam University. He is the author of *The Life of Pakistanis in the Netherlands*. He is currently Head of translation and interpretation services at Stoke City Council.

**Talvinder Gill** is an independent researcher who obtained his PhD in History from the University of Warwick, on the topic of *The Indian Workers' Association Coventry*, 1938–1990.

**Virinder S. Kalra** is Senior Lecturer in Sociology at the University of Manchester. He is the author of *Sacred and Secular Musics: A Postcolonial Approach* (2014). Widely published, his areas of research include Punjabi popular culture, British racism and themes in creative resistance.

**Tahir Kamran** is a notable Pakistani historian, currently the Iqbal Fellow at the University of Cambridge, as professor in the Centre of South Asian Studies. He has authored four books and has written several articles specifically on the history of the Punjab, sectarianism, democracy, and governance.

**Anushay Malik** is currently Assistant Professor in the History department at the Lahore University of Management Sciences. Her PhD thesis focused on the labour movement in Lahore and was completed from the School of Oriental and African Studies, University of London in 2013.

**Ali Raza** is Assistant Professor in History at the Lahore University of Management Sciences. His interests are in radical politics in Punjab in the mid-twentieth century. His PhD focused on the Kirti Kisan Party.

**Shalini Sharma** lectures on colonial and postcolonial history at Keele University. She has written on radical politics in Punjab and is currently working on Indian intellectuals and the USA.

**Benjamin Zachariah** is a historian and postcolonial theorist. He is the Indian Council for Cultural Relations Professor of South Asian History, Orientalisches Institut, University of Halle-Wittenberg, and Senior Research Fellow, Cluster of Excellence 'Asia and Europe', Heidelberg University.

# 1

# State of Subversion: Aspects of Radical Politics in 20th-Century Punjab

*Virinder S. Kalra* and *Shalini Sharma*

Political radicalism has been a constant feature of Punjab politics in the 20th century: from the formation of the Communist Party in the province in the 1920s to the rise of religious sectarianism in Pakistan Punjab in the 1990s, it has been an unsettling, if not a prominent, characteristic of the Punjabi political landscape. Indeed, it is the fact that religious radicalism and communism, often posited on opposite political poles, come together in the space of the Punjab and occasionally in the context of a single political party or political figure that make the region so interesting for those interested in revolutionary change. Yet despite these prominent movements, studies of Punjabi radicalism are few to find. One could argue that the absence of such an assessment is because the Punjab experience does not fit into the nationalist histories of India and Pakistan, nor does it conform to the 'subaltern' histories that have influenced history writing in South Asia since the 1980s. Indeed, the intellectual space for the study of the region in whatever shape tends to require a radical outlook. The chapters of this book, based on a panel on the subject at the European Association of Modern Asian Studies in Bonn, Germany (July 2010), draw together a range of perspectives to cover some of the immense gaps within the history of 20th-century Punjab and provide insight on radical politics in contemporary India and Pakistan.

This collection has deliberately excluded accounts of radicalism in Punjab that already has extensive coverage in academic literature and popular print media, namely the Singh Sabha movement in the early 1920s, the Punjab variant of Naxalism in the 1970s and the militancy and state terror that exploded in Indian Punjab in the 1980s.[1] This is not to deny the enormous importance of these instances in the history of the region — they have left an indelible and enduring mark in the genealogy of radicalism in Punjab. Our aim is to offer an understanding of other movements and events that have been neglected by the disproportionate focus on Indian Punjab in the historical narrative. It is hoped that our selection of radical moments will offer an introduction to little-known movements, as well as a new broader context in which to look at the rise of militancy in the Punjab.

## Context

Radical politics, mostly travelling under the broad umbrella term of 'communism', has been an integral part of the South Asian political scene for almost a century. One of the main arguments of this collection is that radical movements, whether communist, socialist or religious had an important role to play in South Asian politics, not least because the different groups that constituted these movements, in their different ways and in many different arenas, joined in an assault upon the structures of control by which the British Raj and its successors have ruled India and Pakistan. Radical movements in South Asia have had an important impact upon the terms and language of politics more generally. The effect on South Asian politics has not been simple and cannot be measured solely in terms of electoral success or capture of state power, rather it has helped to change these politics in complex and unexpected ways. Indeed, innumerable groups have adopted, and adapted, the language of class struggle and have professed radical, socialist or even communist purposes in their political endeavours. This is particularly the case in Pakistan where

---

[1] On the Singh Sabha and Akalis, see Grewal, *Sikh Ideology*; Tan, 'Assuaging the Sikhs' in *Modern Asian Studies*; Singh, *The Akali Movement*. On Sikh ethno-nationalism, see Wallace and Chopra, *Political Dynamics and Crisis in Punjab*; Brass, *Language, Religion and Politics in South Asia*; Singh, *Ethnic Conflict in India*; Purewal, *Sikh Ethnonationalism and the Political Economy of Punjab*.

the organising structures and rhetoric of the Left was systematically copied by religious parties such as the Jamaat-i-Islami.

Overstreet and Windmiller's *Communism in India*, the authoritative work on the communist movement in India, fails to make due allowance for the extraordinary diversity of Indian politics, the context in which communists and radicals generally had to either adapt or to perish. By placing national politics at the centre the historiography of communism in India, the crucial role of regions in Indian radical politics is ignored. To understand radical movements in South Asia, it is essential to analyse the very different manifestations of the movements in different regions, particularly those where the Communist Party has been relatively strong such as Bengal, Kerala, Andhra Pradesh, and the Punjab. To be sure, a beginning has been made by others, and some regional political histories of the party have been written. These include the works of Pavier on Telangana; Singh, Javed and Josh on the Punjab; Nossiter on Kerala; and all those, whether historians or political scientists, who have looked at the Naxalite movement in Bengal.[2] However, these works still tend to view the regional parties as integral parts of a national machine through which the centre imposed structure and control over the regions. The work of Dilip Menon on Kerala has a somewhat different perspective.[3] His analysis of communism takes full account of its cultural and regional specificities, and Menon recognises that communists were pragmatic and that this pragmatism was the key to the party's success in Kerala. Despite the obvious differences between Kerala and the Punjab, Menon's approach provides some useful lessons for this study of radicalism in the Punjab, the most important being that regions and their characteristics define local politics and have a significant impact upon the relationship between centre and province.

In the pre-partition Punjab, many groups, such as the Kirti Kisan movement, the Hindustan Socialist Republican Association, the Naujawan Bharat Sabha, the Ahrar movement and even the Congress Socialist Party as well as the Communist Party itself, appealed to

---

[2] See Franda, *Radical Politics in West Bengal*; Nossiter, *Communism in Kerala*; Pavier, *The Telangana Movement*; Overstreet and Windmiller, *Communism in India*.

[3] Menon, *Caste, Nationalism and Communism in South Asia*, 188–89.

the peoples of the Punjab through the slogans of communism, class struggle and variants of what they deemed to be Marxism. They were among numerous other groups in India which were linked to the broader international movement that travelled under the name of communism; not all of these different groups subscribed to some common ideology or strategy laid down by international communism. Rather they all deployed the language of class struggle alongside a range of other ideologies, which in hindsight may seem incompatible but in the political moment and to the actors involved were reconcilable. In consequence, it makes good sense to label their politics as 'radical' for the purposes of this collection, however, divided these groups were in their strategies, tactics and even substantive ideologies.

This collection also seeks to go beyond the findings of other works on the history of the organised Left in the Punjab. In 1979, Bhagwan Josh's pioneering book on communism in the Punjab was published; in 1988 and later in 1994, Ajeet Javed and Gurharpal Singh took the subject further.[4] Each of these works has a different focus. Josh belongs to a tradition of historiography in which communism tends to be seen as an unsound project at a time when the only legitimate politics was the dominant nationalism of the Congress movement. Whig (or indeed Congress) interpretations of history have concentrated on why the organised Left failed, inevitably from this angle of vision. By contrast, Gurharpal Singh and Ajeet Javed, by examining a wide range of sources, have added much detail to our knowledge of the political history of the movement. Their works are mainly concerned with the organisation of the party, the factionalism within the Left, trade union activity and peasant or kisan movements in the region. These works tell us much about the inner workings of the Communist Party in the Punjab, but little about the relationship of the Left with the Indian National Congress. Of course, the Congress and the Muslim League in the Punjab were weak, and so the region's political history has attracted little attention from nationalist scholars in India and Pakistan. However, this very weakness led both movements to be linked to the Left more closely than has previously been assumed. The mainly Hindu leadership of Congress looked to the Left to recruit followers in the Punjab countryside and, in

---

[4] Javed, *Left Politics in Punjab: 1935–47*; Josh, *Communist Movement in Punjab (1926–1947)*; Singh, *Communism in Punjab.*

a symbiotic relationship, the leaders of the Left, vilified, arrested and imprisoned though they were, needed Congress to give them an acceptable platform from which they could plan and propagate their ideologies. The communist support for Pakistan provided the Muslim League with a base of activists in the years before independence, and for a short period after independence, the Left played a role in the party. It follows that the institutions of the Punjab and its 'school' of administration, the imperatives of local politics, whether Congress, Akali, Muslim League or others on the margins of dissent, are critical elements in understanding the significance of the politics of radicalism in the Punjab.

The chapters in this book are concerned with a history of radicalism from the perspective of organisations and their leaders. This is in contrast to the work of the subaltern historians who have made a huge contribution to the understanding of radical movements from grassroot level. Nonetheless, the contrast made between subaltern and elite by Guha is perhaps too definitive: 'Mobilisation in the domain of elite politics was achieved vertically whereas in that of subaltern politics this was achieved horizontally. ... Elite mobilization tended to be more legalistic and constitutionalist in orientation, subaltern mobilization relatively more violent.'[5] No doubt this perspective acts as a corrective to nationalist historians. It also, however, directs attention away from regional mobilising and the workings of local leaders. Indeed, the violence associated with the radical movements presented in this collection belie the easy distinction offered by Guha between elite and subaltern. Mobilisation by communist and radical parties was certainly an integral part of the Punjab political landscape and these often led to political violence in direct confrontation with the state or political rivals.

## Radicalism in Punjab

Punjab was partitioned when India gained independence from British rule and divided again because of linguistic and religious differences. On the East and West sides of the borders that divide it, Punjab makes a crucial contribution to the military, economic and administrative structures of India and Pakistan. However, its historiography remains

---

[5] Guha, 'Historiography of Colonial India', 4.

fixated on explicating the religious sectarianism and partitions that have dominated its history. In this framework, Punjabis are deemed either politically backward or opportunist. This characterisation is influenced by two diametrically opposed historiographical trends. The first, initially articulated in colonial accounts but still influential, cast Punjabis as an apolitical people, primarily interested in loyally serving their colonial masters. Writers of the second tendency did not know where to place Punjabis in their Whiggish history of the struggle for Indian independence. So Punjabis were deemed as overly religious and hence less politically acceptable in the new secular state of India and subsumed as de facto rulers in the Republic of Pakistan. Indeed, a post-1947 history of Punjab that is not framed through religious or nationalist discourse is difficult to find. In Indian Punjab, the narrative is dominated by accounts, which emphasise the role of the Sikhs (Singh and Gaur), and in Pakistani historiography, the region is negated at the behest of a religious nationalism. Two recent collections *Sufism in Punjab* and *Punjab Reconsidered* explicitly address the issue of the absence of a Punjab historiography by bringing together accounts that attempt to cross the religious, sectarian and political boundaries that have concerned previous scholarship.[6] This collection is also explicitly concerned with what has been called the 'Three Punjabs': East, West and the diaspora.[7] In that sense, the unifying theme of radical movements allows for the emergence (and submergence) of Punjab as a space of analysis in which the national is also held in question. It is this potency that offers scholars rich veins of material for exploration and insight.

The articles in this collection are still mainly looking at the Left and the history of communist parties, but this is complicated by looking at other aspects of the ideological gamut, especially the issue of religion and culture more generally. While recognising that religion has over determined frames of understanding the Punjab when placed in these other contexts, it also provides a crucial backdrop. Indeed, our use of the term radicalism is to acknowledge its association

---

[6] Singh and Gaur, *Sufism in Punjab*; Malhotra and Mir, *Punjab Reconsidered*.

[7] This term was coined by the Punjab Research Group, see http://theprg.co.uk.

with Marxism and to recognise that in its actual application, the tradition of the Left spawned many and multiple political and social movements. The connections between the Ghadar movement and the Akalis in the 1920s in their anticolonial stance would lead us to indicate both as radical movements even though their ideologies were distinct. Punjabi history and the history of Punjabi migrant networks throughout the world provides the opportunity to interrogate the term 'radicalism'; to explore the relationship between left radicalism and religious radicalism and its relationship with terms such as 'militancy', 'terrorism' and 'extremism' in the Punjab context and elsewhere in the 20th century.

The material developed in this collection spans the colonial to post-colonial, demonstrating the continuing role of radical movements from the unified Punjab to the bifurcated new states.

Though many of the movements under discussion in the chapters have been considered elsewhere, the collection is unique in the substantive accounts of communist parties in Pakistan. Four of the chapters are concerned with the way in which the radical Left was organised in the lead up to Pakistan and in the newly formed state. This is the first time that such a detailed and in depth analysis of the Pakistani Left has been published, in its many shades and meanings. Given that much of the contemporary academic work on Pakistan is concerned with the roots of religious extremism and on the failure of state control, the chapters here provide an indication of the much broader canvas from which those movements emerge. Indeed, to try and understand many of the problems of the Pakistani state without an appreciation of how the Left was treated in the country's formation remains only a partial story as the chapters written here clearly demonstrate.

Far from seeing Punjabis as politically backward or reactionary, the authors in this collection attempt to examine the different genealogies of political radicalism in Punjab in the 20th century. They aim to tease out the ideological moorings that motivated radical politicians and their connections with wider and more long-standing traditions of intellectual thought. Rather than focus on the organisation and practice of particular political groups, the authors, informed by the importance of life-stories and fragmented historical experience, deliver accounts that can potentially transform contemporary Punjab studies from its narrow regionalist and subject focus.

## Contributions

Two chapters are situated in colonial Punjab. Shalini Sharma describes the communist engagement with the Government of India Act of 1935 and its ramifications in Punjab. Despite their small number, the communists transformed the level of debate inside the assembly and public perception of it while changing themselves and their own ideological rigidity to get inside the chamber. The shifting contours of the debate illustrate the way in which Left wing and religious ideologies could be mixed and matched depending on political context. A similar case could be made for a group which was openly religious but mixed in socialist ideas: the Ahrar. Tahir Kamran offers a different perspective on the party that was involved in many major political agitations in Punjab during the late 1920s and 1930s but is often written out of the region's history. His study of the Ahrar Party opens up questions of how Islam and socialist ideas worked together in their discourse. This combination was reflected in their class makeup and along with their Khilafatist origins meant that their relationship with the Muslim League was fraught and for many of the Ahrar leaders an impossibility. This provides a refreshing relief from histories of Muslim politics in Punjab that simply focus on the Unionists and the Muslim League.

Two chapters cover communists and socialists during partition and the first years of Pakistan. Kamran Asdar Ali looks at debates between Punjabi communists and the irreconcilable factions that played a part in policy over partition and how to participate in the Pakistani polity. The relationship between the central leadership of the Communist Party of India (CPI) and local leaders in Punjab is crucial here, exemplified by the particular hazards faced by Sajjad Zaheer during his tenure as a leader. Ali Raza examines the relationship between the Muslim League and the Punjabi communists. His work reflects on the points of similarity between activists of both parties, their mutual dependence in the years before independence, and also the cutting of ties when the Muslim League became the party of power in the new state in 1947. In contrast to Asdar Ali, who draws on internal party documents to make his case, Raza draws on the colonial and official archive. In that sense, a rich tapestry is woven of this period of time from the perspective of the activists and the state's response. It is clear from all of the chapters in this book, but especially from these two that the role of radicals does not depend on their numerical propensity but rather on their ability to generate panic and discomfort in the state.

Anushay Malik's chapter takes up the story of the Pakistani Communist Party in the first few years of the newly formed state and crucially locates her narrative at the local level in the city of Lahore. The erstwhile cultural capital of Punjab and home to many of the most pronounced political events of the colonial period, Lahore after partition was a relatively hollow echo of its colonial 'Coffee House' culture of radical intellectuals and anti-British ferment. Nonetheless, Malik's account of the Punjab elections of 1951 and the Rawalpindi Conspiracy illustrate the way in which the Left was able to maintain its influence despite the activities of an increasingly hostile state. Relying on memoirs and police reports, a picture of the closing down of spaces for radical activity emerges. It is only in the early 1970s, with the emergence of the Mazdoor Kisan Party (MKP), that the radical Left again finds a space in the polity of Punjab. It is this story that is taken up by Kalra and Butt, who look at the mobilising methods of the MKP when it comes to the issue of language. Indeed, the ideology of the MKP was clearly inspired by Maoism and the need to address the peasants and workers in their language, and this point is explored in the context of Punjab. The imbrication of culture and politics is addressed by the authors, demonstrating their practical inseparability in the context of student mobilisation in the setting of a rural college.

Two chapters take us away from the Indian subcontinent. Talvinder Gill writes of the Indian Workers Association that, from its inception in Coventry in 1938, grew to challenge the British state and change the history of race relations in Britain. He describes the activists of the movement as inheritors of the cultural memory of radicalism in Punjab and their work in fighting to participate in British unions and give voice to Asian workers a continuance of that very radicalism. Ben Zachariah ends this volume with a chapter on a person who was a hero to most Punjabi radicals: Lala Har Dayal, leader of the Ghadar Party. However, his chapter challenges the assumptions and myths that have grown around the figure of Har Dayal. His chapter also asks us to rethink the whole genre of biographical history and give more importance to the contingencies of exile and location and Har Dayal's own ideological contradictions rather than cast judgement on his heroic or fickle radicalism.

The chapters in this book narrate the hoops that radicals jumped through in order to be heard to represent the concerns of their imagined or real constituencies, the workers and peasants of Punjab. Three chapters deal with the trials faced by communists in the early years of Pakistan. They each emphasise one particular factor that affected the way communists in Punjab propagated their ideas, namely their engagement with Islam, the leadership of Sajjad Zaheer and their being vilified as state enemies by the official leaders of the new Pakistani nation state. Together the three chapters throw light on the brave new world of the nation and how politics, especially communist politics, was imagined and practised in this context.

All of the chapters have to engage with the language and translation of radical politics. How is a revolutionary agenda articulated in the particular contexts of colonial Punjab, Pakistani Punjab and the diasporic Punjabs of Southall and Coventry? What are the differences and similarities? Zachariah gives the change in Har Dayal's location a significant explanatory role in his ideological shifts. The place of Kashmir is equally important in explaining the Ahrar's strategies in colonial Punjab. Butt and Kalra take this debate to a different level by focusing on the nature of Punjabi as a medium adopted by the Left in Punjab. Thus, the emphasis here is not only a translation of radical ideology but a strengthening and transformation of the Punjabi language by radical activists and authors who made the political decision to reconnect with the working classes of Punjab and recharge the cultural importance of their language.

The definition of a radical that most contributors to this volume demonstrate is a person who wants to change the status quo, who does not keep still. Indeed the story of Har Dayal, the intellectual paragon of the Ghadar Party in California, is told by narrating his 'trip' from India to Europe and the United States, fitting the restlessness of the radical. However, as Benjamin Zachariah describes, Har Dayal's own political convictions seem to swerve from left to right, from atheistic to religious and from secular to spiritual almost arbitrarily. That said, it is perhaps most likely that radical politicians are informed by some Left inspired ideas, either socialist or communist, and are often those who seek a redistribution of wealth and a world based on equitable social justice, as a bare minimum of their political demands. These are the radicals that concern the authors of this volume. Theirs is a history that has been neglected, but as the chapters in this volume demonstrate, they have changed the way that politics is imagined and practised in the Punjab. The story of communists and socialists is not fashionable in our post Cold War era. However, to embark on a life of resistance and often imprisonment was a choice that many radicals made and stuck with in a world that often condemned them as aliens or imposters. Major Ishaque died whilst in prison, Har Dayal was condemned to a life in exile, dying just after the authorities reneged his debarment, while many unknown communists and socialists in colonial and post-colonial Punjab have spent considerable periods of their life either 'underground' or incarcerated. It is hoped that this book will be the first of many that give voice to these unknown people to understand why and how they made their choices to intervene in the politics of Punjab. From the Akali struggle to 1984, from Jallianwala Bagh to partition, from Civil Liberties Union activity to Punjabi Naxalism, radicals have been enmeshed in each turning point of the region's history, if not at their centre. It is their history that we have set out to probe and open up for further research.

---

# References

Brass, Paul, *Language, Religion and Politics in South Asia*, Cambridge: Cambridge University Press, 1974.

Franda, Markus F., *Radical Politics in West Bengal*, Cambridge, MA: MIT Press, 1971.

Grewal, J. S., *Sikh Ideology, Polity and Social Order*, New Delhi: Manohar, 2007.

Guha, Ranajit, ed., 'Historiography of Colonial India', in *Subaltern Studies I: Writings on South Asian History and Society*, New Delhi: Oxford University Press, 1982.

Javed, Ajeet, *Left Politics in Punjab: 1935–47*, New Delhi: Durga Publications, 1988.

Malhotra, Anshu and Mir Farina, *Punjab Reconsidered: History, Culture, and Practice*, New Delhi: Oxford University Press, 2012.

Menon, Dilip, *Caste, Nationalism and Communism in South Asia: Malabar, 1900–1948*, Cambridge: Cambridge University Press, 1994.

Nossiter, Thomas Johnson, *Communism in Kerala: A Study in Political Adaptation*, London: C. Hurst for the Royal Society of International Affairs, 1982.

Overstreet, Gene D. and Marshall Windmiller, *Communism in India*, Los Angeles, CA: California University Press, 1959.

Pavier, Barry, *The Telangana Movement, 1944–1951*, New Delhi: Vikas, 1981.

Purewal, Shinder, *Communism in Punjab*, New Delhi: Ajanta, 1994.

———, *Sikh Ethnonationalism and the Political Economy of Punjab*, New Delhi: Oxford University Press, 2000.

Singh, Gurharpal, *Ethnic Conflict in India: A Case Study of Punjab*, London: Palgrave Macmillan, 2000.

Singh, Manjit, *The Akali Movement*, New Delhi: Macmillan, 1978.

Singh, Surinder and Gaur, Ishwar. *Sufism in Punjab: Mystics, Literature and Shrines*, New Delhi: Aakar Books, 2009.

Tan, Tai Yong, 'Assuaging the Sikhs: Government Responses to the Akali Movement, 1920–1925', *Modern Asian Studies* 29, no. 3 (1995): 655–703.

Wallace, Paul and Surendra Chopra, eds, *Political Dynamics and Crisis in Punjab*, Amritsar: Guru Nanak Dev University (GNDU), 1988.

# ✠ 2

# Progressives, Punjab and Pakistan: The Early Years

*Kamran Asdar Ali*

---

By the mid-1950s, Muslim Nationalism that led to the creation of Pakistan in 1947 had been severely put to test by nationalistic claims by Pakistan's diverse ethnic groups. Foremost among them was the voice of its Bengali citizens, who as the largest demographic part claimed its fair share from the overtly centralising state in Karachi, 1,400 miles away from Dhaka. The March 1954 provincial elections in East Pakistan led to the routing of the Muslim League, the founding party of Pakistan that had dominated its politics since its inception. The coming into power in East Bengal of the United Front government resulted in an upsurge of radical incidents in different parts of the province. A violent incident that left scores dead in the Adamjee Jute Mills near Dhaka in May of 1954 became a catalyst to impose Governor's rule and the banning of the Communist Party of Pakistan (CPP). The government said that it had reacted to the radicalisation of labourers and political workers after the March elections.[1] The CPP had already been weakened since the 1951 attack on it after the Rawalpindi Conspiracy Case, but CPP's partial resurgence during the 1954 elections in the shape of activism within political groups and parties perhaps remained a lingering threat to the central government in Karachi.

The banning of the CPP was a culmination of a series of undemocratic and authoritarian acts by the central Muslim League government. From the very first year of its existence, the ruling elite of

---

[1] A discussion on the riots and its aftermath at the Adamjee Jute Mills in 1954 can be found in American Consul General to Dept. of State, Dacca Despatch no. 123, 22 May 1954, NND 842909 890d.062.

Pakistan remained suspicious of any challenge to its authority. Jinnah and the Muslim League had brought together a range of interests and social classes on its side in support for the call for Pakistan. By avoiding specifics and by not putting forward any concrete economic programme, the Muslim League had succeeded in appealing to 'land-owners, businessmen, lawyers, socialists, intellectuals and the middle classes'.[2] It had also played on the slogan of 'Islam is in danger' to mobilise the more religious groups, the rural masses and of course those large landowners who were linked with religious authority as caretakers of shrines and sacred lineages. However, once Pakistan was created, the lack of clarity on any social and economic policy made the governing of the new state a game of political gamesmanship where the party continued to manipulate colonial laws and legal procedures to stay in power.[3]

Following Jinnah's death, the Prime Minister, Liaquat Ali Khan, openly advocated the supremacy of one ruling party and derided those who opposed the Muslim League as traitors and enemy agents.[4] There is no denying that the new state had enormous economic and social challenges, foremost being the settling of refugees who had poured into the country, mostly destitute and without resources. There were secessionist tendencies in the NWFP politics that were being encouraged by the Afghan government, and the lingering problem of Kashmir was ever present, making the security of the country vulnerable. This said, the government relied on public safety

---

[2] Although the Provincial Muslim Leagues of Punjab and Bengal had put forward progressive manifestos for the 1945–1946 elections. McGrath, *The Destruction of Pakistan's Democracy*, 52–53. Also see, Jalal, *The State of Martial Rule*, 62–63.

[3] Jinnah himself dismissed to two provincial ministries, one in Sindh and the other in NWFP, during his brief tenure of over a year in office as Governor General of Pakistan. During this period, he had consolidated for himself the position of not only the Governor General, but also as the President of the legislature. Disregarding the colonial tradition of Governor Generals remaining above every day politics and not accepting cabinet positions, Jinnah not only handpicked and appointed the entire first Cabinet, over riding the Prime Minister, he also retained two for himself, that of Evacuation and Refugees and Frontier Regions. McGrath, *The Destruction*, 41–42 and Jalal, *The State*.

[4] Jalal, *The State*, 65–68.

acts from the colonial period and other new draconian measures[5] to keep a check on political opponents. The early history of Pakistan is clearly littered with disagreements on a range of issues,[6] but what may have brought the landowners, lawyers and the emerging mercantile elite together was their fear of communist politics that threatened the status quo and demanded radical change.[7] In a developing atmosphere of the Cold War, the bogey of the communist threat was an easy target for the government to deflect from its shortcomings in providing the people of Pakistan political stability.

The CPP was founded in Calcutta when in February of 1948 the Communist Party of India (CPI) held its second Congress. The most important task performed during the Congress was the shift towards a more radical political line by the party and a severe critique of reformist politics of the party leadership during most of the 1940s. In addition, the Congress divided the party into two constitutive parts, the CPI would confine its working to the boundaries of the Indian Union and the post-August 1947 separated territories of Pakistan would be free to form a different Communist Party.

After the passing of the Report on Pakistan by the Party Congress, the delegates from Pakistan met separately and convened the first Congress of CPP.[8] It accepted the Report on Pakistan with amendments and elected its first office bearers. Syed Sajjad Zaheer was elected the General Secretary. After the Calcutta conference, Zaheer came to Pakistan as the leader of the nascent party and his name did not appear again on the CPI's central committee list.[9]

---

[5] For example, Public and Representatives Offices (Disqualification) Act, also known as PRODA, which was introduced by the Liaquat Government.

[6] By the end of 1949, there were 21 new political parties mostly consisting of Muslim League dissenters. See note 4 above, page 64.

[7] Ibid., 53.

[8] Among the delegates to the Congress were three from West Pakistan, Mohammad Hussein Ata from NWFP, Eric Cyprian from Punjab and Jalaluddin Bukhari from Sind. There were 32 delegates from East Bengal, including Kalpana Dutt and Khokar Roy. The discrepancy in numbers of delegates were perhaps because crossing borders between West Pakistan and India even in February 1948 was dangerous because of the lingering effect of the partition riots.

[9] The CPP was organised for West Pakistan, and the East Bengal CP was still under the direction of the West Bengal Party. Chief Event in Past History of Communist Party of Pakistan. Public Record Office, D0 35/2591.

This chapter partly follows Sajjad Zaheer's career (1948–1955) in Pakistan to focus on specific events in the early years of Pakistan's existence as they pertain to the communist movement in Pakistan's Punjab. It will initially discuss CPI's argument on the Muslim question as it evolved during the 1940s and then briefly give an overview of CPI's coalition with the Muslim League during the 1945–1946 elections.

To be sure, this chapter does not dwell on the pre-partition progressive politics in Punjab, but rather concentrates on aspects of communist politics in Pakistan's early history, a historical process that has not received much attention by historians and the public alike. It shows how the CPP with its new 'immigrant' leadership consolidated itself in Lahore and conducted politics under conditions of extreme surveillance and attack from the Pakistani state. Further, this chapter argues that as much as the communists provided for a different vision for the future, there were simultaneous internal tensions on policy issues within the party itself.

In its critical engagement with particular events during Pakistan's early years of existence, this chapter is part of a larger attempt to document the history of the working class movement that offers a perspective beyond the official retelling of Pakistan's history. The aim here is not to rehearse the more prevalent discussions on Pakistan's founding moments, arguments linked to Muslim Nationalism, the refugee question or that of Kashmir. Rather by concentrating on the internal debates within the CPP, it will bring forward events and voices that have remained inaudible or suppressed in history writing on Pakistan.[10] Hence, this chapter necessarily links itself to a recuperative history of various struggles and political aspirations of Pakistani people and challenges the pre-dominant representation of Pakistan in academic writings, such as the continuous discussions on South Asian Muslim nationalism linked to Islam and Urdu language.

---

[10] However, see Ansari, *The Emergence of Socialist Thought*, for a selective understanding of Muslim progressives and their role in the national movement. Leghari, *The Socialist Movement*. Unpublished PhD thesis, Laval University, Montreal. This text is to date the only comprehensive attempt at the history of the Left in Pakistan, yet it remains unpublished. Finally also see Malik, 'The Marxist Literary Movement in India and Pakistan', 649–64, for a detailed discussion on the politics of the Progressive Writer's Movement during Pakistan first 20 years.

## The Muslim Question

By the early 1940s, the CPI had taken a major position on the Muslim question in India and drew a connection linking the Muslim League's demand for a separate state to the ultimate independence from colonialism. Unlike the Indian National Congress, that was opposed to the division of British India almost until the partition of the territory itself, the CPI in a plenary session of the Central Committee in 1942 passed a resolution based on the report by G. Adhikari to accept the Muslim separatist position within its thesis of legitimate right of the multiple peoples of the territory (British India) to secede from the Union.[11]

The thesis on self-determination of different nationalities and the acceptance, in principle at least, of the right to secede from the Indian Union was a bold departure from the arguments that the party itself had adhered to in the past. The right of people living in contiguous territories to create autonomous states if they so desired clearly signalled an acceptance for Muslim separatism, which a year later the party openly supported as evidenced by the writing of Sajjad Zaheer, then a member of the Central Committee. Zaheer, in a pamphlet on Congress-League Unity, forcefully argued that the case for Muslim self-determination and for Pakistan was a just, progressive and positive expression of Muslim political sentiments.[12] Similarly, in November of 1945, the Communist Party's journal, *People's War*, published an article by N.K. Krishnan that followed Adhikari's argument on the social and political backwardness of Muslims in

---

[11] Dr. Gangadhar Adhikari, one of the pioneer members of the Communist Party of India, was member of the Politburo 1943–1951 while also serving on the Central Committee during that period. See Adhikari, *Pakistan and Indian National Unity*, 5–32.

[12] Zaheer, *A Case for Congress-League Unity*. This argument may, however, be a bit different from the one made by Adhikari. In the Adhikari report, Muslims were not given a status of nationality, and it was understood that Muslims constitute the numerical majority among some nationalities, like the Baluch, Pathans, Sindhis and so on. Adhikari argued against recognising Hindus or Muslims as nationalities, rather by giving all nationalities the right to secede the idea was that the various national groups would come together as a commonwealth. Zaheer's point may be a later evolution of the discussion on the Muslim question within the CPI.

relation to their Hindu neighbours. Krishnan gives examples of how Hindus dominate the industries and big capital and also are the large feudal landowners in Punjab and Bengal. Yet the article goes beyond Adhikari's argument in supporting the cause of Pakistan. For Krishnan although there were differences with the Muslim League, the CPI still needed to support the creation of Pakistan as this would enable the Muslim masses to attain equality, freedom and justice. In solidarity with the call for Muslim self-determination, the article rhetorically calls the demand for Pakistan as a demand for freedom that is equal to the demand for India's independence from the British.[13]

Following this argument, indeed the Communist Party's manifesto for the 1945–1946 elections demanded immediate independence and transfer of power to not only two governments (India and Pakistan), but to 17 interim 'sovereign' national assemblies that corresponded to different nationalities that had been defined by the party in 1942 and now also included Baluchis as an additional national group.[14] Hence, in a matter of less than five years, the CPI had moved from a position of considering India as a single nation to a policy of national self-determination in a multi-national India culminating in the right of all nationalities to secede from the union and create their own sovereign states.

## The Communists and Pre-independence Punjab

Given CPI's changed position on the Muslim question, the party encouraged its members to work closely with the Muslim League to organise for the 1945–1946 elections.[15] In Punjab, the Unionist party had remained influential in politics in the inter-war period during the early part of the 20th century. The Unionist party mainly represented the interests of the landed gentry and landlords of Punjab, which included Muslims, Hindus and Sikhs. The Muslim leadership of

---

[13] Krishnan, N.K. People's War, Supplement 18 November 1945. Quoted in Leghari, *The Socialist Movement*. Unpublished PhD Thesis, Laval University, Montreal, Canada. See page 14.

[14] Overstreet and Windmiller, *Communism in India*, 231.

[15] In December 1945 and January 1946, there were elections for the Central and Provincial Legislature in which all political parties participated with much enthusiasm.

the party — Mian Fazl-i-Hussain and then Sir Sikandar Hayat and Sir Khizir Tiwana — although sympathetic to the Muslim League, ruled Punjab through alliances with the Congress and with the Sikh party, the Akali Dal. Despite these broad coalitions, by 1946, the Muslim League had become a major player in Punjab politics. For the 1945–1946 elections, rather than appeal to ideological sentiments linked to Islam to garner support, the Muslim League used the same networks of clan and lineage that had been a Unionist hallmark in earlier years. The large Muslim landowners and Sufi leaders of Punjab, who had previously provided the backbone of the Unionist alliance with Hindu and Sikh landowning elite, jumped ship and sided with the Muslim League during these crucial elections. However, there was also a groundswell of popular rural and middle class support for the Muslim League from quarters that were not even eligible to vote.[16]

The rural enthusiasm for Muslim League may partly be due to the hard work of the communist cadres who joined in the effort for the League's electoral victory. This cooperation was most evident in the Punjab where the League sought to distance itself from the ruling Unionists and worked hard to gain the rural Muslim vote. Muslim communists like Danial Latifi, Ataullah Jehanian, Chaudhary Rehmatullah, Anis Hashmi, Abdullah Malik, Mian Ifitikharuddin and others joined the Muslim League and assisted in its contact with the peasantry and working class and helped in organising and publicising the League's election programme.[17] Activists like Jehanian and Iftikharuddin were land owners, but had joined Congress Committees of their respective districts in the 1930s.

Jehanian was the general secretary of the Multan district Congress Committee. He joined the Communist Party during his 1940–1942 detention at Deoli camp. He was extremely popular among peasants and was elected as the first Muslim general secretary of the Punjab Kisan Committee.[18] Iftikharuddin, who later on served as the publisher of *Pakistan Times* and *Imroze*, two progressive newspapers in post-independence Pakistan and as a member of the Constituent Assembly, had joined the Congress Party in the 1930s. He was active

---

[16] See Talbot, *Pakistan*.

[17] Leghari, *The Socialist Movement*, 27–32.

[18] Grande, *Communist and the Pakistan Movement in Punjab Province*. Unpublished manuscript. See page 12.

in the Kisan front and was instrumental in founding the Congress Socialist Party in 1938. He was, however, 'persuaded' to resign as the President of the Punjab Congress Party by his friends in the Communist Party and made to join Muslim League to further the CPI's agenda of Muslim self-determination.[19]

Among this group of Communist Party members and sympathisers, Danial Latifi, who has had a brilliant career as a constitutional lawyer in India, became the office secretary of the provincial Muslim League headquarters in Punjab and drafted the Provincial Muslim League Manifesto in 1944. From the Muslim League side, younger leaders like Mumtaz Daulatana (who was supported by the communists in his election to become the general secretary of the Punjab Muslim League) and Nawab Iftikhar Husain Khan of Mamdot, although scions of feudal families, encouraged the alliance as the communists assisted them in undermining the hold of the Unionists on rural Punjab.[20] The manifesto itself, as David Gilmartin suggests, was an attempt at radically transforming the relationship between a future state and the masses. It primarily concentrated on rural reform, and in a communist influenced progressive language, the manifesto guaranteed state protection to the peasants against the excesses of feudal power. It remains one of the most progressive documents of Muslim League's pre-Independence history. The document asks for state planning of the economy with nationalisation of key industries and banks, full employment in the industrial sector with minimum wage guarantees, right to strike and acceptance of collective bargaining agents. In the rural areas, it speaks for the landless peasant and the small land holders and pushes for debt relief and ownership of

---

[19] Sibte Hasan in his essays on Sajjad Zaheer details how Zaheer forced Iftikharuddin to resign. Iftikharuddin was very close to Nehru and to Maulana Azad, and he was a nationalist and did not agree with Muslim League's politics, which he thought of being led in most part by feudals and communalists. Yet he was under the ideological influence of the CPI leadership and specially Zaheer who according to Sibte Hasan would taunt Iftikharuddin of being an anarchist by temperament and not able to follow party discipline. He also would speak about how Iftikharuddin's reluctance to resign from Congress was because he would lose contact with his more famous friends like Nehru, Gandhi and Azad. See Hasan, *Mughani-e-Atish-e Nafs*, 39–40.

[20] Gilmartin, *Empire and Islam*, 192–98.

state land by landless peasants, while arguing for progressive taxation on larger holdings.[21]

Hence, through their alliance with the League, the communists sought to raise consciousness among the Muslim peasantry, an area that they had not had much earlier success in, while the Muslim League itself in the mid-1940s benefitted from communist work among the peasantry and strengthened its own secular appeal among a large section of the Muslim masses.

Notwithstanding the progressive manifesto in Punjab or the hard work performed by the communists for the League, the long-term effects of this collaboration did not produce the structural transformation that the communists were pushing for. The weakness of the communist movement in the area itself and the forms in which Muslim League manipulated the situation in its favour by using the communist connections to create a mass base, but eventually not allowing communist sympathisers any formal position in the party, inevitably created misgivings towards the League among the CPI members.[22]

## The Reversal and Partition

Despite the desire to work within the League, by the mid-1940s, there were other competing and vocal tendencies that shaped CPI's outlook on partition of British India and the Muslim League. In a paper on the Cabinet Mission,[23] Rajani Palme Dutt, the British communist leader and influential journalist who also served as the principal advisor to Indian communist politics, emphasised that 'the unity of India is desirable from a progressive point of view and

---

[21] See notes 17 above, page 28. Also see Gilmartin. Empire for detailed discussion.

[22] Ibid. Based on interviews with communists who participated in the Punjab movement in the 1940s, Leghari argues that they felt rejected when prominent communist workers in the Muslim League like Ataullah Jehanian were not given party tickets during the 1946 elections. Work with the Muslim League aided some CPI members to either leave the Communist Party or become more firmly entrenched in Muslim League politics in the post-partition years.

[23] Sent in February 1946 by the new Labour Government of Britain, headed by Clement Atlee, to work out a formula for India's eventual independence.

partition would be a reactionary step'.[24] He went on to argue that the slogan of Pakistan was not one of national self-determination, but of Muslim separatism. However, he conceded that the issue is an internal matter for the Indian people to settle and the resolution could take into account the principle of national self-determination as applied in the Soviet Union. Recognition of this principle, including the right to secession, however, does not mean, Palme Dutt asserted, that separation is desirable.[25]

Still later in August of 1946, the CPI issued a resolution, which while asserting that the Muslim League represents the bulk of the Muslim masses, as evidenced by its victory in the 1945–1946 election in which it won all Muslim seats to the central legislature (30) and 447 of the 507 Muslim seats in the provincial assemblies, the CPI distanced itself from Muslim League's demand for Pakistan. It declared that the demand reflected the feudal and Muslim elite interests that sought to compromise with imperialism for a share in administering divided India.[26] Further, the party acknowledged that unlike the Congress, the Left in the Muslim League was very weak and asked the League to abandon its bargaining tactics with Congress on its demands and unconditionally join the common struggle against the British presence and the princely states.[27] Following Rajani Palme Dutt, the resolution argued that the masses that support the Indian National Congress are correctly against the division of the country on a religious and undemocratic basis and want a single union.[28]

To be sure, the CPI was critical of both the Congress and the Muslim League for accepting the partition plan.[29] Yet, it was at least clear in CPI's analysis that Congress' 'compromise' on partition was more to retain control of the pre-independence popular upsurge by bargaining with the British, while the Muslim League had been

---

[24] Palme Dutt, *A New Chapter in Divide and Rule*, 13.

[25] Ibid., 15.

[26] This section on the 'August Resolution' is from *For the Final Assault: Tasks of the Indian People in the Present Phase of Indian Revolution, 1946*, Bombay: People's Publishing House. Reprinted in Documents of the Communist Party of India, Volume 5, 103–27.

[27] Ibid., 120–21.

[28] Ibid., 103–27.

[29] Palme Dutt, *A New Chapter in Divide and Rule*.

a lackey of the British by forcefully demanding the division of the country on a religious basis and hence weakening the progressive forces of united India. I would emphasise that although the CPI finally accepted the creation of Pakistan by arguing for the division of the party itself, the deep suspicion of Muslim League's politics and the agony over British India's division was the overwhelming sentiment that was shared by a majority of party workers of all religions and ethnicities. Pakistan's creation was, according to the CPI, non-progressive and hence reactionary.[30]

## The Party Line in Pakistan

It is by now well known that the violence that followed the partition of British India was unprecedented in its scale and method.[31] In the summer and autumn of 1947, Punjab burned as millions were uprooted from the ancestral lands and forced to flee across the newly formed borders to previously unknown areas. It was a catastrophe that incorporated killings, arson, disappearances, and rape. Entire communities which until recently had lived together had turned against one another and the carnage that followed had undermined long held practices of shared existence and tolerance. The CPI in its communiqués during that time[32] vehemently condemned the killing and held the British responsible for the breakdown in the law and order situation. The CPI argued that the British had instituted governor rule in the Punjab province five months before the division of the country, and hence its security services and bureaucracy should have been prepared for all eventualities and not allowed religious extremists on all sides of the political spectrum to take advantage of the situation. This partition violence, according to the party, was a conspiracy to weaken the newly emergent nations and for creating discord amongst its people at the moment of independence. The party also blamed the extremists on both sides, the rulers of princely states, the large landowners and industrialists. All of whom for personal

---

[30] See Dyakov, *A New British*, 14–15.

[31] Pandey, Gyanendra, *Remembering Partition*.

[32] Secretary Communist Party 1947. Zaghmi Punjab Ki Faryad (Wounded Punjab's Plea), Lahore: Qaumi Dar-ul-Isha't. Extracts from *Naya Zamana*, 7 September 1947.

gain gave support to communalist tendencies and stoked the fire of hatred. The party praised the national level leadership of Indian National Congress and the Muslim League who in their statements and actions sought to stop the violence. This violence had also taken its toll on the communist movement in Western Punjab. Different estimates are given for the pre-partition party strength in the region, and an unreliable figure of 10,000 is sometimes used out of which almost 90 per cent left for India. Irrespective of the actual counts, the communist workers that were left in Pakistan were much less in number (perhaps less than 50), less trained and limited in experience than those Sikh and Hindu cadres who had migrated.[33]

Sajjad Zaheer, the secretary general of the new party, belonged to a very prominent, educated and respected Muslim family from the United Provinces of the Owadh area. His father Sir Syed Wazir Hasan was once the Chief Justice in Owadh, and his brother Ali Zaheer was the first Indian Ambassador after independence to Indonesia.[34] Sajjad Zaheer had come to Pakistan in December of 1947, soon after the violence had subsided, as a central committee member of the CPI to organise the remaining cadres in the newly formed state. Zaheer toured the country to generate interest among party members who were still present. He came again in May of 1948, this time to lead the CPP.

On his arrival Zaheer opted to make the party headquarters in Lahore as some of his closest associates, the poet Faiz Ahmed Faiz and the Punjab Muslim League leader Mian Iftikharuddin, were based in Lahore.[35] In addition to Zaheer, other Muslim cadres were

---

[33] See, note 17 above, page 35.

[34] See, Chief Event in Past History of Communist Party of Pakistan. Public Record Office, D035/2591. It goes to Zaheer's credit that he never used his family's influence and wealth for his personal gains. Even during moments of extreme financial burdens that the family faced during Zaheer's time in Pakistan and after his return to India in the mid-1950s, he seldom received (or asked for) assistance from his more well off relatives. A glimpse of this relationship can be gauged from Zaheer's youngest daughter, Noor's memoirs. See Zaheer, *Mere Hisse Ki Roshnai*.

[35] Surprisingly enough a person whom Zaheer also saw on a regular basis was Nawabzada Imtiaz Ali Khan, the first cousin of the Prime Minister, Liaquat Ali Khan. The Nawabzada was a friend from Zaheer's Oxford days

sent to Pakistan by the CPI leadership to take charge of the communist movement. Indeed, the CPP's Political Bureau in late 1948 constituted of Sajjad Zaheer, Sibte Hasan and Ishfaque Baig. These were highly educated men from Urdu speaking North Indian *ashraf* (respectable elite)[36] who, in many cases, had university degrees from Europe and possessed previous experience of urban and cosmopolitan life. However, all had minimum cultural or social understanding of or political experience among the working class masses within the territories that became Pakistan. They arrived in a Pakistan where the majority of the population was rural, the level of industrialisation was low and the labour was ethnically diverse and non-organised.[37]

In Pakistan, Zaheer followed the political thesis laid out in Calcutta. At the Calcutta Congress, the Report on Pakistan[38] was presented by Bhowani Sen,[39] who elaborated on the trends of discussion on the Pakistan question within the party. After putting forward the two opinions, one that emphasised that the Indian union was progressive and considered Pakistan politically reactionary, while the other that held the creation of Pakistan as an advance in Muslim freedom from the yoke of Hindu domination, Bhowani Sen gave his own analysis of the situation. He argued that both India and Pakistan were dominated by reactionary capitalists and landlords who were collaborating with imperialists. He went on to criticise how the Muslim League had propagated the false theory of Hindu domination to retain the vested interest of Muslim elite against its richer and more powerful Hindu competitors. To achieve this goal,

---

and remained loyal to him during the entire Lahore period without officially joining the Communist Party.

[36] See note 17 above, page 45–73.

[37] Pakistan in 1947 had an estimated industrial workforce of about 480,000 within a total population of 75 millions in both wings. See Amjad, *Labour Legislation and Trade Unionism in India and Pakistan*, 67.

[38] See Report on Pakistan, Review of the Second Congress of the Communist Party of India, 757–61. Documents of the Communist Party of India. Vol. 5 (1997). Calcutta: National Book Agency.

[39] Bhowani Sen was a major figure in the Bengal Communist Party, he was re-elected to the Central Committee during the 1948 Congress and was also elected to the Polit Bureau. He was considered one of B.T. Ranadive's (who would become the general secretary of CPI during the Calcutta Congress) chief lieutenants.

Sen continued, the Muslim league channelled the anti-imperialist momentum of the poor Muslim masses toward communal politics and played in the hands of imperialist forces that wanted to keep both Muslims and Hindus enslaved. Hence, in his opinion, the central task of communist movements in India and in Pakistan was identical, to radically change the existing social order and struggle toward the creation of people's democratic states in both countries.

This of course was the period (1948–1950) of the radical turn within the CPI under B.T. Ranadive's, the newly elected General Secretary of CPI, leadership. Ranadive had argued for a revolutionary strategy, which sought to bring people together to launch a massive struggle against bourgeois forces and the Congress led government in India (or the Muslim League in Pakistan). The party envisaged a People's Democratic Revolution based on the alliance, led by the working class and the Communist Party, of the workers, the peasantry, the progressive intellectuals and the petit bourgeoisie. This 'democratic front' would form the basis of the new future governance by the toiling masses after the eventual overthrow of the current system.[40] The radical line postulated that the spontaneous industrial strikes and militant peasant struggles (like the one in Telangana) over the entire country would enable the disillusioned masses to join the struggle leading to a mass upsurge. The rank and file members of the party were ordered to radicalise every political front with the hope that this would serve as a catalyst for an insurrectionary action by the people. Hence, working class workers and peasants from a range of different parts of the country were encouraged to face the brunt of state repression. They were also asked to follow the example of the peasant movement in Telangana.[41]

---

[40] Three major documents were produced to defend this new policy. 'People's Democracy', 'Agrarian Question' and 'Tactical Line'; a complete discussion of these texts is beyond the parameters set out for this chapter. See Documents of the Communist Party of India (1997). Letter of the New Central Committee of the CPI Volume VI, 105–41.

[41] Telangana movement was of course historically specific and was the culmination of long-term work among the peasants by communist and radical workers. Further, the various cross cutting forces vying for power in the area allowed the peasant movement to become an armed rebellion. For example, after the transfer of power by the British, there was a tussle between the Nizam of Hyderabad (the area in which Telangana is located)

Following Ranadive's thesis, during the years 1948–1951 when he managed the CPP, Zaheer was extremely critical of even the slightest deviation from party policy. Zaheer's attitude toward Pakistan and the Muslim League initially reflected CPI's radical line, which also saw the need for the Muslim masses to be made conscious of their nationalistic and historic duty and be wrenched away from their communally minded feudal Muslim League leadership. Hence, the militancy in his letters to party comrades was represented often with dictatorial language, giving much importance to the dissemination of the party literature, opposition to the Muslim League leaders (he calls them downright scoundrels) and the building of open political front linked to other progressive forces in the country.

The anti-Muslim League politics was further complicated by CPP's own assessment of Pakistan's political and economic situation. It based its class analysis for a revolutionary change on the argument that Pakistan was a capitalist country where socialism was the next step, and hence the intensification of the struggle against capitalism was a necessary revolutionary goal. This argument was clearly reflected in Sajjad Zaheer's message — which was read out — to the first All Pakistan Progressive Writers (APPWA) Association's conference held in Lahore in November of 1949, a year after his arrival in Pakistan. In addressing the assembled writers and intellectuals, he argues:

> We can only call that literature successful, that knowledge true knowledge, that art real art which benefits the tree of humanity, which

---

and the Central Indian State. There was also an anti-Nizam movement within the princely state by nationalists and a Razakar movement in support of Nizam's rule and against the encroachment of the Nizam's state by the Indian dominion. Finally, there was the struggle against the local Deshmukh's (the name for big landlords in the area) by the peasantry. Taking advantage of these competing and at times overlapping movements, the peasantry of the area forcefully asserted itself for land rights. These same conditions did not prevail in other parts of India, yet the Ranadive Line called for insurrection in India and named it the 'Telangana Way'. Chaudari, Tridb (1950). The Swing Back: A Critical Survey of the Devious Zig Zags of the CPI Political Line (1947–1950). Marxist Internet Archive. Chapter, Since Calcutta Thesis, accessed 15 April 2011. http:// www.marxists.org/archive/chaudhuri/1950/swing-back/ch02.htm.

soldiers against capitalist violence and oppression and is a blessing for
the working class, one which enlightens the minds of the oppressed
classes and fills their hearts with passion and courage to speed up the
path toward social evolution and democratic revolution.[42]

In addition to the rhetorical and polemical flourish of his speech,
Zaheer goes on to state that to accomplish this task, intellectuals,
artists and writers need to forsake all their middle class behaviours
that enable them to follow the dictates of the capitalists and the feudals. Rather, his advice to the writers is that they should be ready to
accept economic, material and bodily pain and also be prepared to
struggle against bourgeois and retrogressive ideas that they harbour
within themselves. These ideals, Zaheer argues, have been inherited
by the middle class writers as the elites have tried to use to keep us
away from revolutionary thought and practice. Hence, the ruling
classes sometimes in guise of spiritualism and at others in the form
of moralistic arguments or nationalism seek try to placate our senses.
He says that these arguments are mere fronts to hide the exploitation and oppression of the capitalistic and feudalistic systems. Yet,
according to Zaheer, in the present moment of history, the industrial
workers are uniting all the socially oppressed classes to lead them
in the revolutionary struggle against capitalism and imperialism.
This was Zaheer's analysis of the situation in Pakistan as well, and
he elaborated on this in the rest of his message by emphasising how
owing to the Russian revolution, the spread of communism in Eastern
Europe, the recent victory of communist forces in China, the day
was not far that the industrial working class in India and Pakistan
would be victorious against the entrenched capitalist system (and
their feudal allies) who were being supported by the US and British
imperialists.[43]

The emphasis on Pakistan being at a level of 'social evolution'
where it could be counted as being a capitalist country with a large
working class, and the struggle was for the next stage of socialist
transformation may have been a rhetorical ploy to energise the various mass fronts, like the APPWA. Despite this rhetoric, it was evident
to Zaheer and others in the leadership of the party that Pakistan

---

[42] Zaheer, Sajaad, 1949, *Paighamat* (Messages), Sawera (Lahore) number
7–8, 10–12.
[43] Ibid.

at independence was primarily a rural country and an agrarian economy. Pakistan at its independence had 9–10 per cent of British India's industrial base and only 7 per cent of its population was employed in the formal work sector.[44] It can be ascertained that in late 1940s, the party itself had not developed its own Pakistan strategy and mostly based its analysis on the 'Report on Pakistan' that was presented in the Calcutta Congress. There was an urgent need in the party to come up with a Pakistan-specific thesis that could elaborate on what was the actual strength of the Pakistani bourgeoisie, its links with the Anglo-American capital and also the effects of the war and post-war economic crisis on the peasantry.

## Purging the 'Punjabis'

The party headquarters for the Punjab Communist Party had already been established at 114 McCleod Road, Lahore. This building belonged to the daughter of Mian Fazl-i-Hussain, the deceased Unionist leader; the CPI in Punjab had rented it from her with the help of Faiz Ahmed Faiz in the early 1940s.[45] One of the first tasks that Zaheer put to himself was the reorganising of the party structure and the formation of the West Pakistan Regional Committee, the Provincial Committees and the District Organising Committees. In addition to the original members that formed the Central Committee after the Calcutta Congress, Sajjad Zaheer, Muhammad Hussain Ata, Jalaludin Bokhari, and Mirza Ibrahim, six more members were added: Shaukat Ali (Punjab), C.R Aslam (Punjab), Mirza Ishfaque Baig (Centre), Ziarat Gul (NWFP), Abdul Khaliq Azad and Hasan Nasir (both from Sind). This regional committee initially served as the new Central Committee; while Zaheer, Shaukat Ali and Ishfaque Baig constituted the new Central Secretariat, Zaheer, Baig and Sibte Hasan formed the Politbureau.[46] It is clear that Zaheer kept his most trusted colleagues from his Bombay days, Ishfaque and Sibte Hasan,

[44] See note 4 above, page 64.

[45] Fazle Hussain was the founder of the Unionist Party in Punjab. His daughter was married to Manzur Qadir, a constitutional lawyer and one time Pakistani Foreign Minister in the Ayub Cabinet; he was also Chief Justice of the Punjab High Court in the 1960s. Also see Interview with C. R. Aslam, Atish Biyan (weekly), Volume 12(13), 22 May 2000.

[46] Ali, Mian Anwer, 218.

close to him in the party hierarchy. Despite criticism of favouring people who had come from India, it also needs to be stressed that Lahore was a new place and also an entirely new cultural milieu for Zaheer, and he needed to rely on people whom he could trust and work with to perform his task.

Historically, Punjab had several peasant-based organisations and some had over the years come under the CPI's influence. For example, in Punjab since the 1920s, there were Ghadar Party influenced peasant and workers groups.[47] The most prominent among them were the Kirti-Kisaan Party (peasant-workers party), the Kisan Sabha and Naujawan Bharat Sabha. Most had a large percentage of Sikh membership, and they also dominated the leadership positions, although they were 14 per cent of Punjab's population, in relation to 56 per cent Muslims and 26 per cent Hindu. In the early 1940s, two dominant tendencies of Left activism, primarily the factions in the Kirti Party in Punjab, had been brought together by the CPI headquarters in Bombay to constitute the Communist Party of Punjab. The Provincial Communist Party in Punjab by 1947, however, still had two dominant groups. These factions were led by Teja Singh Swatantar and Sohan Singh Josh, respectively, and included prominent Muslim communists like Ferozuddin Mansoor and Fazal Elahi Qurban within its fold.[48]

By mid 1947, the difference between Teja Singh faction, which included Qurban, and that of Sohan Singh (which was more closely aligned with the CPI central leadership and had Mansoor in its ranks) became more acute. Iqbal Leghari, based on interviews with some of the actors involved in the split, argues that Teja Singh Swatantar

---

[47] The Ghadar Party was formed by migrant Sikh workers in the United States who during the early years of WWI decided to come back to India and overthrow the British government by violent means.

[48] Mansoor and Qurban had left British India in 1919 after the demoralising affect at the defeat of Turkey in WWI and the end of the Khilafat movement. They went to Afghanistan and from there to Tashkent, where they were given military training in a school organised by M.N. Roy with Soviet assistance. Mansoor who came back to India in 1921 was arrested and convicted on conspiracy charges. But Qurban went on to attend the Moscow University of Eastern Toilers and did not return unitl 1926, when he was promptly arrested (Leghari 1979, 24 also see Overstreet and Windmiller).

and Fazal Elahi Qurban were against the central leadership of the CPI about the change of position on the Pakistan question. The new party position under P.C. Joshi (prior to the Calcutta Conference) which considered Muslim League and its demand for Pakistan as reactionary was resisted by Qurban in his discussions with Ajoy Ghosh, who was the central leader in-charge for Punjab. When the central party leadership did not pay heed to their arguments, Qurban and Swatantar along with their colleagues decided to form an independent Pakistan Communist Party in June of 1947, basing it on the old thesis of national self determination of the Muslim populace.[49]

The Bombay based CPI took serious note of this disciplinary breach and immediately made preparations to sideline the new party from its remaining cadres in West Pakistan. Ajoy Kumar Ghosh, a member of the Central Committee of the CPI and, as mentioned above, in-charge for Punjab, came to Pakistan in October of 1947 and reorganised the various provincial committees that had been left leaderless due to the migration of most non-Muslim members, the majority. In Punjab, the provincial committee consisted of Mirza Mohammad Ibrahim, Shaukat Ali, Chaudhary Rahmatullah, Ferozuddin Mansoor, and Eric Cyprian. Because of the differences with the Swatantar group, the name of Fazal Elahi Qurban, one of the senior most party members in the province, was left out of this list. Further, keeping in mind the opposition to the central party's view on the division of British India among some members of the Punjab (and Sind) party, it may be possible that Sajjad Zaheer's election as the leader for the newly formed West Pakistan party had already been decided before the Calcutta Congress by the CPI in India. Hence, the number of delegates was kept at a minimum from this part of Pakistan, only three as opposed to more than 30 from East Bengal. Soon after Calcutta Congress, on 18 March 1948, Qurban was presented with a chargesheet that expelled him from the common membership of the party. The signature on the document was of Ferozuddin Mansoor, a rival of Qurbans in Punjab's communist politics, yet also his comrade during their travels in the Soviet Union

---

[49] They rented a house on Montgomery Road in Lahore, an address distinct from the one used by the CPI on Macleod Road. See note 17 above, page 34–36. Also see Communism and Communist Activities in Pakistan (10 October 1949, Communism in West Punjab. PRO FO-1110/210).

earlier in the 20th century. With the removal of Qurban, Zaheer could now come to Pakistan as the only legitimate leader of the new party. The chargesheet[50] itself is an interesting document that rhetorically invoked the new Ranadive line of the CPI, but primarily concerned itself with the formation of a new Pakistan Communist Party by Qurban and Swatantar. In the chargesheet, Qurban is accused of siding with the Swatantar faction who on reaching India had already flaunted the authority of the CPI by organising a new Communist Party by the name of Red Flag Communist Party in Jullundhar. The chargesheet continuously reprimands Qurban for not following party discipline by associating himself with Swatantar, who is called a traitor, anti party and antiworking class. Qurban is also accused of calling his dispute with the central committee as only technical in nature as it was a quarrel between two factions within the Punjab communist movement. After this main charge, several points are added that further accuse Qurban of facilitating dissension in the party ranks and among the trade union workers close to the party. The chargesheet calls Qurban a malicious liar as he is alleged to have told workers of the Attock Oil Company in Rawalpindi that the communists were allied to the CPI and were working as 5th columnists for India, seeking to break Pakistan into pieces. Qurban is then compared to Teja Singh Swatantar and told that his activities are exactly similar to that of Teja Singh, which could lead to collaboration with communal and reactionary forces to disrupt the revolutionary people's movement.

These were extremely serious charges addressed to one of the most senior Muslim party members in the newly formed state. Despite his two long rebuttals of the charges against him, Fazal Elahi Qurban was expelled by the CPI and a circular was sent out in October of 1948 to all party members with Sajjad Zaheer's signature as General Secretary attesting to the dismissal.

Qurban in his defence uses the rhetorical ploy of denying all charges and then pleads for inclusion in the party recalling his 27 years of service to the cause. In this sense he was correct, as he was senior to all who had come from India to take on the leadership and also to most who were already working in Pakistan after the

---

[50] The following discussion is based on seized Communist Party documents reproduced in Anwer Ali, M. The Communist Party, 7–17.

departure of other senior Hindu and Sikh members. He also criticised the party leadership for not giving him a fair hearing and a chance to plead his case. Qurban argues that his expulsion is like a death sentence to him, and it has been carried out in an arbitrary fashion without any regard to his seniority and service to the party itself. In both his responses, one as an answer to the chargesheet and the other a letter in Urdu to Sajjad Zaheer, Qurban retains a veiled criticism of the Calcutta Congress as being undemocratic and representing a clique within the party. In his responses, he resists his expulsion by decree and calls for a meeting of all the members of the party so that the decision could be made in a transparent fashion as he deserved this hearing after his long dedication to party. He also reiterates that sane communists in Pakistan wanted an independent Pakistan Communist Party, which should work with all democratic minded and progressive elements to form a real Democratic Government in Pakistan. Here again, he was forwarding a criticism of CPI's line on radicalising the movement. Qurban's removal did indeed pave the way for Zaheer to establish his authority on the fractured and demoralised Communist Party in Pakistan's early years. However, he continued to receive internal pressure from comrades like Eric Cyprian and Mirza Ibrahim, who had a longer history in Lahore and were more historically and culturally linked with Pakistani society from pre-Independence days.[51]

## The Internal Debate

The CPP's confrontational politics, under the influence of the Ranadive line, harmed the day-to-day working of the trade unions, affected the selling of literature and also resulted in periodic arrests of the more committed cadre, leaving the offices to be run by junior colleagues. For example, by 1948, the major communist-supported labour federation was Pakistan Trade Union Federation. Its elected president was Mirza Ibrahim, a veteran leader of the Railway Workers' Union in Lahore. In Lahore, the largest concentration of labour force in the country lay within the Moghalpura Railway Workshop, a public sector enterprise. Prior to the partition of British India, the government of India had set up a Pay Commission to study

---

[51] Ali, Anwer. Report to India. The Communist Party, 355.

the working conditions of the railway workers. This had come about due to a sustained pressure exerted by the railway workers under Mirza Ibrahim's leadership through strikes and stoppages. Both Congress and Muslim League had accepted the Pay Commission's recommendation, but after independence, the Muslim League due to its economic problems did not address this issue. To pressure the government on the Pay Commission issue, there were major strikes in Lahore in December of 1947, which led to Ibrahim's arrest. Faiz Ahmed Faiz, the poet and intellectual, was thrust into the position of leading the PTUF as he was the elected Vice President. The government's repressive machinery sensing further disturbances arrested Faiz (in April of 1948), while other communist leaders connected to the labour movement, Eric Cyprian, Ferozuddin Mansoor, Dada Amir Haidar (from Rawalpindi) and Mirza Ibrahim (again), were picked up in September of 1948. Scores of workers would be arrested for selling the banned CPP paper, *Naya Zamana*, and dismissal from work or arrests by the security agencies of the rank and file members and industrial workers under one law and order pretext or the other was extremely common.[52]

The blind following of the radical line by the CPP central leadership had created some dissension among the party members. One of the dissenters was a senior party colleague, Professor Eric Cyprian. Cyprian, a pre-partition member of the party, had received a BA from Oxford and had taught in the Punjab (including Murray College in Sialkot). He was member of Regional Committee of the CPP and worked on the trade union and peasant (kisan) front.[53] Although agreeing with the party's general radical line, Eric Cyprian, who had travelled to the Party Congress in Calcutta as one of three members from West Pakistan, argued in a memo that militancy without organised and coherent party discipline could lead to anarchy on the one hand and severe repression by the state on the other.

His seniority allowed him to speak openly in Party meetings and send letters critical to the leadership, criticising them on their policies. For example, Cyprian seriously supported the training of new cadres

---

[52] See note 17 above, page 53. Also see *Pakistan Times*, 17 April 1948, 1 and *Pakistan Times*, 27 April, 3.

[53] He was originally from Allahabad, but had settled in Lahore for some years prior to partition.

and the purging of those who were of doubtful use or had 'reformist' tendencies, which may have included people like Fazl Elahi Qurban, Jalaluddin Bokhari (from Sind) and Kazi Mujtaba (also from Sind).[54] However, in terms of Punjab politics, he particularly identified Mian Iftikharuddin (mentioned above, an ex-Congress worker who was close to the CPI and was asked to enter Muslim league before the 1946 elections). Just after independence, Iftikharuddin was the Provincial Minister of rehabilitation of refugees (August–November 1947) and had resigned from the post arguing that he had not been given a free hand in the implementation of his ministerial duties. He had also advocated for land distribution and for putting a ceiling on land holdings in West Punjab to absorb the rural refugees who had entered Pakistani Punjab after the partition of British India. He was clearly a major progressive voice in Muslim League politics and was creating a political space to radicalise Muslim League from within. Iftikharuddin was also close to Sajjad Zaheer.

Eric Cyprian perhaps sensing the closeness and personal friendship between Zaheer and Iftikharuddin[55] opposed Ifitikharuddin's argument for changing the Muslim League from within and called it nothing more than an opportunistic manoeuver to capture power

---

[54] We have met Qurban above. Bokhari and Mujtaba were pre-partition CPI members from Sind. Both had begun to show tendencies to support the Muslim League after partition. Mujtaba had taken on a position within the Muslim League by 1948, while Bokhari would occasionally make speeches in trade union gatherings in favour of Jinnah.

[55] It was an open secret that Eric Cyprian resented the fact that the Central Committee was dominated by people from the United Provinces (UP). See Ali Anwer, The Communist Party, Memo to Sajjad Zaheer by Mohammad Ata, 328–29. Zaheer and Iftikharuddin were of course old friends from their joint work in the 1930s and early 1940s with the progressive wing of the Indian National Congress. Both had also studied at Oxford, Iftikharuddin predating Zaheer by a few years. He went to Balliol College at Oxford (1927–1930), joined the Indian National Congress in 1936 and was elected to the Punjab Assembly in 1937 and later was a founding member of the Congress Socialist Party (1938). As noted above, he joined the Muslim League in 1945, most probably under pressure from friends in the Communist Party of India. See, Biographical Note in Malik, Abudullah, ed. 1971. Selected Speeches and Statements. Mian Iftikharuddin. Lahore: Nigarishat.

while keeping the state machinery intact. Perhaps on policy grounds or due to his own apprehensions about those who came from India to lead the party, like Zaheer, Cyprian remained suspicious of Iftikharuddin's politics and deemed all Muslim League and other nationalist leaders (like the Pashtun leader, Ghaffar Khan) as either representatives of landlords (like the Nawab of Mamdot in Punjab) and painted them, either Punjabi, Sindhis or Pathans, as reactionaries who may raise progressive slogans and criticise the central government, yet in fact were quarrelling about their right to hold on to their power bases and their right to exploit the masses.[56] In putting forward this analysis, he insisted that Iftikharuddin, who was thought of as the CPP's man in the corridors of power due to his past personal and political association with the CPI, should pay serious attention to the changed party policy as put forward by Ranadive line and more closely follow the party dictates.[57]

However, the most significant break from party line that Cyprian puts forward was his suggestion to shift the party line toward organising rural areas as opposed to concentrating on industrial labourers and the trade union front. Cyprian argued that because of continuous repression of communist workers and the closeness of Lahore

---

[56] Anwer Ali, Eric Cyprian's Impression of Mian Iftikharuddin (June 1948). The Communist Party, 242 and Eric Cyprian on Ghaffar Khan (August 1948). Ibid., 247.

[57] Anwer Ali, Cyprian's Impressions of Mian Iftikharuddin. The Communist Party, 242. Mian Iftikharuddin was the President of the Punjab Muslim League for a few months in 1948. Because of his progressive views and general political disagreements with the Muslim League leadership in Karachi and in Lahore, he resigned from the party presidentship in November of 1948. Zaheer criticised this move in a memo to the CPP's Punjab Provincial Committee. The CPP, on the one hand, had kept a distance from Muslim League and had been unrelenting in its criticism, yet also wanted to retain a hold on the progressive elements in the Muslim League structure; Iftikharuddin was their foremost supporter within Muslim League. However, he had to work with his own constituency and within the limits of party politics. His decisions were at times not completely in accord with the CPP line, which would then irk the CPP leadership. Hence, Zaheer, despite his friendship, in the memo mentioned above calls Iftikharuddin unreliable and a person who continuously vacillates. See ibid. Zaheer on Daulatana, Siddiqui and Iftikharuddin (28 November 1948), 281–83.

to the border (a geographical argument), the trade union activity alone could not lead to a radical change in the political status quo.[58] The price that the workers would pay for even a partial struggle would be more than what the party could sustain in state repression. Following this, he called for the party to move its organising to landless peasants and recent refugees all over West Pakistan, while concentrating initially on the peasantry in the Multan and Rawalpindi divisions in Punjab. His arguments were based on his assessment that there was widespread poverty among the non-organised and non-political peasants, and they would join the struggle out of desperation to see a better future for themselves. Hence, the trade union front should have minimum cadres working in it and the party should send members to the rural areas to the two named divisions, to establish party centres, contact local leaders who have conducted spontaneous peasant struggles, form kisan (peasant) committees and start leading small struggle on day to day issues, which may then cohere to form larger movements.[59]

Although Cyprian shifted the discussion to peasant mobilisation from the struggle of the industrial workers in cities, his radicalisation and argument on agitational politics remained very similar to the Ranadive line of intensifying the struggle,[60] the difference was in tactics as Cyprian was advocating a shift from urban to rural milieu. This shift was a precursor to some of the debates in Indian communism as well (the Andhra Committee), albeit at a later date,[61] he may well have been influenced by the advancing Maoist forces in China or was in communication with the Andhra Committee itself.[62]

---

[58] Meaning that the already security conscious Pakistani state would not allow civic disturbances in Lahore, so close to the Indian border.

[59] Ibid., 142.

[60] See note 40.

[61] Letter of the New Central Committee of the CPI to All Party Members and Sympathisers. In Documents of the Communist Movement in India. Volume VI (1949–1951), 105–42. Calcutta: National Book Agency (1997). First issued, 1 June 1950.

[62] The Andhra Committee in Spring of 1950 created a new consensus against Ranadive's leadership and forced him out of the Secretary General's position. There is a longer discussion about Soviet pressure based on the editorial titled, 'Mighty Advance of the National Liberation Movement in the Colonial and Dependent Colonies' in the Cominform weekly *For a*

## Conclusion

The CPP agreed with the CPI analysis of Muslim backwardness and considered the territories of the new state as economically underdeveloped, lacking industrialisation and under entrenched feudal control. In this they were not off the mark. For example, as mentioned above, Pakistan, at its independence in 1947, inherited only 9 per cent of the total industrial establishment of British India, and the industrial workforce was estimated to be around half a million within a total population of 75 millions in both wings. Following this assessment, many have argued that the fragmented and low concentration of industrial capital was mirrored by the weakness of organised industrial labour.[63] Given the cultural 'backwardness' thesis on Muslims and the economic underdevelopment of Pakistan, it was obvious that in the progressive and somewhat developmentalist narrative of the Communist Party, as exemplified by Bhowani Sen's position on Pakistan, there was much work to be done to educate, motivate and organise the citizens of the new land about their historical task toward 'true' liberation.

Given this background, the initial insistence by the CPP leadership (following the CPI line) on an urban insurrectionary model was rightly critiqued by Eric Cyprian. His argument on the peasant question was the seed that later matured in the 1960s, after the international Sino-Soviet rift, into a major division in the progressive forces on the question of revolutionary praxis. Of course in the late 1940s, with the success of the Chinese Revolution and the support it received from the Soviet Union, these arguments had not yet surfaced. But the shift in a political strategy in a country where the majority still lived in rural areas was already being imagined by some in the Communist Left.

---

*Lasting Peace, For a People's Democracy* on 27 January 1950. This editorial and another lead article by P.N. Pospelov (commemorating the 26th death anniversary of V.I. Lenin) together created a major shift in the political thesis of the Communist Party of India with major reverberations on the CPP. The editorial did not directly criticise the Ranadive line, but for the CPI it created a major crisis of leadership and policy.

[63] Alexeyev, 'The Political Situation in Pakistan', 9–12.

Cyprian's intervention is one of the many criticisms and suggestions that were being offered right from the very beginning of Zaheer's arrival in Pakistan. As much as they show the inner party debate on what the correct line should be, it also makes us aware that Zaheer was not entering a space that he was culturally and politically that familiar with. His lack of experience in trade union work (in Bombay (now Mumbai) he was linked with literature and publication issues and the Muslim front for the CPI) and his lack of knowledge about the cultural and geographical terrain of the new country did not make it easy for him to settle into his new task.

Given this background, and as suggested in the introduction, within the first few years of its existence, the ruling elite of Pakistan became suspicious of any challenge to its authority. The Prime Minister, Liaquat Ali Khan, openly advocated the supremacy of one ruling party and derided those who opposed the Muslim League as traitors and enemy agents.[64] Pakistan, very soon after its independence, also became a political stage for Cold War politics. British and US intelligence agencies periodically worked closely with the higher echelons of the Pakistani state apparatus to help them in their efforts to curtail the real or imagined communist threat from within or across the border.[65] Public Safety Acts and other draconian measures from the colonial period were reinvigorated and used to arrest and harass party workers and sympathetic trade unionists. Important members of CPP's central committee were periodically put in jail, and communist publications were routinely banned or confiscated. Even literary journals linked to the Progressive Writers Association — *Sawera*, *Adab e Latif* or *Nuqush* — were constantly asked to stop publication for disseminating anti state literature. Further, the state also started using Islam as a political weapon to counteract various democratic forces. Islamic doctrine was employed in the media to persuade people against the antireligious (meaning anti-Islam) and, linked to it, anti-Pakistan political stance of the communists.[66] Public gatherings by communists were occasionally attacked and disrupted by mobs claiming Islamic tendencies or love for Pakistan.

---

[64] McGrath, *The Destruction of Pakistan's Democracy*, 65–68.

[65] See Communist and Communist Activities in Pakistan, 1949 FO 1110/210. Public Record Office, UK.

[66] Ibid.

Despite such pressures, Zaheer, working under semi-legal conditions and after the collapse of the party structure and loss of able cadres and members along with the constant harassment and arrests of party members, worked hard toward rebuilding the party by holding of cell meetings, sending out assignments to individuals and groups (while checking up on their completion), seeing to it that the work is performed according to time and schedule, creating opportunities for regular study groups and education and yet being cautious enough so that the leadership and other members are not exposed and arrested leading to a stoppage of the party's basic functioning. These were not the easiest of tasks where a new kind of individual trust had to be formed between him and those who had a longer history in Pakistan. It is obvious that in these circumstances he relied heavily on people whom he knew from his Bombay days, like Sibte Hasan and Ishfaque and those he had known earlier from his own political, personal or literary connections, people like Faiz Ahmed Faiz and Mian Iftikharuddin.

Further, with constant government surveillance, as Secretary General of the CPP, Zaheer remained underground throughout his tenure until his arrest in February–March of 1951 in connection with the Rawalpindi Conspiracy Case. In February–March of 1951, the Pakistan Government brought charges of sedition and of plotting a military coup against certain leaders of its own military[67] and members of the Central Committee of the CPP, Sajjad Zaheer and Mohammad Ata.[68] The poet and progressive intellectual Faiz Ahmed Faiz (Faiz was never a card carrying member of the Communist Party)

---

[67] The conspiracy was exposed by the government on the eve of the first post-independence provincial elections in Pakistan (Punjab). Liaquat Ali Khan, the Prime Minister, was touring Punjab and his party was facing a stiff challenge from newly formed parties, the Jinnah Muslim League of Nawab of Mamdot and the Azad Party of Mian Iftikharuddin. There are indications that the announcement of a threat to the country was used as a cynical ploy to consolidate votes by the Muslim League leadership in its own favour. See Dawn, 10 March 1951 and also see Inward Telegram to Commonwealth Relations Office from UK High Commissioner in Pakistan. FO-371-92866 (Public Records Office).

[68] Major General Akbar Khan, Chief of the General Staff of Pakistan Army, was deemed the leader of the coup attempt. His deputy in this alleged

was also accused of being a co-conspirator and was jailed along with the others.

Whether this was a real conspiracy or the Party was holding a tentative dialogue with some army officers is a question that still makes the rounds in intellectual circles. Following the announcement of the conspiracy, there were widespread arrests and blanket clampdown on the Communist Party's activities. The entire process crippled the movement and demoralised cadres. The discussions with the disaffected military leaders that became the basis of the Rawalpindi Conspiracy Case, howsoever tentative, did expose the political stance of CPI's leadership: a party position that may have thought of relying on the military to bring about social change from above. These discussions could themselves be interpreted as an elitist move by the CPP to short circuit a future popular revolution. This 'change from above' model was based on the CPP's analysis of Pakistan's economic development. It showed the CPP's leadership's understanding of 'Muslim masses', as being socially backward due to religious influence and susceptible to manipulation by Muslim League's politics. It may also be a sign of the non-rootedness of the CPP's immigrant (*mohajir*, Urdu speaking) leadership that could not completely link itself with the cultural politics of the masses and commit itself to the task of building a popular movement from below. Irrespective of the cause, the communist movement in Pakistan, nascent as it was, took years to recover from this suppression.[69] When the communists in

---

conspiracy was Brigadier M.A. Latif, who was a Brigade Commander at Quetta. Mrs. Nasim Akbar Khan, daughter of a prominent female Muslim League politician Begum Shahnawaz, was also accused of being a co-conspirator.

[69] Zaheer spent the next several years in jail and soon after his release in 1955 he went back to India. Tufail Abbas, who later became the secretary general of the party in the late 1950s, among other criticisms addressed the Rawalpindi Conspiracy Case as a process that showed haste on the part of the leadership (personal interview). He argued that people were in a hurry to bring about the revolution and could not wait for the Party to develop its roots among the masses. Whether this is a serious analysis or not, it does seem that the CPP leadership in the early 1950s had decided to keep all options for capturing state power open. Similar views were expressed by Eric Cyprian, member of the CPP's central committee at the time of the

East Bengal tried to regroup, they were again crushed and the entire party banned in 1954: a legal stricture that remained in force for almost four decades.

—

# References

Adhikari, G. M., 'Pakistan and Indian National Unity', *Labour Monthly*, March 1943, 29.

Alexeyev, A., 'The Political Situation in Pakistan', *New Republic* 47 (1951): 9–12.

Amjad, Ali, *Labour Legislation and Trade Unionism in India and Pakistan*, Karachi: OUP, 2001.

Ansari, Khizar Humayun, *The Emergence of Socialist Thought among North Indian Muslims (1917–1947)*, Lahore: Book Traders, 1990.

Anwer Ali, M., *The Communist Party of West Pakistan in Action*, Punjab: Criminal Investigation Department (CID), 1952.

Aslam, C. R., *Atish Biyan* (weekly), Volume 12(13), 22 May 2000.

Chaudari, Tridb, The Swing Back: A Critical Survey of the Devious Zig Zags of the CPI Political Line (1947–1950), Marxist Internet Archive. Chapter, Since Calcutta Thesis, 1950. http://www.marxists.org/archive/chaudhuri/1950/swing-back/ch02.htm, accessed 15 April 2011.

Dyakov, A, 'A New British Plan for India', *New Times*, Moscow, 13 June 1947.

Gilmartin, David, *Empire and Islam*, Berkeley: University of California Press, 1988.

Grande, Robert W., 'Communist and the Pakistan Movement in Punjab Province', unpublished manuscript, 1977.

Hasan, Sibte, *Mughani-e-Aatish Nafs*, edited by Syed Jaffar Ahmad, Karachi: Maktab Danyal, 2005.

Jalal, Ayesha, *The State of Martial Rule*, Cambridge: Cambridge University Press, 1990.

Joshi, P. C., *Congress and Communists*, Bombay: People's Publishing House, 1944.

---

'conspiracy', in his interview with Hasan Zaheer in 1995. See Zaheer, *The Rawalpindi Conspiracy Case 1951* (Specially see chapter 4). Also see Inward Telegram to Commonwealth Relations Office from UK High Commissioner in Pakistan. FO-371-92866 (Public Records Office).

Krishnan, N. K., 'People's War', Supplement 18 November 1945. Quoted in Leghari, Iqbal, 1979. The Socialist Movement in Pakistan: An Historical Survey, (1940–1974). Unpublished PhD Thesis, Laval University, Montreal.

Leghari, Iqbal, 'The Socialist Movement in Pakistan: An Historical Survey (1940–1974)', unpublished PhD Thesis, Laval University, Montreal, 1979.

Malik, Abdullah, ed., *Selected Speeches and Statements*, Mian Iftikharuddin, Lahore: Nigarishat, 1971.

Malik, Hafeez, 'The Marxist Literary Movement in India and Pakistan', *Journal of Asian Studies* 26, no. 4 (1967): 649–64.

McGrath, Allen, *The Destruction of Pakistan's Democracy*, Karachi: Oxford University Press, 1996. 'Might Advance of the National Liberation Movement in the Colonial and Dependent Colonies' in the Cominform weekly *For a Lasting Peace, For a People's Democracy*, 27 January 1950.

Overstreet, G. and M. Windmiller, *Communism in India*, Bombay: Perennial Press, 1960.

Palme Dutt, Rajani, *A New Chapter in Divide and Rule*, Bombay: Peoples Publishing House, 1946.

Pandey, Gyanendra, *Remembering Partition*, Cambridge: Cambridge University Press, 2001.

Talbot, Ian, *Pakistan: A Modern History*, London: Hurst and Company, 1998.

Zaheer, Hasan, *The Rawalpindi Conspiracy Case 1951*, Karachi: Oxford University Press, 1998.

Zaheer, Noor, *Mere Hisse Ki Roshnai*, Karachi: Sanjh Publishers, 2006.

Zaheer, Sajjad, *A Case for Congress-League Unity*, Bombay: People's Publishing House, 1944.

———, Paighamat (Messages), *Sawera* (Lahore) no. 7–8 (1949): 10–12.

## Newspapers

*Dawn*, 10 March 1951, 1.
*Pakistan Times*, 17 April 1948, 1.
*Pakistan Times*, 27 April 1948, 3.

## Archival Material

American Consul General to Dept. of State, Dacca Despatch no. 123, 22 May 1954, NND 842909890d.062.

Chief Event in Past History of Communist Party of Pakistan. Public Record Office, D0 35/2591. Communism and Communist Activities in Pakistan. 10 October 1949, Communism in West Punjab, Public Record Office, FO 1110/210.

Documents of the Communist Party of India. 1997. Letter of the New Central Committee of the CPI Volume VI, 105–141. Calcutta: National Book Agency. First issued, 1 June 1950.

For the Final Assault: Tasks of the Indian People in the Present Phase of Indian Revolution, 1946, Bombay: People's Publishing House. Reprinted in Documents of the Communist Party of India, Volume 5. Calcutta: National Book Agency.

Inward Telegram to Commonwealth Relations Office from UK High Commissioner in Pakistan 1951. Public Records Office. FO-371-92866.

Report on Pakistan. 1997. Review of the Second Congress of the Communist Party of India, 757–761. Documents of the Communist Party of India, Volume 5. Calcutta: National Book Agency.

Secretary Communist Party. 1947. *Zaghmi Punjab Ki Faryad* (Wounded Punjab's Plea). Lahore: Qaumi Dar-ul-Isha't. Extracts from Naya Zamana, 7 September 1947.

# ✖ 3

# Majlis-i-Ahrar-i-Islam: Religion, Socialism and Agitation in Action

*Tahir Kamran*

---

Radical history has often become synonymous with Left-wing movements and communist parties. However, in the South Asian context the infusion of religion with politics during the colonial era means that radical movements were often contradictory in terms of whether they were Left wing or right wing. The Majlis-i-Ahrar movement,[1] with its street-level agitation politics in the 1930s and the 1940s, and in particular, its key ideology of *Hakumat-i-Illahia* (rule through the dictates of Allah), is perhaps the best example of a radical movement that embodies multiple traditions. Indeed, even the name Ahrar, as the movement was usually referred to, is a plural form of the Arabic word *hur* or *har*, which means become to be free. The Ahrar movement has yet to find any space in the national discourse of Pakistan. From the very outset Pakistan's historiography was dominated by the official version of freedom, which excluded those movements and parties that had been pitched against the All-India Muslim League. The conspicuous absence of parties like Khudai Khidmatgar Movement in NWFP (presently Khyber Pakhtun Khawah), Jeeya Sindh in Sindh and the Awami League in East Bengal from the mainstream political discourse leaves a vacuum in the mainstream scholarship on Pakistan. The works of the two most prominent historians of Pakistan, Ishtiaq Husain Qureshi and Sheikh Muhammad Ikram, set the historiographical trend for the

---

[1] For details on the correct usage of the word 'Ahrar', see Steingass, *Arabic–English Dictionary*, 269.

later generation by reducing these movements to the margins.[2] Yet they all, in different ways, played extremely important roles in Indian Muslim politics of the late colonial era. The history of the future Pakistan areas cannot be completely understood without reference to their careers and legacies.

This chapter highlights a particular aspect of agitation that the Ahrar came to epitomise in the 1930s and the 1940s, which sets it apart from other studies, conducted so far. Samina Awan's book, *Political Islam in Colonial Punjab: Majlis-i-Ahrar, 1929–1949*[3] is the first in-depth study in English of the movement. The outline that Awan provides offers a foundation from which this chapter will consider the agitational mode of politics that the Ahrar deployed. Similarly, Awan has based her study mostly on archival sources, which obscures the points of view of the Ahrar ideologues. Hence, this chapter aims to unravel the ideology and methods of the Ahrar politics through original sources not used before, such as the writings of Chaudhary Afzal Haq, Janbaz Mirza, Shorish Kashmiri, Master Taj-ud-Din, and Mazhar Ali Azhar. All of them were the frontline leaders and ideologues of the Ahrar. They wrote extensively on the Ahrar; however, their writings have not been fully tapped in academic histories. In this chapter, an attempt has been made to draw on these vernacular sources.

## Origins and Ideology

All the individuals who later constituted the Ahrar were exponents of the Khilafat Movement in the Punjab during the 1920s. The history of the Khilafat movement, its components and the reasons why the movement fizzled out in 1924 have been well documented by South Asian historians.[4] Whilst the Ulema-i-Deoband was in the vanguard

---

[2] Ishtiaq Hussain Qureshi calls 'Ahrars' a minor and insignificant non-League group like the Momins, the Shia Conference and the Jamiat Ulama-i-Hind in one of his important books. For full reference, see Qureshi, *The Struggle for Pakistan*, 241. Similarly Ikram in *Modern Muslim India and the Birth of Pakistan* does not mention Ahrar at all. For full reference see Ikram, *Modern Muslim India 1858–1951*, 202–38.

[3] Awan, *Political Islam in Colonial Punjab*.

[4] See for details Minault, *The Khilafat Movement* and Qureshi, *Pan-Islam in British Indian Politics*.

of the Khilafat movement, they were not the only people striving for its sustenance. The Modernist Muslim section, spearheaded by Muhammad Ali and Shaukat Ali, mostly referred to as the Ali brothers, also had its representation in the movement. Both groups worked superficially well together in the early stages of the struggle. However, a schism soon appeared. It was in this context that Majlis-i-Ahrari Islam came into existence. As Shorish Kashmiri states:

> Undoubtedly Ahrars were the outcome of the Khilafat Movement, the ideas of *Al Hilal* and the pen of the *Zamindar* put together. It was a combination of an anti-British outlook, love for Islam, patriotism, hatred of capitalism, enmity with superstition, love for sacrifice ... ambition to bring about revolution and enthusiasm for conducting *jihad*.[5]

This heady combination of religion and politics, communism and patriotism means that the Ahrar would ultimately agitate in multiple political arenas. For example, because of its Khilafatist background the Ahrar was close to the Indian National Congress, although it differed from it on such issues as separate electorates. Syed Ata Ullah Shah Bokhari, one of the founders of the Ahrar, is quoted in a few Ahrari texts as saying that Abul Kalam Azad asked him to set up Majlis-i-Ahrar the organisation, although Azad himself did not relinquish his position as a top Muslim leader of Congress to join the organisation. To solve this conundrum, a thorough appraisal of the political scenario in the 1920s is required: both at the national level and in the Punjab.

Before Kemal Attaturk's abolition of the office of caliph, the Khilafat Movement had been dealt a series of blows. These included Gandhi's calling off of civil disobedience after the Chauri Chaura incident in 1922 and the movement's own internal crisis. The embezzlement to the tune of ₹1.6 million in the Khilafat fund resulted in the erosion of trust that millions of Muslims had reposed in the leadership. Muhammad Ali Jauhar and Shaukat Ali (Ali brothers) also took some of the blame. The Enquiry Committee set up for investigating the matter held them equally responsible for the mismanagement of the fund. It was headed by Maulana Abdul Qadir Qasuri and comprised all Punjabi members branded as loyalist to

---

[5] Kashmiri, *Bou-e-Gul, Nala-e-Dil, Dood-e-Charach-e-Mahfil*, 310.

Abul Kalam Azad. Maulana Muhammad Ali harboured suspicion and ill will towards the Committee, and ensured that the Central Khilafat Committee ostracised it. The Committee itself split into two factions: namely the Muslim Nationalist Party under the leadership of Muhammad Alam, which could not keep its distinct character for long and subsequently submerged into Congress, and the Majlis-i-Ahrar-i-Islam. Zafar Ali Khan (editor of *The Zamindar* newspaper), Maulana Daud Ghaznavi, Syed Ata ullah Bokhari, Chaudhri Afzal Haq, Maulana Mazhar Ali Azhar, Khawja Abdul Rehman Ghazi Sheikh Hassam ud Din and Maulana Habibur Rehman Ludhianvi constituted the core leadership of the Ahrar. Afzal Haq writes as follows regarding the background to the Ahrar movement's emergence:

> Punjab Khilafat Committee was the soul of the Central Body, unintentionally and unconsciously it had two distinct factions in itself. Khilafat Punjab had an elite faction and a downtrodden faction. The elite, like the son of a prostitute and the horse of a trader, had been sluggish and enjoyed the easy life. All the laborious work was the fate of the downtrodden faction. The elite were conscience of their distinctness as a class whereas the downtrodden had no such realization, they thought of themselves as a part of the totality . ... When Majlis i Khilafat Punjab severed its link with Central body, the elite formed its organization by the name of Muslim Nationalist Party and the downtrodden constituted Majlis i Ahrar.[6]

This explicit division of the movement along class lines perhaps reveals why the author Afzal Haq Razi Wasti was widely known as Mufakir-i-Ahrar or 'the brain of Ahrar Party'. Haq undoubtedly created a stir amongst the Muslim *ulema* by writing a pamphlet *Islam mein Umara Ka Wajud Nahin* (The rich have no existence in Islam). Iftikhar Malik therefore contends that the Ahrar imbibed the 'impact of the October Revolution in Russia (1917) and the communist ideas that it had disseminated'. In 1931, addressing the annual meeting of the Ahrar, Sahibzada Faizul Hassan enunciated that socialism was not at all different from the Islamic concept of *musawat* (equality):

> The unjust distribution of production is the real root-cause of all maladies and social injustice. To control it properly will be the actual

---

[6] Haq, *Tareekh-e-Ahrar*, 70.

cure of a big problem faced by human beings. Such control can be called *musawat*, too. Socialism is an ideology brought out after a thorough research, and to me, is better than capitalism, fascism and other contemporary ideologies.[7]

However, it would be a mistake to perceive the Ahrar as solely a Left-wing party influenced by communist ideology. Although many of its members came from poor backgrounds, they displayed religious zeal and conviction. Hamza Alvi regards the humble origins of many of its leaders as a source of strength. 'Its main assets were the devotion and zeal of its members and the eloquence of its leaders. Some of them could cast spell bound influence upon their audience. In spite of a lack of material resources, the Ahrars, within a short period, became one of the strongest political parties in the Punjab.'[8]

The Ahrar had the following aims: to work for complete Indian freedom through peaceful means; to provide political guidance to the Muslims; to strive for ensuring betterment of the Muslims in the fields of religion, education, economic and social plight; to promote indigenously manufactured products; to organise peasants and workers on the economic principles and to set up voluntary organisations by the name of *Jayush i Ahrarul Islam* throughout India. The working Committee of Ahrar approved its party's red-colour flag with a white crescent and a star in the middle. The Ahrar leaders decided on a red-coloured uniform for the Ahrar volunteers who regularly drilled with a band and a drum and carried hatchets.[9] The decision to wear red was made in the memory of those *Khudai Khidmatgars* who died in an armed clash with the British in *Qisa Khawani Bazar,* Peshawar on 23 April 1930.[10] During the early days, Ahrar volunteers were widely known as *surkhposh* (people in red outfit) but subsequently that appellation became specific to the *Khudai Khidmatgars*. All of these symbols nonetheless were representative of the Ahrar leadership's aim to imbibe influences not only from Islam but also from socialism. Samina Awan provides a succinct account of the

---

[7] Ibid., 9; also see Malik, *Sikandar Hayat Khan*, 55.
[8] An interview with Hamza Alvi at Lahore in 2004.
[9] Mirza, *Karwan-e-Ahrar*, Vol. IV, 150, quoted in Javed Haider Syed, 'Pakistan Resolution and Majlis-e-Ahrar', 402.
[10] For details, see Taqi-ud-Din, *Pakistan ki Siyasi Jamatain*, 105.

ideological mix underpinning the Ahrar's ideology. The movement not only aimed at eradicating the 'darkness of imperialism and feudalism' but also 'stood for equal distribution of wealth; eradication of untouchability; respect for every religion; and freedom to live according to the Sharia'.[11]

Majlis-i-Ahrar-i-Islam-i-Hind expounded the concept of *Hakumat I Illayia* in, its annual meeting held at Sahranpur on 26 April 1943. *Hakumat i Illayia*[12] had its conceptual basis in unequivocal opposition to the British Raj, as the very first clause of the resolution put forward at Saharanpur explicitly suggests: 'we cannot support any political move or settlement for which one has to go to London obsequiously and cringingly'.[13] *Hakumat I Illayia* called for more powers to be devolved to the provinces and considered the schemes like *Akhand Bharat* (United India), and the establishment of Pakistan or Independent Punjab as lethal for communal harmony. The organisation laid optimum stress on inter-communal peace and so the Ahrar would not oppose any effort aimed at forging an alliance between Congress and Muslim League but the Ahrar itself would not have any alliance with any political group. Most significant was the Ahrar's avowed stand against any machination professing division on the basis of geographical, ethnic or linguistic considerations as, to them, this was not a religious obligation of the Muslims.

The concept of *Hakumat i Illayia* suggests a complete disparity between the Ahrar's ideals and those of the Muslim League. Nevertheless, the two organisations briefly allied in 1936.[14] This alliance reflected Jinnah's marginalisation in the Punjab politics on the eve of the Provincial elections, and the Ahrar's declining popularity in the wake of the Shahid Gunj affair (as explained later in this chapter) rather than any coming together of ideologies. The alliance could not survive because of the inherent contradictions between the separatist stand of Muslim League and Ahrar's aversion for any division based on linguistic or ethnic differentiation. Therefore, the issue of fees for party tickets, which drove a wedge between the components of the

---

[11] Awan, *Political Islam in Colonial Punjab*, 15.

[12] See Hassan, *Legacy of Divided Nation*, 66; also see Kashmiri, *Bou-e-Gul, Nala-e-Dil*, 305–21; and Afzal, *Political Parties in Pakistan*, 27.

[13] For a brief reference, see Haq, *Tareekh-e-Ahrar*, 61.

[14] Afzal, *Political Parties in Pakistan*, 27.

alliance, took nobody by surprise. When the Muslim League Central Committee at once raised the fee for the party ticket from ₹50 to ₹500, the Ahrar registered its discordant note and the 'marriage of convenience' was over.[15] Despite falling out in the Khilafat committee, in terms of religious ideology the Ahrar were clearly inspired by Dar-ul-Ulum Deoband (established in 1867 near Sahranpur). The Deobandi ulema professed a puritanical version of Islam that called for strict adherence to the *sharia* and attacked the intercessory activities of the Sufi shrines. This was most apparent in the Ahrar's opposition to the Ahmadis. *Khatam-i-Nabuwat* or finality of the prophet-hood[16] assumed extraordinary significance ever since the *Ahmaddya*[17] sect emerged in the late 1890s. The Ahmadis refuted the very idea of the last prophet, considered as one of the five fundamentals of Islam. Ahrar leaders, through the eloquence of such speakers as Ataullah Shah Bokhari, whipped up so much of an enthusiasm for *Khatam-i-Nabuwat* that it became one cornerstone of its agitational politics. Indeed, the Ahrar became increasingly sectarian in their various stances on religion and perhaps their ideological legacy will be that of providing inspiration to the sectarian movements in contemporary Pakistan. However, in

---

[15] Conversely, Ashique Hussain Batalvi states in his celebrated book *Iqbal Key Akhree Do Saal* that Ahrar had an impression that the Nawabs of various Muslim princely states and Muslim traders and Seths (businessmen) from Bombay had contributed generously in the League fund, specifically for the elections. Its leadership, therefore, was expectantly looking towards the League to bear the election expenses of the Ahrari candidates. Chaudhri Afzal Haq and Maulana Habibur Rehman were hoping that the exorbitant sum to the tune of at least ₹100,000 would be set aside for the election expenses exclusively for Ahrar candidates. When the reality dawned on them (that the League had no lavish funds), they decided to part ways and resigned from the Muslim League Parliamentary Board. For details, see Tajud Din Ludhyanvi, *Majlis-e-Ahraraur Tariekhi Tahrief ki Yalghar*, 5–13; and Batalvi, *Iqbal key Akhri Doo Saal*, 321.

[16] According to the concept of *Khatami Nabuwwat*, 'Prophethood (nabuwwat) ceased with the death of the Holy Prophet and that no new prophet (nabi) shall appear hereafter is said to be deducible from the following verses of the Quran: Sura XXX111, verse 40, Sura III, verse 81, Sura V, verse 4'. See for reference, *Report of the Court of Inquiry*, 185.

[17] For detail, see Ali, *The Ahmadiyyah Movement*. Also see Friedmann, *Prophecy Continuous*.

the context of the late colonial Punjab their activities were much less easy to confine solely within the religious domain.

## The Ahrar's Relations with Congress

If relations with the Muslim League were strained then things were not much better with the Congress. While describing the election of the All India Congress Committee at Karachi in 1931, Nehru says:

> Some Muslim members of the A.I.C.C. objected to this election, in particular to one (Muslim) name in it. Perhaps they also felt slighted because no one of their group had been chosen. In an all-India committee of fifteen it was manifestly impossible to have all interests represented, and the real dispute, about which we knew nothing, was an entirely personal and local one in the Punjab. The result was that the protestant group gradually drifted away from the Congress in the Punjab, and joined others in an 'Ahrar Party' or 'Majlis-e-Ahrar'.[18]

That observation evoked an incisive response from Afzal Haq. Nehru's calling the Ahrar, the representative of the lower middle class, in Afzal Haq's opinion, amounted to an attitude of insolence perpetrated by a rich bourgeoisie socialist leader. He narrated the details of the 'election' more exhaustively and differently too. In fact, Dr Muhammad Alam was nominated to the All India Congress Committee at the recommendation of Abul Kalam Azad and Abdul Qadir Qasuri. That nomination caused a stir among the people gathered in the *pandal* (a place of public meeting) and some voices of dissent in particular were raised from amongst the members of the Working Committee. However, Nehru was not all that wrong in his observation. The nomination of Muhammad Alam at the AICC was one of the reasons that alienated the members of the erstwhile Punjab Khilafat Committee from the All India Congress Committee. The Ahrar had been constituted in 1929, two years earlier than the Karachi session of AICC, and its leadership had till this point enjoyed close ties with the Congress. When Gandhi gave a call for Civil Disobedience, the Ahrar leadership had participated with full enthusiasm and many, including Afzal Haq, were incarcerated. Subsequently, after the conclusion of the Gandhi-Irwin Pact in 1931,

---

[18] Nehru, *Jawaharlal Nehru: An Autobiography*, 269.

Ahraris along with all other political prisoners were released. The final break with All India Congress eventually came about in 1931. A renowned Ahrari, Abu Yusuf Qasimi, while drawing on Afzal Haq's narrative 'Tarikh i Ahrar' sheds light on the break-up. The foremost reason for the 'parting of the ways' between Congress and the Ahrar was the issue of separate electorates and the misgivings they created on all sides. The Punjab Khilafat Committee, right from the very beginning, was in favour of separate electorates, a weak centre with a federal form of government ensuring complete autonomy to the provinces. When Nehru's Report proposed adult franchise in its recommendation for the Indian Constitution, the Punjab Khilafat Committee found its thrust quite consistent with the interests of Punjab Muslims. Therefore, it acceded to the joint electorate.[19] However, the Nehru Report soon ran into trouble and protests on the question of other minorities and could not muster enough overall support. Even Gandhi did not approve of it, particularly on the question of the representation of Sikhs. As J.S. Grewal explains:

> The report prepared by the committee (Nehru Committee) recommended separate electorates for Muslims in provinces other than Punjab and Bengal. When the report was taken up in the All Parties meeting at Lucknow in August, the Sikh delegates raised the issue regarding their position in the Punjab. Some of them demanded that if separate electorates or weightage was to be maintained for minorities in other provinces then a similar provision should be made for the Sikhs. Most of the Sikh leaders dreaded the prospect of universal suffrage without reservation of seats for the Sikhs as a minority.[20]

Because of these reservations, the Sikh leadership (The Central Sikh League in particular) rejected the Nehru Report and decided to boycott the Lahore Session of Congress. Gandhi, Moti Lal Nehru and M. A. Ansari met Master Tara Singh and Kharak Singh and persuaded them to attend the Session with the promise of safeguards for minority communities. The Nehru Report was also suspiciously viewed by Punjabi Hindus. If adopted, the provision of separate electorates would definitely have a negative bearing on their political status in the Punjab, where Muslims were in a clear majority.

---

[19] Ibid., 159–60.
[20] Grewal, *The Sikhs of the Punjab*, 168.

On the Muslim side, Afzal Haq and Jan Baz Mirza had altogether different views vis-à-vis those expressed by the Sikhs and Hindus. In the end, it was clear that though Punjabi Hindus and Sikhs had endorsed the Nehru Report, both communities held serious reservations about the 'Joint Electorate' as proposed by the Nehru Committee. It is likely that the commotion engendered by the Nehru Report among the minority communities, particularly the Sikhs, convinced the Congress high command to dump the Nehru Report at its All India session held in Lahore on 28 December 1929.[21] While discarding the Nehru Report, the Congress leadership did not even bother to consult those individuals who had lent unequivocal support to it, that too at the behest of Congress itself.

Such treatment gave rise to grief and dismay in the ranks of the Punjab Khilafat Committee, who ultimately decided to chart their own course of action. When the participants of All India Congress Committee were disposing off the copies of the Nehru Report in one corner of the same *pandal,* the leaders of the defunct Punjab Khilafat Committee were holding a meeting to form a new party, Majlis-i-Ahrar-i-Islam, on 29 December 1929 in Lahore.[22]

Another factor leading to the alienation of these people from Congress was the election of the Amritsar Congress Committee. Dr Saif-ud Din Kitchlew and Ghazi Abdul Rehman were the two contestants and Ata-ullah Shah Bokhari was the polling officer. Those elections were held based on joint electorates. Dr Kitchlew won the elections, much to the chagrin of Afzal Haq and Ata-ullah Shah Bokhari. Afzal Haq narrates the situation, prevailing on the eve of that election and also the estimate of the two candidates:

> Dr. Saifud Din was undoubtedly a selfless but articulate person. He had established his writ among Hindus and Sikhs more than Muslims. Therefore, he was not quite well known in the circle of Muslims. Since the zeal about freedom was very pronounced in him, that prevented him from becoming unpopular among the Muslims also. Ghazi Abdul Rehman on the other hand enjoyed an enviable reputation that he earned through serving the interests of the local Muslims. He was an eloquent speaker and well versed in the art of luring people to his side. Kitchlow won the contest because Hindu capitalists made

---

[21] Haq, *Tareekh-e-Ahrar,* 86.
[22] Taqi-ud-Din, *Pakistan ki Siyasi Jamatain,* 176.

substantial investment for Kitchlow, which proved to be a decisive factor in those elections. Ghazi did not have such clout, so he lost. After seeing the effect of the joint electorate in practice, Ata-ullah Shah Bokhari prepared a resolution in favour of separate electorate. Ghazi also supported the move.[23]

That resolution worked as a catalyst in the formation of Majlis-i-Ahrar as a separate political organisation. Therefore, in July 1931, the Ahrar Conference was convened in the Habibia Hall of Islamia College Lahore. It was presided over by Maulana Habibur Rehman Ludhianvi and Maulana Daud Ghaznavi was its secretary. Addressing the audience, Maulana Habibur Rehman declared: 'I want to tell all the nations of Hindustan in clear words that the Ahrars do not want to do any injustice to any other nation. However they are not prepared to live as a scheduled caste either. The Muslims are equally entitled to the share in the Indian affairs.'[24] The assertion of Maulana Habibur Rehman that Muslims must not be deemed 'scheduled caste' provides a context to Afzal Haq's reference recurrently made in both of his representative works, namely *Tarikh-I-Ahrar* and *Meira Afsana* to the *chootchaat* (untouchability) practiced by the Congress Hindus against Muslims.[25] That factor also provided sufficient basis for the Ahrar leaders to chart their own course. The Conference passed a unanimous resolution in favour of separate electorates for Indian Muslims.

The Ahrar Conference at Lahore drew a lot of criticism from the pro-Congress section of the press. Nevertheless, the umbilical cord providing a link between Congress and Ahrar remained intact, largely because of its leadership's reverence for Abul Kalam Azad and Gandhi.

## The Ahrar Movement in the Punjab

Although the Ahrar aspired to all-India support, its greatest influence was in the Punjab. It played an important role in the Muslim politics of the province during the 1930s. This is not always acknowledged

---

[23] Qasmi, *Mufaker-e-Ahrar*, 160–61.

[24] Malik, *Sikandar Hayat Khan*, 55.

[25] Haq, *Mera Afsana*. Also see Qasmi, *Mufaker-e-Ahrar*, 160–61.

by Pakistani scholars because of its chequered relationship with the Muslim League. Immediately after the Lahore Conference, where it assumed the formal status of a political party, Majlis-i-Ahrar plunged into political work. Until the setback of the Shahid Gunj affair in 1935, it posed the only major challenge to the Unionists in urban Muslim politics.[26] The Unionist Party was an agriculturalist party.[27] All the major landlords and tribal *Sardars* (chieftains) had gathered under its banner. The Ahrar had to contend not only with fortified landed interests but also with Mian Fazl-i-Husain's (a Unionist leader) tenacity in the realm of politics. Interestingly, this leading exponent of Muslim Punjabi interests initially revered Chaudhri Afzal Haq because of the rectitude and forthrightness, which he had demonstrated in the Punjab Legislative Council. Afzal Haq too held Fazl-i-Hussain in high esteem. In *Tarikh-i-Ahrar*, Haq rates him as the best political figure among the Muslims. Even M.A. Jinnah was not considered a match for Hussain's sagacity and ingenuity in the political arena.[28] This mutual respect and reverence turned into avowed hostility when Fazl-i-Hussain recommended Sir Zafarullah Khan, an *Ahmadi* leader from the Punjab, for a vacant slot in the Viceroy's Executive Council. The Ahrar party's uncompromising stand on the issue of *Khatam i Nabuwat* meant that any association with the *Ahmadiya* sect was considered out of bounds. Following the selection of the Ahmadi leader, Hussain, became a special target for Ahrar wrath. Deploying the tactics of religion did not however disturb the Unionists' rural powerbase.[29] Local power relations connecting shrines and their incumbents, the *Sajjada Nashins*, to a form of Sufi Islam infused an added vigour through thousands of their devotees to the already impregnable Unionist Party. They successfully countered the religious appeal of the Ahrar, who had among their leaders, religious scholars from all the sects of the Islamic faith.[30]

---

[26] Azhar, *Masala-e-Shaheed Gunj*, 38.

[27] See for details on Unionist Party, Talbot, *Punjab and the Raj*.

[28] Haq, *Tareekh-e-Ahrar*, 209.

[29] For details, see Husain, *Fazal-i-Husain: A Political Biography*, 226–66. Also see Batalvi, *Iqbal key Akhari Do Saal*, 320.

[30] The Ahrar leader included representatives of other sects, like Dawud Ghaznawi from the Ahl-e-Hadith and Maulana Mazhar Ali Azhar, who were of *Shii* descent, a cooperation that was based less on common doctrinal

It was the other dimension of the Ahrar that had more success in the rural areas, that of socialism. Majlis-i-Ahrar's radical economic programme carried more impact because of agricultural depression in the Punjab. Nevertheless, similar to the Kisan Sabhas, the Ahrar found that the Unionists were still able to deflect rising discontent by blaming the harsh conditions on the depredations of the *bania* (money lending) class. Even so, the Ahrar success in a by-election to the Central Assembly in 1934 revealed that the Punjab's depressed conditions had opened up at least some chinks in the Unionists' armour. Sir Fazl-i-Hussain selected Khan Bahadur Rahim Baksh as the Unionist candidate for a constituency comprising four districts, namely Lahore, Amritsar, Ferozepur, and Gurdaspur. Ahrar fielded Khalid Latif Gabba (he was the son of Lala Harkishen Lal, a famous Punjabi entrepreneur; he embraced Islam just to renounce it afterwards) as their candidate. As the time for the election drew near, the propaganda for an Ahrar candidate gathered momentum, rightly causing panic to the Unionists as the Ahrar won the seat. This was at a time when the party was at the peak of its popularity, the basis of which came from their activities in Kapurthala and Kashmir.

## The Kashmir Agitation

The Ahrar's agitation for the rights of the Muslims of Kashmir who were suffering under the oppressive rule of Maharaja Hari Singh is not as fully acknowledged in contemporary Pakistani historiography as they deserve to be. Indeed, their contribution is surprisingly omitted in the otherwise excellent studies by Victoria Schofield and Alastair Lamb into the Kashmir issue.[31] The 1931 agitation was important also because it raised the Ahrar party's popularity in urban Punjab to an unprecedented degree.[32] This was due to the presence of large Kashmiri Muslim communities in such cities as Amritsar, Lahore and Sialkot. In combination with the Ahrar's efforts in Kapurthala, a Muslim majority Punjabi state with a Hindu leader

---

ground than on shared allegiance to the Congress. For details, see Reetz, *Islam in the Public Sphere*, 78.

[31] For the details of Glancy Commission, see Mirza, *Karwan-e-Ahrar*, Vol. I, 314–15; and Haq, *Tareekh-i-Ahrar*, 125–26.

[32] For details, see Ludhyanvi, *Ahrar Aur Tehrik-e-Kashmir 1932*.

(as explained later in this chapter), this agitation was to provide electoral dividends in the assembly elections of 1934. In some senses the mode of mobilisation in Kashmir was very similar to the model subsequently followed in Kapurthala: a series of incidents that took a communal tinge were exploited for political mileage by the Ahrar.

The Kashmir case first. Dogra rule in Kashmir (1847–1948) was notorious for its 'autocratically wayward methods of administration' and its religious intolerance. Killing a cow was a cognisable offence punishable with seven years of rigorous imprisonment. A special tax was levied on the slaughter of goats and sheep, even on *Eid*. A Hindu in case of embracing Islam had to forfeit all his inherited property. The State had usurped many Muslim places of worship and pilgrimage, which the Glancy Commission subsequently restored to the Muslims in 1931. Such discrimination reflected quite conspicuously on the distribution of economic resources, especially those at the behest of the state. Suddans of Poonch and the Sandans from Mirpur were the only people among the Muslims recruited into the army but in the subaltern positions. They were culturally different from the Kashmiris of the valley and therefore the Maharaja believed he could use them to quell any uprising stirred by the valley people.[33]

Punjabi Muslim newspapers in the 1920s and the early 1930s consistently highlighted the miserable plight of the Kashmiri Muslims. The daily *Inqalab* and its editor Abdul Majid Salik were particularly critical on the discriminatory policies of Maharaja Hari Singh towards the Muslims. Its circulation in the state of Kashmir was accordingly disallowed.[34] A series of incidents were then highlighted by the Ahrar indicating discrimination against the Muslim population.[35] The arrest of Abdul Qadeer, from Amroha District Muradabad who was in Srinagar as a guide to a few English travellers, provided the catalyst for violence, when he urged Muslims to launch an active struggle against the Maharaja's rule. The State authorities promptly arrested him. When his trial began in the Sessions Court of Srinagar on 6 July 1931, Muslims assembled there in such a huge number that proceedings were shifted to the securer environment of Srinagar Central Jail. When the trial commenced at

---

[33] Schofield, *Kashmir in the Crossfire*, 100.

[34] Salik, *Sar Gazasht*, 264.

[35] For the general details, see Mirza, *Karwan-e-Ahrar*, Vol. I, 236–37.

the newer venue, people thronged again and the police ruthlessly baton-charged them. The violence escalated and the police opened firing, thus killing 22 demonstrators. Therefore, 13 July 1931 came to be known as 'Martyrs Day'.[36]

The killings immediately triggered clashes between Muslim demonstrators and the state police throughout Jammu and Kashmir. The violence took a communal turn when a procession of demonstrators forced a Punjabi Hindu shopkeeper to close his shop in protest. When he refused the protestors ransacked his and other Hindu-owned shops. 'In terms of casualties and damage to property', concludes Ian Copland, 'it was possibly the most serious communal outbreak in India between the Moplah rebellion of 1921 and the Calcutta riots of 1946'.[37] Consequently the law enforcement agencies of the state arrested more than 300 Muslims, including Chaudhri Ghulam Abbass and Shiekh Abdullah. Sporadic processions, strikes and riots kept the tension soaring in Kashmir.

During the last week of July, leading Muslims assembled at Nawab Sir Zulfiqar Ali's residence at Simla and formed the All India Kashmir Committee.[38] The head of the Ahmadiya community, Mirza Bashir Ahmed, was the Kashmir Committee's President and Sir Muhammad Iqbal, Sir Zulfiqar Ali, Khawja Hassan Nizami, Syed Mohsin Shah, Khan Bahadur Sheikh Rahim Baksh, Maulana Ismael Ghaznavi, Abdul Rahim Dard (an Ahmadi and secretary of the committee), Maulana Nurul Haq (owner of the English daily '*Outlook*') and Syed Habib Shah (owner of the daily '*Siasat*') were its members. The Committee pledged to redress the grievances of Kashmiri Muslims through peaceful and constitutional means. Therefore, it called for the appointment of an impartial Commission of Enquiry to determine the causes leading to the crisis. It also proposed to observe 14 August as a special Kashmir Day in the memory of the martyrs of 13 July 1931.[39] Bashir ud Din Mehmud also had some important local contacts in Srinagar — notably Jamal-ud-Din, the Director of Public Instruction, and Sheikh Abdullah, the emerging Kashmiri leader.[40] More so Qadian was made headquarters of 'the freedom

---

[36] Ibid.
[37] Copland, 'Islam and Political Mobilization in Kashmir', 231.
[38] Mirza, *Karwan-e-Ahrar*, Vol. I, 181.
[39] Ibid.
[40] Copland, 'Islam and Political Mobilization in Kashmir, 1931–34', 231.

movement' for Kashmiri Muslims. The prominence of the Ahmadiyas was too much for the Ahrars, who were both ideologically opposed to the Ahmadis but also aware of the political mileage that the new group could take from them. Afzal Haq, Ata-ullah Shah Bokhari and Mazhar Ali Azhar excoriated the Ahmadis and the ruler of Kashmir alike. They evoked considerable response from the masses in support of their stand.[41]

The Ahrar leadership became proactive and requested the Government of the Kashmir for an inquiry committee to be permitted into the valley. After getting no response, it forced its entry into the Kashmir. On their way Ata-ullah Shah Bokhari, Afzal Haq and Mazhar Ali Azhar addressed huge rallies at Gujranwala and Sialkot, which caused a lot of concern for the state government. Despite this, however, on the advice of Prime Minister Hari Kishan Kaul,[42] they received free passage, whereupon they put forward their demand for the establishment of a responsible government in the state. They also unsuccessfully attempted to woo Sheikh Abdullah, the leader of the National Conference.

Failing on all these fronts, they organised *Jatha*s (bands of Ahrar volunteers) with the aim to enter Kashmir from Sialkot on 6 October 1931 onwards. The *Jatha*s were detained by the *Darbari* police (those loyal to the Maharaja). Nevertheless 'the stream of volunteers kept flowing — 2376 had crossed the border by the beginning of November'.[43] Soon afterwards, batches of 21 Ahrar volunteers sneaked into Kashmir. From the Punjab alone, according to one estimate, 45,000 volunteers entered and courted arrest. Such a massive invasion by Ahrar volunteers paralysed the state machinery.

David Gilmartin notes that the agitation expanded so rapidly that 'the sheer number of those arrested embarrassed the jail department and forced the opening of special camp jails'.[44] The Maharaja found

---

[41] Ahmed, *From Martial Law to Martial Law*, 129.

[42] Raja Hari Kishen Kaul was the prime minister of Kashmir. Previously he was civil servant from Punjab and had replaced G.E.C. Wakefield as prime minister. The Government of India characterised him as 'a noted intriguer' and urged his replacement by another British officer. In February 1932, Lieutenant Colonel E.J.D. Colvin was appointed prime minister by Maharaja of Kashmir. See Huttenback, *Kashmir and the British Raj*, 140–42.

[43] Copland, 'Islam and Political Mobilization in Kashmir, 1931–34', 234.

[44] Gilmarten, *Empire and Islam*, 47.

it expedient to replace Hari Kishan Kaul with a new Prime Minister, Colonel E.J.D. Colvin, who was approved by the Indian Political Department and remained in office until 1936.[45] Hari Singh, in order to lower the political temperature, also constituted an Enquiry Commission into the 13 July episode headed by a senior officer in the Political Department of India, Sir Bertrand Glancy. Prem Nath Bazaz and Ghulam Abbass were amongst the co-members of the Commission. This step did not go far enough to appease the Ahrar, but owed much to their agitation.

The agitation in Kashmir proved to be a stepping-stone in the Ahrar's political ascent in Punjab. The Kashmir movement was closely mirrored in the subsequent Ahrar action in Kapurthala and this level of influence in local politics in these two states was rewarded with a foothold in legislative politics. By 11 February 1934, the Ahrar had three representatives in the Punjab Legislative Council, namely Chaudhri Afzal Haq from Hoshiarpur, Chaudhri Abdul Rehman from Jullundur and Maulana Mazhar Ali Azhar from Lahore.[46] Although this was only a small beginning and revealed the limit of their influence to the urban middle class, the Ahrar were emerging as a serious rival to the Muslim League in appealing to this section of the Punjabi Muslim society.

### The Kapurthala Agitation

Along with Kashmir, the Ahrar were involved in a powerful agitation in the Sikh princely state of Kapurthala.[47] It was situated west of the River Beas and although it had a Sikh ruler, Maharaja Jagjeet, 57 per cent of the population was Muslim. The vast majority of the Muslims were poor peasants. Sixty per cent of the state income accrued through the taxes they paid, but the state expended a meagre sum of ₹8440 on poor Muslims as stipends and charity whereas ₹68,338 was allocated for the welfare of non-Muslims.[48] The agitation in Kashmir stirred the Muslim Rajputs who resided in the Begowal area of Kapurthala who suffered exploitation at the

---

[45] For details, see Mirza, *Karwan-e-Ahrar*, Vol. I, 255–79.

[46] Ibid., 411–12.

[47] For details, see Mirza, *Karwan-e-Ahrar*, Vol. I, 324–29.

[48] Haq, *Tareekh-e-Ahrar*, 165.

hands of Hindu moneylenders.[49] Since the Land Alienation Act (1900) was not in place in the princely states of the Punjab, moneylenders operated freely at the expense of peasants. Following a Muslim rally in Begowal, a boycott of Hindu shopkeepers was enacted. Hindu moneylenders and shopkeepers vociferously condemned this action and announced a two-day-long strike. Consequently, Muslims seized the opportunity by setting up their own shops in Begowal and Bholeth areas. This development exasperated the Hindu shopkeepers who were moneylenders as well as retailers. They refused to advance further loans to Muslim peasants and pressed them for the immediate return of the money.

One of the first individuals to respond to the emerging crisis in Begowal was Chaudhri Abdul Aziz, Vice President of the Majlis-i-Ahrar, who voiced his concern over the crisis that the Muslim peasantry had been plunged into; he formed an umbrella Zamindara League organisation early in 1931. It gained momentum when it was joined by Ahrar volunteers, who, following their release by the Kashmir Government in February–March 1932, crossed over to Kapurthala. As in Kashmir, they fell foul of the State authorities. Abdul Aziz of Begowal was arrested and sentenced to five years of rigorous imprisonment for inciting trouble and disrupting peace. Despite these harsh measures, the Ahrar continued lending unequivocal support to the peasants.

In June 1932, the Muslims of Bholeth submitted a list of demands calling for the implementation of all those reforms that had already been carried out in other parts of India. Among their demands was the call for the introduction of the Punjab Land Alienation Act, the reduction in land revenue and the security of the non-transferable land of labourers and artisans against any act of forfeiting or confiscation.[50] The Maharaja, after sensing the gravity of the situation, constituted a committee headed by the magistrate of that particular area. It made little progress, with the result that communal tensions intensified. The Prime Minister of Kapurthala State, Sir Abdul Hameed, next invited the representatives of both the peasants and the commercial castes for parleys. The agriculturists mistrusted Hameed, who they thought was in league with the Hindu moneyed classes. As

---

[49] Qasmi, *Mufaker-e-Ahrar*, 174–75; and Haq, *Tareekh-e-Ahrar*, 142–46.
[50] Qasmi, *Mufaker-e-Ahrar*, 187–90.

the Secretary General of Ahrar, Dasoha, District Hoshiarpur stated in the *Daily Zamindar*:

> The peasantry and labourers of this Tehsil (Bholeth) are passing through a very critical phase. The Northern part of the Tehsil which is largely inhabited by the Muslims has fallen prey to the atrocities of the Police and Civil officers, who have made the lives of these poor fellows so miserable, that many of them are ready to migrate from the area.[51]

Disquiet caused by the upsurge among the ranks of Begowal Muslim peasantry remained unabated in the southern belt of Kapurthala State when another event that heightened communal tension was unfolding, adding to the gravity of an already inflammatory situation.

When in the first week of January 1934, the Land Alienation law was enforced in Kapurthala mostly because of the pressure exerted by the Zamindara Movement, moneylenders and shopkeepers in response began their own civil disobedience.[52] They also put forward a demand for the establishment of an Executive Council to take care of the state's administration. Maharaja Jagjeet acquiesced to the demand and established a six-member Council, two of whose representatives were to be Muslims. This relative marginalisation of Muslim opinion in a Muslim-majority state caused disquiet amongst the local population, although it inevitably pleased the *banias* (money lenders). The Ahrar was now provided with a new Muslim cause in the state.

At an Ahrar Conference held on 3–4 April 1934, the representatives called for the establishment of a responsible Assembly, in addition to job opportunities for the Muslims in proportion to their population. The State's prime minister responded positively,[53] which duly agitated the non-Muslims. As Abdullah Malik, a known sympathiser to the cause of Ahrar explained 'in a bid to foil any such attempt to ameliorate the lot of the peasants, subjected to the exploitative modes of the affluent class (comprising of Hindu Moneylenders and Sikh officials, who were also engaged in the practice of lending money as a side business) it fanned the flame of communalism'.[54]

---

[51] Qasmi, *Mufaker-e-Ahrar*, 186–87.

[52] For details, see Haq, *Tareekh-i-Ahrar*, 164–66; and Malik, *Punjab ki Siyasi Tahrikain*, 188–89.

[53] Haq, *Tareekh-e-Ahrar*, 166.

[54] Malik, *Punjab ki Siyasi Tahrikain*, 202.

On 22 April 1934, Kapurthala State police baton-charged the Muharram procession at Sultanpur Lodhi. However, the real tragedy was yet to occur. In the month of *Muharram* (the first month in the Islamic calendar) in Sultanpur District, the *Tazia* procession (the procession that is taken out on the 10th day of Muharram in commemoration of Hussain's martyrdom) had a prescribed route through a particular street where a huge oak tree was obstructing its smooth passage. Apart from Hindus, Sikhs also revered that very tree, which according to them Bibi Nanaki (sister of Guru Nanak) planted many centuries ago. It was a situation ripe for mischief. Mindful of this, Master Tara Singh and Prof. Jodha Singh, the honourable members of the Gurudwara Parbandah Committee, Amritsar, published a joint statement in the daily *Tribune* on 30 April. In it, the two leaders categorically denied the sacrosanct status of the tree and also questioned its age. Unfortunately, that statement came when all the damage had already been done.[55] The Muslim processionists were adamant in passing through the contentious route with their *Tazia*, Hindus and Sikhs vowed to resist any attempt to cut the overhanging branches of the oak tree. The state authorities, rather than encouraging negotiations to resolve the dispute, sought to limit its impact by pre-emptive arrests of some 450 people in the days before the procession. They did not however manage to prevent the violence on the 10th day of Muharram in which 20 Muslims were shot dead and 33 were injured.[56]

On 2 May, the Working Committee of Majlis-i-Ahrar met at Lahore and expressed its grief over the tragedy of Sultanpur. Ironically, no one but Ahrar took a serious note of the incident with the exception of the daily *Inqalab*. The Ahrar constituted a deputation comprising Abdul Ghaffar Ghaznavi and Abdul Gaffar Akhtar on 27 April 1934. It went to Phagwara, Begowal and Sultanpur to investigate the whole affair. It laid the blame squarely on the Hindus and the Sikhs and the negligence of the state authorities. The Central Majlis-i-Ahrar announced that it would commemorate 11 May as the Sultanpur day.[57] The State Government published its own report on 7 June 1934. It held that the Inspector General Police, Major Kothewala, was guilty for the massacre and he was immediately

---

[55] For further details, see Haq, *Tareekh-e-Ahrar*, 154–57.

[56] Ibid., p. 164; and Malik, *Punjab ki Siyasi Tahrikain*, 197–201.

[57] Malik, *Punjab ki Siyasi Tahrikain*, 203–4.

dismissed. Nevertheless, this hardly brought any gratification to the Ahrar. Its leadership demanded far sterner action and claimed that the State authorities had enacted a travesty of justice.[58] The Kapurthala Movement was a very important link in the chain of events that enhanced the credibility of the Ahrar. Just as in Kashmir, it established its credentials as an organisation that reposed firm belief in the politics of activism and agitation combining socialist ideals in a Muslim framework. The Ahrar were however stopped in their tracks in the July 1935 Shahid Gunj affair in Lahore.

## The Shahid Gunj Affair

Ahrar volunteers never flinched from courting arrest, taking out processions in protest or resorting to civil disobedience. However, the Ahrar was involved in not only agitational activities but also social service. In this respect, it displayed similarities with the Khaksar movement, which was also active in the Punjab at this time. The social service dimension of the Ahrar's activities was especially evident at the time of the 1935 Quetta earthquake. After the calamity had hit Quetta, 'Ahrars performed outstanding service in connection with the relief work ... Among the camps set up by non-government agencies the most organised and helpful was that of the Ahrars'.[59] Nonetheless, their primary mode of mobilising support was through public agitation and it was this that was to ultimately result in their decline, most notably around the issue of the Shahid Gunj mosque.

The issue of Shahid Gunj revolved around a Mosque (Abdullah Khan Ki Masjid), located in the *Landa* bazaar at some distance from Lahore Railway Station. Khan-i-Saman of Dara Shikoh (the kitchen in-charge of the Crown Prince of the Mughal Emperor Shah Jehan), whose name was Abdullah Khan, built the mosque in the 17th century. Before the onset of the Sikh rule, the mosque was in use. When the Sikhs rebelled against the Mughals, the Governor of the Punjab Nawab Moin-ul-Mulk was entrusted with the task of quelling the resistance. During those days, adjacent to the Mosque was a *kotwali* (a police station), where criminals or dissidents were executed. One of those fighting against the Mughal state was Tara Singh who was brought to this *kotwali*, tortured and executed. The

---

[58] Ibid., 204.
[59] For details, see Mirza, *Karwan-e-Ahrar*, Vol. II, 193–201.

Sikhs subsequently built a *samadhi* (a monument for the dead) on the spot where Tara Singh had breathed his last and named it as Shahid Gunj, which was subsequently converted into a Gurudwara. Before Maharaja Ranjit Singh's assumption of power in the Punjab in 1799, three *Bhangi* Sardars (Gujjar Singh, Lehna Singh and Sobha Singh) established their writ over Lahore (1765–1799). At this time, the Sikhs occupied the mosque and the *granthi* (priest) of the Gurudwara started using it as his residence and took rent for the shops attached to the building. The arrangement remained the same even after the annexation of the Punjab by the British in 1849.

The promulgation of the Gurudwara Act in 1925 caused a considerable change in the Shahid Gunj scenario. That Act nullified the control of the *Mahants* (priests) over the Gurudwaras and the trust properties worth *crores* of rupees. The Shiromani Gurudwara Prabandhak Committee (SGPC) assumed control over the Gurudwaras as laid down in the Act. Soon after the Act was invoked, the Sikh occupants of the mosque and the property attached to it approached the tribunal set up under the Act and 'prayed for exemption from this regulation under the plea that the Mosque building and the attached shops were their personal property'. In these circumstances, the secretary *Anjuman-i-Islamia* (Islamic Association) of Punjab, Syed Mohsin Shah, also filed a petition claiming the Anjuman's right over the mosque and the property attached to it. However, the tribunal dismissed the claims of both parties and declared the mosque and the building as the property of the Gurudwara. The Sikh occupants challenged the tribunal's verdict in the High Court, but *Anjuman-i-Islamia* did not file any appeal. A division bench of the High Court affirmed the decision of the tribunal in December 1934 and the building was transferred to the Lahore branch of SGPC in March 1935.[60]

After securing the possession of the building, SGPC embarked on an extensive renovation of the compound. Initially the reaction of Muslim leaders was quite moderate. They constituted a committee, the Anjuman-i Tahaffuz-i Masjid Shahid Gunj (committee for the protection of the Shahid Gunj mosque).[61] As the work

---

[60] For details, see Ahmed, *From Martial Law to Martial Law*, 130–31.

[61] A wide spectrum of Unionist Muslims, lawyers, journalists, and biradari leaders like Mian Abdul Aziz became the members of the committee, to find legal means to protect the mosque and press for the peaceful settlement

progressed, Muslims started thronging to the place of work; some of them came there to protest and some just to watch. Mala Singh, one of the masons, fell to his death. Muslim newspapers claimed that his death was a punishment for perpetrating a sinful act of demolition of a mosque. Thereafter, the site drew larger crowds of Muslims and the tension with the Sikhs palpably increased. The Deputy Commissioner forbade the Sikhs to touch the mosque. He also persuaded the Muslims to disperse and posted a police guard around the compound. Nevertheless, the tension continued to mount despite the Deputy Commissioner's assurance that the structure of the mosque would not be 'torn down until a final settlement was made'.[62] Governor Emerson also after meeting the Muslim notables agreed to consider the proposals put forward by them. However, to the chagrin of the Muslims, the mosque was razed to the ground by the morning of 9 July. Muslims felt cheated by the Governor and tempers rose to crescendo proportions. Notable by their absence from this mobilisation were the Ahrar.

On 14 July a public meeting at Mochi Gate was held, Zafar Ali Khan being the main speaker. He chastised the Ahrar's opportunism and said 'despite great efforts to bring the Ahrar leaders to the assemblage they had refused to come'. Thereafter the bubble of Ahrar's popularity was said to have burst. Immediately after the meeting, Zafar Ali Khan formed a group, the Majlis Ittehad-i Millat (association for unity among the Muslims) and the enrolment of the *Niliposh Razakars* (blue shirt volunteers) began with the intention of embarking upon a civil disobedience movement.[63] Consequently, four persons were externed from Lahore: Zafar Ali Khan, Syed Habib, Malik Lal Khan, and Mian Ferozuddin. On 15 July public meetings were banned by the British and press censorship was stiffened.

The Ahrar leaders perceived the Masjid Shahid Gunj issue as a conspiracy against them. They also saw Zafar Ali Khan as a stooge

---

of the issue. Report on the Shahid Gunj affair by Mian Abdul Aziz, n.d. (Abdul Aziz collection); F.H. Puckle, chief secretary, Punjab to deputy commissioners, 19 July 1935 (NAI, Home Political, file 5/14/35), quoted in Gilmartin, *Empire and Islam*, 100. Also see Gilmartin, 'The Shahid Gunj Mosque Incident', 146–68.

[62] Ahmed, *From Martial Law to Martial Law*, 132.

[63] Gilmartin, *Empire and Islam*, 101.

of the Unionists who had been their arch enemies.[64] The Shahid Gunj incident remained unresolved, despite the popular protests. Feroze Khan Noon, in his correspondence to Fazl-i-Hussain, divulged that some Ahrar leaders, wanting to forge an electoral alliance with the Sikhs in the forthcoming elections, kept quiet about the Shahid Gunj issue.[65] Abdullah Malik contends that the Ahrar stayed away from that contentious issue because joining the fray could have put its leadership in jail, which would have amounted to handing over the electoral victory to the Unionist party in a silver platter.[66] Malik also asserts the collusion of Zafar Ali Khan with Governor Emerson against Ahrar because of its soaring popularity.[67] Zafar Ali Khan and his newspaper *Zamindar* along with Sayyid Habib's the Daily *Siyasat* launched a condemnatory campaign against the Ahrar even though the *Zamindar* had previously been such a staunch supporter. Consequently, the Ahrar movement was permanently undermined in its Punjab heartland.

## Sectarianism and Decline

The Ahrar's major impact came in those political moments where it was able to mobilise the peasantry and the exploited through a religious idiom against the existing powers of the state. However, there was always an undercurrent of sectarianism in their politics, particularly when it came to the *Ahmediyya*. As Indian politics became increasingly communalised, the Ahrar seemed to also become increasingly sectarian. Although its mobilisation in Kapurthala ignored the Shia–Sunni divide (as it was defending a Muharram march), and its last large-scale mobilisation ostensibly carried on this practice by preaching Muslim unity, it was always nevertheless within an overarching framework of Sunni hegemony. Ultimately, this strategy backfired.

The Ahrar were involved in a movement called *Madeh-i-Sahaba*, which translates as eulogising the companions of the Prophet in United Provinces (UP).[68] Its main target was the Shia practice of

---

[64] See for details Haq, *Tareekh-e-Ahrar*, 242–46.
[65] Malik, *Book of Readings*, 559.
[66] Malik, *Purani Mahfilain*, 102.
[67] Ibid.
[68] Haq, *Tareekh-e-Ahrar*, 218–43.

revering Ali to a higher status than the other Caliphs (companions). One of the Ahrar spokesperson Atta-ullah Shah Bokhari, while addressing a public gathering in Lucknow (a city with a Shia majority among the Muslims), referred to the second Caliph Umer with a suffix *Raziallaha* (may Allah be pleased with him). Someone from the gathering told him: 'alluding to the first three caliphs with so much of deference is legally proscribed here in Lucknow'.[69] But Bokhari kept on quoting the companions of the Prophet reverentially. He also said, 'to respect some personality is not crime though abusing him is definitely a crime'. His speech ended peacefully and Bokhari went back to Lahore and broached the issue in the meeting of the Ahrar working committee. The working committee deputed Maulana Mazhar Ali Azhar to investigate the issue. The report he presented is summarised below:

> Before 1905 Shias and Sunnis lived like brothers and participated in the Tazia procession, in which Hindus also took part without any sectarian misgivings. As Shias were in majority so most of the municipal committee members adhered to *Asna Ashari* faith. It was in 1905 that a split occurred between them and one faction called in a Shia *Maulvi* (religious Scholar) by the name of Maqbul Ahmed from Rampur. He exacerbated the sectarian difference. Consequently, Shia-Sunni riots took place for the first time in the entire history of Lucknow. Therefore, Hindus stopped joining Muslims in the *Tazia* procession. And Sunnis set up their own *Karbala* outside the city and started taking out their own procession. To investigate Shia-Sunni riots the government set up a commission under a British officer Mr. Piggot and thereby the sectarian divide got perpetuated.[70]

In these circumstances, the Ahrar decided to launch a movement against the UP government. From the different cities of UP and Punjab, Ahrar volunteers started pouring in to Lucknow. After disembarking from the trains, they used to enter the city by reciting these verses:

Hain Kirnain Eik hi Mushal ki
Abu Bakar, Umer, Usman Ali
Hum Martaba Hain Yaraan-e-Nabi

---

[69] Taqi-ud-Din, *Pakistan ki Siyasi Jamatain*, 195–97.
[70] Farouqi, *Imam e Ahl e Sunnat Hazrat Allama Muhammad Abdul Shakoor Farooqi Lucknavi*, 214–55.

Kuch Farq Nahin in Charoon Main[71]
(Rays emanating from the same lamp
Abu Bakr, Umer, Usman and Ali
Companions of prophet have equal status
There is no difference in these four.)

While reciting these verses they courted arrest in large numbers. Concurrently, the 5th Shia political conference was held in Lucknow in December 1937, which was presided over by Prince Ikram Hussain, son of the last Nawab of Awadh. A Resolution was passed that added further fuel to the fire in which it was said: 'we warn the Government and Sunnis to respect the rights and sentiments of Shias. Our status and rights are practically ignored and *Madha-i-Sahaba* movement is anti-Shia which aims at extirpating Shia political influence'.[72]

More than 1000 people were imprisoned during the agitation. Eventually the governor of UP intervened and with the help of Sunni notables of Lucknow the Majlis-e-Ahrar was pleaded to stop that movement, which it did, although unrest kept resurfacing from time to time throughout the 1940s. In the long term, the movement intensified the sectarian division within the Muslims and its impact is explicitly visible in the present-day state of Pakistan. Indeed, sectarian militants such as Haq Nawaz Jhangvi (1952–1990), the founder-leader of *Sipah-e-Sahaba* (Army of the Companions of the Prophet) Pakistan, have acknowledged the legacy of Atta-ullah Shah Bokhari and his colleagues in *Majlis-e-Ahrar*. By organising solely on a religious issue and without any base in the peasantry, the legacy of the Ahrar in this context is the exacerbation of religious conflict rather than decline in exploitation.

The Ahrar decline, according to Shorish Kashmiri, began as early as in 1931 with the desertions of its founding members like Zafar Ali Khan and Ghazi Abdul Rehman. It was however the Shahid Gunj affair that began the rot and this was completed by the changes in all-India politics in the 1940s. The Pakistan demand in the Punjab, as elsewhere in India, changed the terms of political discourse.[73] The

---

[71] Quoted in Taqi-ud-Din, *Pakistan ki Siyasi Jamatain*, 196.

[72] Ibid., 197.

[73] Ahrar vehemently opposed the Lahore Resolution. They were particularly opposed to the idea of transfer of population based on religion. For Ahrar's point of view, see Azhar, *Humarey Firkawarana Faysaley ka Istadraj*, 162–69.

Ahrar opposed the Pakistan demand but also became estranged from Congress and *Jamiat Ulema-i-Hind* (JUH).[74] It tried hard to bounce back to the political mainstream by passing the *Hakumat-i-Ilahiyya* resolution, but no gains accrued.[75] That resolution meant promulgation of the Islamic System as ordained by Allah and his Prophet. *Hakumat-i-Ilahiyya* deprecated any geographical or ethnic solution to the communal problem that confronted India at the time.[76] It also widened the gulf between Congress and the Ahrar because the latter chose to focus on this aspect instead of lending support to the Quit India Movement in 1942.

Consequently Congress turned its back on the Ahrar and so did its political ally JUH, thus marginalising the movement and leaving its leadership little option but to quit politics. Yet, its brief political career — its capacity to mobilise the peasantry and its mixed ideological appeal on economic and religious registers — provide an important case study in the politics of late colonial Punjab.

—

# References

Afzal, M. Rafique, *Political Parties in Pakistan*, Islamabad: National Commission of Historical and Cultural Research, 1976.

Ahmed, Syed Nur, *From Martial Law to Martial Law: Politics in the Punjab, 1919–1958*, trans. by Craig Baxter, Lahore: Vangaurd Books, 1985.

Ali, Maulana Muhammad, *The Ahmadiyyah Movement*, trans. and ed. by S. Muhammad Tuffail, Lahore: Ahmadiyyah Anjuman Ishaat Islam, 1973.

Awan, Samina, *Political Islam in Colonial Punjab: Majlis-i-Ahrar*, Karachi: Oxford University Press, 2010.

Azhar, Mazhar Ali, *Humarey Firkawarana Faysaley ka Istadraj: Judagana Intakhabatsey Pakistan Tak*, Lahore: Maktaba-i-Ahrar, 1944.

———, *Masala-e Shaheed Gunj*, Lahore: Bukhari Academy, 1978.

---

[74] Kashmiri, *Sayaad Ataullah*, 117.

[75] Afzal, *Political Parties in Pakistan: 1947–1958*, 27. For *Hakumat-i-Ilahiyah* and its conceptual exposition, see Azhar, *Humarey Firkawarana Faysaleyka Istadraj*, 244–47.

[76] Azhar, *Humarey Firkawarana Faysaleyka Istadraj*, 247.

Batalvi, Ashique Hussain, *Iqbal key Akhri Doo Saal*, Lahore: Idara-i-Saqafat-e-Islamia, 1989.

Copland, Ian, 'Islam and Political Mobilization in Kashmir, 1931–34', *Pacific Affairs* 54, no. 2 (Summer, 1981): 228–59.

Farouqi, M., *Imam e Ahl e Sunnat Hazrat Allama Muhammad Abdul Shakoor Farooqi Lucknavi: Hayat aur Khidmat*, Lahore: Idarai Tehqiqati Ahl e Sunnat, 2009.

Friedmann, Yohanan, *Prophecy Continuous: Aspects of Ahmadi Religious Thought and Its Medieval Background*, New Delhi: Oxford University Press, 2003.

Gilmartin, David, *Empire and Islam: Punjab and the Making of Pakistan*, London: I.B. Tauris, 1988.

———, 'The Shahid Gunj Mosque Incident: A Prelude to Pakistan', in *Islam, Politics, and Social Movements*, Edmund Burke, III, and Ira M. Lapidus (eds), Berkeley: University of California Press, 1988.

Government of Punjab, *Report of the Court of Inquiry Constituted Under Punjab Act II of 1954 to Enquire into the Punjab Disturbances of 1953*, Lahore: Printed by the Superintendent, Government Printing, Punjab, 1954.

Grewal, J. S., *The Sikhs of the Punjab*, Cambridge: Cambridge University Press, 1995.

Haq, Afzal, *Tareekh-e-Ahrar*, Lahore: Maktaba Majlis-e-Ahrar Islam, 1968.

———, *Mera Afsana*, Lahore: Kutabnuma, 1991.

Hassan, Mushirul, *Legacy of Divided Nation: India's Muslim Since Independence*, New Delhi: Oxford University Press, 1997.

Husain, Azim, *Fazal-i-Husain: A Political Biography*, New Delhi: Longman, Green & Co. Ltd, 1946.

Huttenback, Robert A., *Kashmir and the British Raj: 1847–1947*, Karachi: Oxford University Press, 2004.

Ikram, S. M., *Modern Muslim India and the Birth of Pakistan (1858–1951)*, Lahore: Sh. Muhammad Ashraf, 1965.

———, *Bou-e-Gul, Nala-e-Dil, Dood-e-Charach-e-Mahfil*, Lahore: Chattan, 1972.

Kashmiri, Shoresh, *Sayaad Ataullah Shah Bokhari, Swanehwa Afkar*, Lahore: Matbuaat-i-Chattan, 1969.

Ludhyanvi, Tajud Din, *Ahrar Aur Tehrik-e-Kashmir 1932*, Lahore: Maktaba-i-Majlis-e-Ahrar Islam, Pakistan, 1968.

———, *Majlis-e-Ahraraur Tariekhi Tahriefki Yalghar*, Lahore: Markazi Maktaba Majlis-e-Ahrar-e-Islam Pakistan, 1968.

Malik, Abdullah, *Punjab ki Siyasi Tahrikain*, Lahore: Nigarshat, 1982.

———, *Purani Mahfilain Yaad A Rehi Hein*, Lahore: Takhliqaat, 2002.

Malik, Iftikhar H., *Sikandar Hayat Khan: A Political Biography*, Islamabad: National Institute of Historical and Cultural Research, 1985.

Malik, Ikram Ali, ed., *A Book of Readings on the History of the Punjab*, Lahore: Research Society of Pakistan, 1970.

Minault, Gail, *The Khilafat Movement: Religious Symbolism and Political Mobilization in India*, New York: Colombia University Press, 1982.

Mirza, Janbaz, *Karwan-e-Ahrar*, Vol. IV, Lahore: Maktaba-i-Karwan, 1972.

———, *Karwan-e-Ahrar*, Vol. I, Lahore: Maktaba-i-Karwan, 1975.

———, *Karwan-e-Ahrar*, Vol. II, Lahore: Maktaba-i-Karwan, 1975.

Nehru, Jawaharlal, *Jawaharlal Nehru: An Autobiography*, London: John Lane the Bodley Head, 1936.

Qasmi, Abu Yusuf, *Mufaker-e-Ahrar: Chaudhary Afzal Haq*, Lahore: Basat-e-Adab, 1991.

Qureshi, Ishtiaq Hussain, *The Struggle for Pakistan*, Karachi: University of Karachi, 1965.

Qureshi, Naeem, *Pan-Islam in British Indian Politics: A Study of the Khilafat Movement, 1918–1924*, Karachi: Oxford University Press, 2009.

Reetz, Dietrich, *Islam in the Public Sphere: Religious Groups in India 1900–1947*, Delhi: Oxford University Press, 2006.

Salik, Abdul Majid, *Sar Gazasht*, Lahore: Al Faisal, 1993.

Schofield, Victoria, *Kashmir in the Crossfire*, London: IB Tauris & Co Ltd, 1996.

Steingass, F., *Arabic — English Dictionary*, Lahore: Sang-e-Meel Publications, 1979.

Syed, Javed Haider, 'Pakistan Resolution and Majlis-e-Ahrar', in Kaniz Fatima Yusuf, Saleem Akhtar and Razi Wasti (eds), *Pakistan Resolution Revisited*, Islamabad: National Institute of Historical and Cultural Research, 1990.

Talbot, Ian, *Punjab and the Raj*, Delhi: Manohar, 1988.

Taqi-ud-Din, Hafiz, *Pakistan ki Siyasi Jamatainwa Tehreekain*, Lahore: Fiction House, 1995.

# ✠ 4

# An Unfulfilled Dream: The Left in Pakistan c. 1947–50

*Ali Raza*

On the 9th anniversary of the Lahore Resolution, which enunciated the Muslim League's formal political demand for the creation of Pakistan, Faiz Ahmed Faiz penned an editorial on the 'progress of a dream'. Speaking of the 'common man' and his vision for Pakistan, Faiz wrote:

> The devotion and fervour that he so plentifully offered to the national cause sprung from other connotations of the term Pakistan and it connoted above all, freedom and independence ... Everyone felt, however, that Pakistan meant freedom from the poignant humiliation of being governed by an alien people; it meant freedom from the economic strangle-hold of a ruthless class of exploiters whose class antagonism to the victims was reinforced by differences of culture, creed and outlook; it meant freedom from the tyranny of officials big and small who derived their authority from a foreign source; it also meant freedom to speak one's language without feeling abashed. It means freedom from perpetual affront and insult at the hands of men not as good as oneself; it meant freedom from the constant violence that one's integrity and intelligence was subjected to, by men who had risen to power through fraud and treachery or birth and riches ... Once we get rid of this destructive combine, the people said, we shall be able to sweep all minor obstructions aside — the stupid, vainglorious, feudal grandee, fub-thumping obscurantist demagogue, the tyrannous policeman, the grasping rent-racketeer, the incompetent corrupt official, the censor and the CID.[1]

---

[1] Editorial in the *Pakistan Times,* 23 March 1949. Majeed, *Coming Back Home,* 23.

More than the mythical 'common man', this tract perhaps better represented the hopes and aspirations of Faiz and other like-minded Leftist activists. Much like the varied understandings and visions of *swaraj*, the call for Pakistan too offered hope and succour to those on the progressive end of the political spectrum. This partly explained why the Communist Party of India (CPI) and its affiliates initially greeted the call for Pakistan as a just and progressive demand. This in turn was a reflection of what decolonisation meant for those political actors whose understanding of identity, sovereignty and socio-political objectives was at variance with the inheritors of the colonial state. With its understandable emphasis on the themes of Empire, Nation and Community, dominant accounts of Partition and Independence have usually served to further marginalise these political actors in historiography. This is especially true insofar as the Punjab is concerned, given that it was one of the two fault lines on which the two independent states emerged.

The Left of course is one of the more prominent victims of this historiographical blind spot.[2] This gap is even more striking when it comes to the Left's engagement with the Muslim League and the challenges it faced after it was reduced to a much weakened 'Pakistani' Left in the wake of Partition.[3] This absence is both understandable and inexplicable. Viewed from the former perspective, the Leftist movement in Pakistan, or at least its western variant, could never claim the relative strength enjoyed by their counterparts in India. On the other hand, Pakistan's leftist movement, unlike any other political

---

[2] Nevertheless, there are a few accounts that have touched on this issue. Nearly all of these, however, have exclusively focused on the trajectory of the Leftist movement in post-colonial India. For the earliest wide ranging work in this genre, see the second half of Overstreet and Windmiller, *Communism in India*. With respect to East Punjab, see the second half of Singh, *Communism in Punjab*, which explores the movement up until the late 1960s.

[3] A notable exception is the recent paper published by Ali, 'Communists in a Muslim Land', 501–34, in which he skillfully charts the intellectual and cultural exchanges between prominent Leftists that were a response to the dilemmas they faced in the nascent state. Ali's article, then, provides an essential intellectual backdrop to this piece, which is largely concerned with the newly 'decolonised' political landscape. These and later debates along with their wider political backdrop are also covered in Toor's, *The State of Islam*.

force at the time, was constantly persecuted by a paranoid state that was fearful of the Left's overblown image and its 'subversive' potential, rather than the actual movement itself. Not only did this policy point towards the survivability of the colonial state — along with its institutional outlook and its coercive apparatus — but it also clearly demonstrated the political and ideological priorities of those who inherited it. Viewed this way, the Left, despite its political impotence, cannot be neglected in a commentary on the post-colonial state of Pakistan.

This chapter, therefore, aims to partially fill that gap by charting the Left's experiences in the immediate aftermath of Partition. This narrative is important for a number of reasons. First, it shows how the space for progressive politics rapidly shrunk owing to the devastation wrought by Partition and the onslaught of triumphal nationalist chauvinism, which invoked religion and suppressed dissenting voices that were deemed to be 'anti-Pakistan'. In so doing, the nascent Pakistani polity defined an arena of legitimacy in which the Left was perpetually at or beyond the margins of what counted as acceptable politics. Second, this narrative provides insights into how various political actors were attempting to mould the post-colonial state in their own image in the immediate aftermath of decolonisation. Additionally, these formative years set the stage for the divisive political debates of the ensuing decades in which the state played a decidedly partisan role. In what follows therefore, I mostly situate this narrative in the Punjab as its Leftist tradition had a richer pedigree in comparison to other regions in West Pakistan. Moreover, the province's Leftist movement, again in comparison to other regions, was profoundly affected by Partition. It was also here that the Left actively engaged with the Muslim League in the years leading up to 1947.[4]

There are, however, a few points that should be clarified at the very outset. The first relates to the term 'Left'. As should be obvious, this was a broad category that encompassed a number of organisations and individuals who were associated with what counted as 'progressive' or 'leftist' politics. These labels too were perpetually contested and redefined by individuals within the 'Left' as well as by a paranoid state, which kept a close eye on what it considered to be 'communist' or 'leftist' politics. Clearly then, the 'Left' was a

---

[4] See Ali's piece in this volume.

broad and slippery political category that shifted according to time and context. It is for this reason why I refer to a number of individuals and organisations in this chapter, and in particular, the nascent Communist Party of Pakistan (CPP), which was the most prominent of Leftist parties operating in this period.

The second clarification relates to the sources used in this chapter, which are mostly drawn from the official archive. In part, this imbalance is necessitated owing to this chapter's focus on the post-colonial state and the political arena it crafted. In so doing, this narrative provides a useful contrast to Kamran Asdar Ali's chapter in this book, which closely examines the Left's politics and provides an insight into its internal debates. Still, there are some obvious problems associated with the reliance on official sources. That said, these sources are valuable for offering certain insights into the contours of a state and a political landscape that outlasted the formal transfer of power. Like its predecessor, the post-colonial state also closely observed Leftist politics. Its reporting thus had the 'immediacy' that Ranajit Guha identifies in his discussion on 'primary' discourse.[5] The contemporaneous nature of this reporting, therefore, provides a fascinating glimpse of everyday politics that the Left was engaged with. And while these reports are inevitably coloured by state imperatives, they also betray the anxiety with which the Left and its politics was viewed in the nascent country. Given the backdrop of a developing Cold War, this nervousness was also shared by the former colonial power, which kept a close watch on Leftist politics. Viewed another way, these sources provide greater insights about the priorities and outlooks of the institutions which produced them; then they do about the subjects of their reporting. Put together, these documents provide an intimate view of the Left, which is further supplemented by their meticulous reporting of publications, speeches and intercepted correspondences that are otherwise lost to the historical record. Notwithstanding its problems then, the official archive still remains the largest repository of sources relating to Leftist activities within the colonial as well as the post-colonial state.[6] This fact alone is a telling reminder of the level of scrutiny and persecution the Left was regularly subjected to.[7]

---

[5] Guha, 'The Prose of Counter-Insurgency', 47–50.

[6] It should be added, however, that the official record of Leftist politics beyond these formative years is still largely inaccessible.

## A 'Leprous Daybreak'[8]

The first intelligence report after Partition remarked at very outset that 'the inauguration of Pakistan, which had been so eagerly awaited by the Muslims, brought very little joy'.[9]

As far as observations went, this was perhaps understating the widespread sense of disillusionment that marked the birth of Pakistan. From the highest echelons of a struggling government to wider society as a whole, this sense has been emotively immortalised in much of the literature that has been devoted to Partition and perhaps none more so than in the renowned poet and Leftist Faiz Ahmed Faiz's poem, *Subah-e-Azadi*. But Faiz's lament and his call for continuing the search 'for that promised Dawn' resonated more with the Punjabi Left or, at the very least, the section of it which had been left behind in Pakistan. The horrific scale of the communal massacres gradually saw to it that the majority of Punjabi Leftists, Hindu and Sikh, were compelled to either migrate to or stay in East Punjab. One of these was Teja Singh Swatantar, who founded the first, albeit short lived, Pakistan Communist Party in mid 1947. What remained was an isolated and embittered group of Leftists who had not joined the Muslim League and were still affiliated with a few labour unions and either the CPI or the Socialist Party. Nevertheless, the perennial (if misplaced) optimism that was a hallmark of the Left soon expressed itself in the determination of the remaining radicals to work in Pakistan. The Pakistan flag was hoisted alongside the red banner on party offices, while resolutions were passed offering cooperation to the Pakistan Government in solving the 'problems of the people', appealing for acceptance of minority rights and suggesting

---

[7] Moreover, Leftist activists frequently destroyed incriminating documents themselves. According to popular anecdotes retold by Leftists today, many individuals literally ate such documents owing to a fear that the security services would be able to retrieve them if any other method of disposal was used.

[8] Approximate translation of '*yeh daagh daagh ujala*', which is part of the first verse of Faiz's iconic poem *Subah-e-Azadi* (Dawn of Freedom). This verse has also been literally translated as the 'stain-covered daybreak'. Translation by Victor Kiernan in the book *Poems by Faiz*, http://www. outlookindia.com/article.aspx?212904.

[9] Lahore, 23 August, No. 34, PPSAI — West Punjab (WP) 1947, 419.

cooperation between Pakistan and India in economic, defence and foreign policy questions. Further appeals were made for Pakistan to be a secular democratic republic and not a communal state or British Dominion.[10] Plans were also made for overcoming the dearth, partly through killings, of Muslim workers by encouraging the employment of Sikhs converted as Muslims and calling for the 'import' of Muslim workers from Delhi and other provinces of India.[11]

Viewed in a broader context, the Left in Pakistan was clearly faced with seemingly insurmountable challenges. The immediate issue facing the nascent state was resettling millions of refugees who had mostly flooded into West Punjab. Deprived of their material possessions and sources of income, the refugees were an enormous burden on the scarce resources of both state and society. Additionally, there were other problems that threatened to engulf the new government. For one, there was a food grain shortage across the Province, which resulted in an astronomical rise in the prices of foodstuffs, particularly in the black market.[12] There was also a concurrent shortage of cloth and other commodities, while criminal incidents also increased manifold. More crucially, the political uncertainty surrounding the new state was an invitation for various groups — ranging from Islamists to communists — to fill the vacuum through their respective articulations of socio-political visions for the new state. In doing so, they were seeking to address the prevailing discontent and opposition to a seemingly indifferent government and, in many cases, to the idea of Pakistan itself. Thus, one Qazi Ahmed Jan, Imam of a mosque in Thata, Attock district, spoke for many when he was reported to declare at a public gathering that:

> Hindustan and Hindu Government were better than Pakistan and Muslim Government, as under the latter Government, the people could not even get enough to eat. He (Qazi Ahmed Jan) shouted slogans of *Pakistan Murdabad* and *Muslim League Murdabad* and said the Pakistan Government was encouraging corruption and doing injustice.[13]

---

[10] Lahore, 16 August, No. 33, PPSAI — WP 1947, 417.
[11] Lahore, 23 August, No. 35, 426; Lahore, 13 September, No. 38, PPSAI — WP 1947, 454.
[12] Lahore, 14 February, No. 7, PPSAI — WP 1948, 47.
[13] Lahore 14 February, No. 7, PPSAI — WP 1948, 48.

The Left, however, was in no position to channel this discontent, much as it tried or wanted to, into a more progressive direction. The experience of Partition had divided Leftist groups, with many of their best cadres and leaders migrating to East Punjab. Even the strongholds of union and kisan activity had been weakened by the migration of non Muslim workers and kisans. Most strongholds had also become part of East Punjab. To add to that, there was no united Leftist party operating in Pakistan, let alone the Punjab. Rather, Leftist groups exhibited the established norms of infighting between and within themselves. As a result, and in a continuation from the pre-Partition period, there were a number of Leftist groups that often ended up working in cross purposes to each other. Aside from the famous Pakistan Progressive Writers Association (closely allied to the Communist Party), the most significant of these was the All Pakistan Trades Union Federation, which was set up by the now 'Pakistani' representatives of the 'communist controlled' All India Trades Union Federation. The Federation was led by Mirza Muhammad Ibrahim, a veteran labour leader of the North Western Railways Union in Lahore. Other than this, there was also a Pakistan Socialist Party, led by Munshi Ahmed Din, former member and leader of the Punjab Congress Socialist Party (CSP), and a parliamentary 'Pakistan Peoples' Party'. There were also a slew of parties and agrarian movements operating in Sindh, East Pakistan, and, to some extent, the NWFP. Finally, there was a scattering of Leftists within the Muslim League, such as Mian Iftikharuddin who was the party's Punjab President.[14]

Added to this milieu was the Pakistan Communist Party that was established (again) in 1948. Typically though, the Party was born out

---

[14] *Despatch No. 90 (Secret) from Office of the High Commissioner for the United Kingdom, Karachi, dated 27th March 1948, POL 7416 1948* (henceforth referred to as 'Despatch from Office of HCUK, Karachi') *Communist Activities in India and Pakistan, Jan 1947–Oct 1949* (henceforth referred to as CAIP) IOR/L/P&J/12/772, 127–30. Iftikharuddin, however, did not last long in the Muslim League. He was unceremoniously expelled from the party in 1950. As a Leaguer and later as a prominent politician, he regularly criticised the ruling party for introducing draconian policies and betraying its imagined progressive principles. See, for example, his statement following his expulsion from the League: Malik, *Selected Speeches and Statements*, 173.

of heated debates, which provided a revealing insight into how the prevailing political situation was understood by many activists. The debate centred between two prominent Punjabi Leftists, Fazal Elahi Qurban and Ferozeuddin Mansur. Qurban was in favour of setting up a party that would be independent of the CPI and reflective of a political reality in which the two dominions of India and Pakistan were functioning independently of each other.[15] F.D. Mansur, on the other hand, did not agree with Qurban's assessment as he felt that the two Dominions would be reunited soon. F.D. Mansur then was representing a substantial section of the Left and the initial line of the CPI, which felt that the two autonomous states were a temporary reality. This line was also pursued by the envoy of the CPI, Sajjad Zaheer, who was deputed by the party to visit Lahore and assist and guide the Leftists there in pursuing the directives issued by the All India Party.[16] These debates were an indication of the uncertainty prevailing after Partition and a reflection of the various visions that political actors held, and not just in Leftist circles, over the future direction and political orientation of the two states. Soon though, the CPI at its Second Party Congress held at Calcutta in March 1948 relented to its branches in Pakistan forming a separate party, the headquarters of which were in Lahore.[17] Sajjad Zaheer was entrusted to organise the Party but he was soon forced to go underground to escape state persecution.[18] The founding principles of the party had already been laid and were similar to the demands and political principles articulated by other Leftist groups. These

---

[15] It should be added that Qurban was a member of Teja Singh Swatantar's group, which argued for and even established a separate 'Pakistan Communist Party' a few months before Partition actually happened. This line of argument then was consistent with Qurban's thinking on the seemingly irreversible reality of Partition.

[16] Lahore, 4 January, No. 7, PPSAI — WP 1948, 7. Zaheer was also the founder of the All India Progressive Writers Association and one of the leading lights in colonial and post-colonial Leftist politics. For an English translation of his account *Roshnai*, see Zaheer, *The Light.*

[17] *From the High Commissioner for the UK in Pakistan, Karachi, to Commonwealth Relations Office, London, No. 61, dated 31st March 1948, POL 7069 1948,* CAIP IOR/L/P&J/12/772, 138.

[18] *Communism in the West Punjab,* CAIP, IOR/L/P&J/12/772, 356–57.

included the nationalisation of key industries, radical agrarian reform and the repeal of regressive and repressive laws. More interestingly, a proposal was also made for reorganising the new state on a linguistic basis, in which the resulting federating states would be granted the principle of self-determination.[19] This demand reflected an understanding and recognition of the ethnic and linguistic cleavages within the new nation as much as it was a continuation of the standard communist line of self-determination.

## The Threat of Communism

The communists or the broader Left though was handicapped from the start in pursuing these objectives. For in addition to organisational problems and external events beyond its control, Leftist activists soon became the favoured target of state persecution. Indeed, in this regard, the post-colonial states of both India and Pakistan showed a remarkable degree of continuity in criminalising the very same groups that had been the primary target of their predecessor. Both states clung onto a larger than life image of the Left, and this official hysteria led to a series of repressive measures being put in place. This was as much an outcome of a political movement that had fallen foul of the ruling parties in both countries in the run-up to independence as much as it was of a bureaucracy, which had been institutionalised and habituated into imagining the Left as a seditious movement that was a proxy of the Soviet Union. Thus, in India for instance, the party was banned under a variety of pretexts between 1948 and 1951 in all its major strongholds. This was foreshadowed by hundreds of arrests and the search of party and union offices.[20] The extent of this official hysteria was reflected in the statement of an East Punjab minister who accused the communists of being involved in Mahatma Gandhi's assassination as well as being partly

---

[19] *Letter from the High Commissioner for the United Kingdom in Pakistan, Karachi to the Commonwealth Relations Office, London dated 3rd March 1948*, CAIP IOR/L/P&J/12/772, 81.

[20] See for instance, *Extract from the 'Economist' dated 22 November 1947* POL 12015 1947 and *Reuters India and Pakistan Service 29.3.48*, CAIP IOR/L/P&J/12/772.

responsible, owing to their support for Pakistan, for the recent massacres in the Punjab.[21] In this persecution Pakistan soon followed suit, and in ways that suggested at most, a suspicious degree of coordination between the two states or, at the very least, one of the rare instances when the official policies of both states were perfectly aligned with each other. This was especially the case in East Bengal, which clamped down on communist activity immediately after a ban had been imposed on the party in West Bengal.[22]

Unlike in India, however, where the communists were still a substantial force and involved in agrarian agitation and uprisings against the state, the Left in Pakistan was hardly equipped to withstand the onslaught of state repression. If anything, the paranoia in Pakistan was much worse than that exhibited in India. This primarily had to do with the fear that Pakistan, in the words of the British High Commissioner, 'abound(ed) with excellent material for communist agitation'.[23] Indeed, British representatives were petrified at the possibility of communist activism within the new state and closely liaised with their former colleagues within the Pakistan bureaucracy to get a better sense of the 'threat' it faced. The 'danger', as was acknowledged time and again, and reported by the head of the CID to a British consular official in Lahore, did not come from the present state of organisation of the Left, rather it 'lay in the misery which could be so easily exploited'.[24] There were potentialities for agrarian unrest in the Bengal[25] and NWFP,[26] while there was also cause for apprehension in Sindh and West Punjab of peasant and labour agitations. However, by far, the biggest 'reservoir of discontent and potential agitation' was the mass of refugees who had flooded into

---

[21] 'Sixty nine Communists arrested in Punjab Simla', *Reuters India and Pakistan Service 3/4/48*, CAIP IOR/L/P&J/12/772, 146.

[22] *Communist Movement in East Bengal*, CAIP IOR/L/P&J/12/772, 345.

[23] *Despatch from Office of HCUK, Karachi*, CAIP IOR/L/P&J/12/772, 132.

[24] *Extract from letter from Deputy UKHC, Lahore, dated 22nd February, 1948 Pol. 7071/48*, CAIP IOR/L/P&J/12/772, 83.

[25] See for instance, *Communist Movement in East Bengal*, CAIP IOR/L/P&J/12/772, 345, 349–50.

[26] See for instance, 'NWFP Peasantry Asks Government to End Feudal Tyranny', *Extract from Pakistan Times Date 20th February 1948*, CAIP IOR/L/P&J/12/772, 136.

West Punjab. Those already resettled provided a potential audience for Leftists, while those still in camps, 'living in conditions of appalling squalor and discomfort, demoralised by what they have suffered and by lack of employment, provide(d) even more fertile material'. Thus, according to a report given by a former Indian Army officer who volunteered for service with the refugees:

> The refugees themselves say, 'we were promised Pakistan, what we got is *Qabristan* (cemetery)' and from the thousands and thousands who have died from exposure one can but sympathize with them. I have met quite a number of wealthy people who lost their all owing to partition, (and) they, as a class, all complain that nothing is done for them and they are the bitterest critics of most of the 'tops' now in office. The wish for Communism — which is so foreign to the nature of the Mussalman — is very freely expressed and particularly by the former wealthy classes, the more educated types. Of one thing I am certain, and that is that unless the refugees are very speedily rehabilitated Pakistan will have a permanent problem of hundreds of thousands of *ghoondas* (criminals).[27]

Further compounding the problem was the feared encirclement of Pakistan by international communism. This anxiety of course has to be viewed in the broader context of the Cold War and the joint Anglo-American efforts to check the spread of communism in Asia. For this was a period when the communists were on the verge of victory in China and the advance of the Revolution was anticipated in South East Asia and especially in Malaya, Burma, Indonesia, and French Indo-China. In this regard, conversations were reported to have taken place between Britain and the United States expressing the desirability of 'sustaining and siding with the stable nations of Asia, particularly India and Pakistan, as their examples offer the best counter-irritant to the "co-prosperity sphere" kind of propaganda that is likely to be increased once a communist regime is established in China'.[28] The reality, however, was that Pakistan, as the worried dispatches of the British representatives indicated, was anything but

---

[27] *Despatch from Office of HCUK, Karachi*, CAIP IOR/L/P&J/12/772, 133.

[28] *Reuters Indian and Pakistan Service 20/1/49 POL 10496 1949*, CAIP IOR/L/P&J/12/772, 259.

stable. There was thus a danger that Pakistan could provide 'a fertile field for Soviet intervention'. Already in an ominous development for West Pakistan, the Soviet Union was active in fomenting 'unrest' in Central Asia, and more worryingly Sinkiang, and it was feared that the northernmost princely states of Hunza and Nagar had pro-Soviet inclinations.[29] On the Eastern front, communist infiltration from Burma, or more realistically West Bengal, remained a threat.[30] Unexpectedly enough, this fear was also echoed by the Pakistani establishment itself. Thus, Mian Anwer Ali, head of the CID, wrote later that:

> Communism is the most inexorable and momentous political force in the contemporary world: it's strength and potentialities are often under-estimated. In Pakistan the complacency is partly due to the common belief that Islam and communism are incompatible. How many people realize that the Muslims of the southern states of the USSR and China could not avert its advent? Malaya, despite its Muslim population, is engaged in a gruelling life and death struggle; in Iran, the Tudeh Party is gathering strength: in Egypt, the horizon becomes marked with red streaks. Strangest of all, Afghanistan, in spite of its despotic masters, has a nucleus of a party whose leader, at any rate, hopes to overthrow the existing regime ... The threat of the Red expansion is now turning towards India. Guerrillas battled for years with armed forces in the States of Hyderabad and Madras and kept them at bay. In certain provincial assemblies enough communist MLA's have been returned as to hold the balance of power. These factors must have their effect in Pakistan.[31]

Both this passage and the report given by the former Indian Army officer gave an insight into the hopes within certain official and British circles about what they thought to be the ultimate defence against communist advances: the 'Musalmaan' and his faith.

---

[29] *Despatch from Office of HCUK, Karachi*, CAIP IOR/L/P&J/12/772, 130–1.

[30] *Communist Movement in East Bengal*, CAIP IOR/L/P&J/12/772, 353.

[31] Preface of M. Anwer Ali, *The Communist Party of West Pakistan in Action* (Lahore: CID, Govt of Punjab, 1952). I am grateful and indebted to Kamran Asdar Ali for his generosity in giving me a copy of this report.

## The Rhetorical Deployment of Islam

Even though the formation of the Republic of Pakistan did not include (at that time) Islam in its title, the issue of religion was never far from colonial and post-colonial discourse. Indeed, in some sections, it was felt that communism was 'largely beyond the Muslim mental grasp'.[32] Additionally, one of the reasons why the godless communist 'virus' was believed not to have attained a strong growth in 1948 was of the 'discipline inherent in an Islamic State', which had been augmented by the strength of a victorious political party machine whose appeal had been primarily religious and reinforced by a fear of India and communal hatred of Hindus and Sikhs. It was thus felt that the expansion of secular Government would naturally weaken Muslim League Party discipline and gradually diminish the strength of the religious bonds that were helping ward off imagined communist advances.[33] This was particularly so where the population was strongly bound to 'custom' and 'tenets of Islam', like Baluchistan and the NWFP,[34] while in Sindh, the 'extreme backwardness' of the Sindhi *hari*[35] made for 'poor subversive material'.[36] In addition to these sentiments, the official establishment and the vernacular press were only too eager to replicate these colonial tropes in their pronouncements. The daily 'Dawn' for instance felt that 'the spiritual force of Islam' could play its part in repulsing 'the false philosophy of Communism', for the Muslim people were 'naturally embattled' against the onslaught of communism.[37] Nevertheless, it was still felt, as Mian Anwer Ali's report indicated, that Islam itself won't be a sufficient deterrent against communist advances. Indeed, there was no

---

[32] *Despatch from Office of HCUK, Karachi*, CAIP IOR/L/P&J/12/772, 129.

[33] Ibid., 127, 133.

[34] *Communism in the NWFP*, CAIP IOR/L/P&J/12/772, 363.

[35] Peasant.

[36] *Despatch from Office of HCUK, Karachi*, CAIP IOR/L/P&J/12/772, 128.

[37] *Extract No. 28, from High Commissioner for the UK in Pakistan, Karachi to Commonwealth Relations Office, Dated 4th February 1949, Pol. 10825/49* CAIP, IOR/L/P&J/12/772.

discounting 'the ease with which ignorant Muslim crowds (could) be swayed by unscrupulous orators assisted by real economic distress'.[38]

However, Islam was still an absolutely necessary tool in the defence against communism. In this, sufficient groundwork was already being laid by the Islamist parties, who, much like any other political movement during this time, attempted to direct the prevailing uncertainty towards their imagined polity. While demands for making Pakistan an Islamic State had been raised in the run-up to Partition, these calls grew more vociferous after the state had been established and, especially, as it set itself to agreeing on a Constitution. The implementation of Shariat law and the establishment of a *Hukumat-I-Ilahia* (Divine Rule) were held to be the solution to the manifold problems plaguing the new state. Instead, the incumbent Muslim League leadership was (perceived to be) preventing this from happening.[39] The League leadership was accused of protecting an immoral, indecent (particularly with regard to women) and corrupt system and of not adopting the 'Muslim mode of life' and allowing their women to disregard the observance of *purdah*. Even the Premier, Nawab Liaqat Ali Khan, was urged to 'become a true Muslim, say prayers five times, and give up drinking, instead of exhorting others to become true Muslims'. Nevertheless, the 'Mullahs', as they were derogatorily called, saved their special ire for the Left. In part, this was due to their perceived secular or even 'godless' credentials. This was particularly damaging in a situation in which the place of secularism was the most contentious issue facing the state. In this regard, the *Jamaat-i-Islami* had publicly declared that its loyalty to Pakistan was only contingent on its being an Islamic State.[40] Indeed, the more extreme form of this dichotomy was found in Islamist posters declaring: 'Islam *Zindabad*, Pakistan *Murdabad*'.[41] In attempting to remake Pakistan into a secular state, the communists were of course especially culpable. It was in recognition of this 'threat' that the prominent Islamist, Maulana Maudoodi,

---

[38] *Despatch from Office of HCUK, Karachi*, CAIP IOR/L/P&J/12/772, 130.

[39] Lahore, 6 March, No. 10, PPSAI — WP 1948, 78.

[40] Lahore, 13 November, No. 46, PPSAI — WP 1948, 370.

[41] Lahore, 4 December, No. 49, PPSAI — WP 1948, 396.

characterised communists as dangerous as they were gradually getting a hold in Government departments, and particularly in the Press and Broadcasting Departments.[42] For others, the Left's demands for abolishing the *zamindari* system and nationalising industry were particularly pernicious, while Islam and its system of *zakat*[43] were considered sufficient to resolve the present inequalities of the system.[44] It was also argued that the promulgation of Shariat law was the only way to 'build a bulwark against the advancing tide of Communism'.[45] Despite this fierce rhetoric though, the 'Mullahs' still implicitly recognised some of the legitimacy of the Left's claims as speeches calling for the establishment of an Islamic State contained frequent references to the excesses of the 'capitalist' system, inequity of the prevailing agrarian structure and the imperialist slant of the incumbent leadership.[46] If anything, these acts of ventriloquism indicated that the Left commanded an influence that was starkly disproportionate to its actual presence or political clout.

---

[42] Lahore, 24 April, No. 17, PPSAI — WP 1948, 143. Despite its opposition, it has been argued by Humeira Iqtidar that in these initial years, the Jamaat viewed the Left as a 'tactical ally' against the Muslim League. To support her contention, she quotes from an interview of C.R. Aslam, one of Pakistan's most venerated Leftist leaders, in which he recalled an occasion (in 1948) when the Communist Party organised a joint rally with the Jamaat against the Muslim League. See Humeira Iqtidar, 'Jama'at-e-Islami Pakistan', 250. Notwithstanding the fact that this account is short on specifics, I do accept her argument that in certain periods, 'differences were not so intense so as to prevent a coming together by some groups for specific aims' (248). Indeed, transitory and strategic accommodation was as much a part of Leftist politics as it was of other varieties. That does not, however, detract from the broader argument that despite occasional dalliances, the Jamaat was largely opposed to the Left, a fact that is amply confirmed by its rhetoric and political mobilisation in this period. And as Iqtidar shows, this opposition only became more vocal and intense in subsequent decades.

[43] Under Islamic law, this is an obligatory tax levied on the rich for the uplift of the poor.

[44] Lahore, 10 April, No. 15, PPSAI — WP 1948, 121.

[45] Lahore, 18 December, No. 51, PPSAI — WP 1948, 412.

[46] See for instance, Lahore, 24 April, No. 17, 143; Lahore, 29 May, No. 22, 181; and Lahore, 28 August, No. 35, PPSAI — WP 1948, 318.

This relationship, though, inevitably went both ways as even the Left was compelled to incorporate some of the Islamist discourse to counter the accusations made against it and to remain politically viable, and more crucially, legitimate in the eyes of the state. As a result, individuals like Mian Iftikharuddin, along with their standard demands of nationalisation, were also compelled to declare their support for the imposition of Quranic laws.[47] It was an entirely different matter though that his understanding of 'Quranic laws' was far removed from orthodox interpretations. While it could be tempting to view Iftikharuddin's statements in light of his position as a Leaguer till 1950, the fact nevertheless remained that the pressures to conform to a particular type of Islamic discourse extended to other sections of the Left as well. Within labour circles for instance, the necessity for the imposition of Sharia law was frequently invoked,[48] while Kisan meetings were inaugurated with recitations from the Quran.[49] Audiences were also asked 'not to get startled at the word "Communism" as it advocated equality, which was also the essence of Islam'.[50] And yet, invocations to Islam were the supreme tactics used to delegitimise Leftist politics. The potency of this tactic is reflected in a report filed by a British High Commissioner on a May Day rally:

> In Lahore ... where a meeting under the auspices of the Progressive Writers Association was presided over by Faiz Ahmed Faiz, the Acting President of the Pakistan Trades Unions Federation, an openly communist note was struck. Revolutionary messages from the West Punjab Committee of the CPP and from Sajjad Zaheer, the Communist leader at present in hiding, were read out to the meeting, which followed the Moscow line in pledging itself against war and condemning the Marshall Plan and the Atlantic Pact. The cry of 'Islam in danger' was however, promptly and successfully raised against the organisers of the meeting. The Lahore Press carried a series of articles alleging that speakers at the meeting had proclaimed the superiority of Communistic over Islamic doctrines, and widespread indignation culminated in the passage of resolutions condemning Communist

---

[47] Lahore, 15 May, No. 29, PPSAI — WP 1948, 167.
[48] See for instance, Lahore, 14 February, No. 7, PPSAI — WP 1948, 52–53.
[49] Lahore, 6 March, No. 10, PPSAI — WP 1948, 81.
[50] Lahore, 29 May, No. 22, PPSAI — WP 1948, 188.

activity on over 40 mosques in Lahore on the Friday following May Day. This encouraging demonstration of the ease with which the Pakistan public can be rallied to the defence of Islam against attacks by Communist agitators is not likely to have been lost on the authorities.[51]

Indeed, the success of this delegitimising tactic was such that even within labour circles, invocations to Islam were frequently employed to discredit other factions and leaders. For instance, the leadership of Mirza Muhammad Ibrahim was challenged by his opponent with the demand that he should convince them that 'he was a Muslim and not a Communist'.[52] The same individual later asked the workers to choose between communism and Islam.[53] This was, therefore, an indication of the powerful influence that Islamist discourse came to wield within Leftist politics — both as a legitimating and delegitimising force — almost immediately after Partition.

The uncomfortable relationship with religion was of course a conundrum that the Left was all too familiar with, particularly within the context of Punjabi politics. Similar (and successful) attempts at delegitimisation had been made against Sikh Leftists by the Akali Party from the late 1930s onwards. These mirrored efforts by the former to link the ideals of 'Communism' with the egalitarian tenets of Sikh religious doctrine. Similarly, 'Islam' too was no exception to these attempts at translation and creative appropriation. Such efforts had been made soon after the Bolshevik Revolution by Maulvi Barkatullah and activists from the *Hijrat* movement who founded, along with M.N. Roy, the first CPI in Tashkent in 1920.[54] Roy himself made these connections in his famous pamphlet on 'The Historical Role of Islam'.[55] Indeed, these linkages were repeatedly made in the

---

[51] *Despatch No. 305, Office of the High Commissioner for the United Kingdom Karachi, dated 3rd June, 1949 POL 13980 1949*, CAIP IOR/L/P&J/12/772, 341.

[52] Lahore, 27 November, No. 48, PPSAI — WP 1948, 391.

[53] Lahore, 18 December, No. 51, PPSAI — WP 1948, 414.

[54] See, for example, the second and sixth chapter of Ali Raza, 'Interrogating Provincial Politics'. For specifically the Hijrat movement, see for instance, Ansari, 'Pan Islam and the Making of the Early Muslim Socialists', 509–37.

[55] Roy, 'Historical Role of Islam: An Essay on Islamic Culture', Marxists Internet archive, http://marxists.org/archive/roy/1939/historical-role-islam/index.htm.

run-up to independence[56] and well beyond, which only served to disturb the ostensible dichotomy between religion — particularly 'Islam' — and 'Communism'. These exercises then were as much a function of political pragmatism as they were of convictions held by certain activists who saw no contradiction in their professed faith and the allegedly godless ideology they claimed adherence to.[57] If anything, many considered the fundamental principles of 'Communism' and 'Islam' to be the one and the same. Nevertheless, the mere association with the Soviet Union and 'Communism' was enough for those who wished to appropriate the religious idiom to discredit Leftist politics.

In this respect, the State too was not above employing Islam to denigrate the Left, though its tactic also involved using the 'anti-national' or 'anti-Pakistan' card. Indeed, the State and the ruling Muslim League provided the ultimate sanction for legitimising the use of Islam[58] and 'Pakistan' to discredit the Left and other regional, linguistic and ethnic movements that sought to challenge the hegemony of the prevailing state ideology. With respect to labour politics, for example, the state suppressed trade unions, which had been 'infiltrated' by communists, and replaced them with other unions who worked under the auspices of the Muslim League with the express purpose of 'working for Pakistan' rather than exploiting the Government's difficulties. Quite often, this meant directly supporting or encouraging a trend towards 'Islamizing trade unions'.[59] For instance, a 'Muslim Employees Association' was established as a counterbalance to the more radical unions working within the North Western Railways, which was considered as a hotbed of radical labour activism. Thus, this 'Association' was reported to be issuing posters in Urdu, replete with quotations from the Holy Quran,

---

[56] David Gilmartin also highlights this connection in his discussion of the Left and the Muslim League, 196–99.

[57] In this regard, see, especially, the debates between Sajjad Zaheer and Nadeem Ahmad Qasmi, which Kamran Asdar Ali has highlighted in his MAS paper.

[58] The standard had been set by Liaqat Ali Khan who lectured that 'the people of Pakistan should follow the teachings of the Prophet and not those of Marx, Stalin or Churchill'. Jalal, *The State of Martial Rule*, 281.

[59] *Extract from Weekly Report No. 43 for the Period Ending 31st October 1948, from the Deputy High Commissioner for the United Kingdom in Pakistan*, CAIP IOR/L/P&J/12/772.

'advising the workers to work hard and in an upright manner'.[60] Similar tactics were also employed at the local level to undercut any influence that local Leftist organisations may have had. In districts like Gujranwala, for example, the local Muslim Leaguers set up a rival Labour Party staffed by cadres of the Muslim League National Guard to counteract communist influence within local politics.[61] Most effective, however, was the use of the 'anti-national' label against the Left. Often this was dovetailed with the use of Islam, but increasingly, and in the context of a developing Cold War, the potency of this allegation grew all the more effective as the Left was long suspected, even before Partition, of having dual loyalties. This rhetoric was even used by the highest personality of all, Mohammad Ali Jinnah, who expressed his determination to root out all 'enemies of the state', who were officially described as saboteurs, fifth columnists, socialists and communists.[62]

## Repression and Survival

State rhetoric was naturally a signal for state persecution. Accordingly, a prolonged campaign to suppress Leftists was initiated in which techniques of harassment, intimidation, appeals to Nation and Religion, searches of party and union offices, and arrests proved to be the norm. The most prominent casualties of these tactics were prominent Leftists like Sajjad Zaheer, Dada Amir Haider Khan and M.M. Ibrahim. Sajjad Zaheer was compelled to go underground while Khan and Ibrahim were arrested a number of times.[63] The arrest of M.M. Ibrahim was in particular quite ironic as he was one of the first labour leaders to declare his loyalty to the Pakistani state on the eve of Partition. He had promised Jinnah full support 'in the establishment and progress of Pakistan and given the assurance that no strikes will be organized by the Railway employees to the

---

[60] Lahore, 3 April, No. 14, PPSAI — WP 1948, 117.

[61] Lahore, 27 November, No. 48, PPSAI — WP 1948, 392.

[62] *Communist Movement in East Bengal*, CAIP IOR/L/P&J/12/772, 351.

[63] Khan in particular remained a favoured target for state persecution over subsequent decades. Being a prominent and revered Leftist, his life epitomised the political trajectories of many within the Left. For an autobiographical account of his early political life see Gardezi, *Chains to Lose.*

detriment of the new Dominion'.[64] And yet, this assurance was not enough to protect both Ibrahim and the Union he represented from state repression. Like other Leftists, Ibrahim felt that independence had hardly proved to be a panacea for the problems faced by labourers and peasants. He thus soon accused the government of apathy[65] and stated that Pakistan had not been achieved by 'Quaid-e-Azam, Gandhi and Pandit Nehru, but by the individual sacrifices of labourers, kisans, military men and policemen'. In so doing, 'the workers had expected that with the establishment of Pakistan they would get better treatment, but their legitimate demands had not been accepted'. He, therefore, feared a confrontation between the Government and labourers.[66] His prediction came true as he was soon arrested for fomenting unrest and 'disaffection' amongst railway workers.[67] As an instance of state repression, this was but one of many arrests that took place across Pakistan. This was particularly the case in West Punjab and East Pakistan where the Left had a significant presence in relation to other regions. Indeed the fear of arrest and suppression was so acute that many workers went underground and destroyed their party and union records.[68] Ironically enough, these tactics of survival had been learnt and perfected during the height of colonial persecution.

The Left was also compelled to adopt other means to ensure its survival and remain a viable and legitimate political entity. As in the 1930s during the height of state persecution, Leftists were again compelled to deliberately eschew the terms 'communism' and 'communist', especially as they were loaded with the connation of being an 'enemy of the state'. Indeed, these labels were also pejoratively used by 'loyalist' unions to denigrate their more radical counterparts. These bodies warned labourers to present their demands in a constitutional manner and not to succumb to the machinations of 'Russian agents'.[69] Faced with the dual assault of the state and its supporters or proxies, the more radical element within Leftist circles was soon compelled to publicly defend itself against the charge of

---

[64] Lahore, Extract, 31 July, PPSAI 1947, 406.

[65] Lahore, 14 February, No. 7, PPSAI — WP 1948, 47.

[66] Ibid., 52–53.

[67] Lahore, 31 February, No. 8, PPSAI — WP 1948, 55.

[68] Lahore, 2 October, No. 40, PPSAI — WP 1948, 343.

[69] Lahore, 1 May, No. 18, PPSAI — WP 1948, 154.

being 'anti-national' or an 'Indian' or 'Russian' agent. Time and again they had to protest their innocence against the suspicion that they were 'set out to destroy Pakistan'.[70] This tendency spread to ordinary workers as well who were left to meekly protest against the travesty of being labelled as 'communists' merely for demanding a living wage.[71] Conversely, there were even concerted attempts by certain Leftists to consciously adopt nationalist symbols and publicly affirm their patriotism, which was at the same time a tactic to escape immediate state repression as well as wider public censure. Thus, quite frequently, in labour rallies, the red banner and the Pakistani flag were raised alongside each other. Moreover, M.M. Ibrahim for instance, after being suitably chastised during his first stint in jail, felt compelled to declare after his release that he was a 'faithful citizen of Pakistan and not a citizen of a foreign country'.[72] Interestingly enough, following his release, he was also bestowed with the title of 'Quaid-e-Azam Mazdooran'[73] by his fellow workers; a tongue in cheek attempt perhaps at signalling that the appropriation of nationalist symbols was not the prerogative of the ruling dispensation alone. Viewed differently, these attempts indicated the extent to which the Left was under pressure by a State that sanctioned the use of a hegemonic discourse that effectively criminalised dissent against the prevailing socio-economic inequities and a political system that sought to preserve them.

This repression only intensified in subsequent years. The Left, and specifically the Communist Party, was relentlessly persecuted and found to be implicated in the famous Rawalpindi Conspiracy Case in 1951.[74] As with its colonial predecessor, the post-colonial state also clung onto an image of the Left that was far greater than the strength it actually had, which was in any case never more than a few hundred active members.[75] An indication of this can be found

---

[70] See for instance, Lahore, 20 November, No. 47, PPSAI — WP 1948, 377.

[71] Lahore, 10 April, No. 15, PPSAI — WP 1948, 22.

[72] Lahore, 8 May, No. 19, PPSAI — WP 1948, 162.

[73] Literally translated as 'Great Leader of Workers'.

[74] This concerned an attempted coup that was planned by army officers against the government of Liaqat Ali Khan with the alleged support of prominent leaders of the Communist Party. For a rare insight into this landmark event, see Zaheer, *Times and Trial of the Rawalpindi Conspiracy 1951*.

[75] *Communism in West Punjab*, CAIP IOR/L/P&J/12/772, 357.

in the report filed by M. Anwer Ali, head of the CID, in 1951. While freely admitting that 'very little is known about the working of the party machine, its underground methods, its insidious technique, the fanatic zeal of its followers and their single mindedness of purpose', he nevertheless felt confident enough to state that:

> After the partition, the communist party in Pakistan lost all its veteran workers and was left without financial resources; yet within three years, a powerful party machine has been built up. The budget of the party is perhaps only next to that of the Muslim League. It employs more paid workers than any other political party. New links have been forged and work organized amongst students, factory workers, other laborers, kissans and writers, including journalists. Two candidates were put up for the last assembly elections. Innumerable strikes, processions and demonstrations have been organized. Class consciousness, which was unknown in these parts, has been developed and a distrust of the British created. Sajjad Zaheer, at any rate felt so sure of himself that in February 1951, he decided to plunge his party into the conspiracy hatched at Rawalpindi.[76]

Viewed within the backdrop of the Cold War in which Pakistan had decisively aligned itself with the Anglo-American power bloc, this extract was typical of the mindset prevailing within the official establishment, which succeeded in convicting and imprisoning prominent leaders like Faiz Ahmed Faiz and Sajjad Zaheer in the Rawalpindi Conspiracy Case. Indeed, the latter was later extradited to India at Nehru's personal intervention, which was a profound commentary on how far the ruling dispensation had come in its relationship with its erstwhile supporters. As for the Communist Party itself, it was banned along with its sister organisations in 1954 but only, and in a process starkly reminiscent of the colonial era, to remerge in various shapes and forms in response to the almost consistently acrimonious relationship that the Left had with the State.

## Conclusion

It is important to bear in mind though that the Left was but one of many political movements that were persecuted by the State and a vindictive Muslim League leadership. Faced with political uncertainty,

---

[76] Preface of *The Communist Party of West Pakistan in Action.*

geo-strategic and security concerns, economic and social problems, a refugee crisis, regional opposition, and above all, a desire to consolidate power in the hands of a select few, the incumbent leadership sought to suppress dissenting voices. Liaqat Ali Khan, for instance, regarded those who formed other political parties as 'traitors, liars and hypocrites'. Political rivals were regularly characterised as 'dogs of India', while any opposition to the Muslim League was considered equivalent to opposing Pakistan itself.[77] Convinced that 'Pakistan was beset by enemies on every side and menaced by saboteurs within',[78] the League leadership wasted little time in reintroducing the infamous 'Safety' and 'Security' Acts that were a legacy of colonial rule. These draconian laws served to restrict civil liberties and target political dissidents. Ironically, this was the very same Muslim League that had made the imposition of these laws a pretext for their agitation against the Unionist Ministry in late 1946, early 1947. With 'independence', however, the boot was firmly on the other foot. Mian Iftikharuddin then spoke for many when he questioned the Minister of Interior: 'in what manner has the State of Pakistan changed today for the ordinary people from what it was when the British ruled over us?'[79]

This reality of Pakistan then was the exact opposite of the Pakistan that progressives had hoped for. In an attempt to hedge its bets with the expected winners of the colonial end game, the CPI affiliated Left had worked with the League in an ultimately futile attempt to influence its politics.[80] Many joined the League and played an active role in the 1945–1946 election campaign in the Punjab.[81] Indeed,

---

[77] Cited from Grath, *The Destruction of Pakistan's Democracy* in Kazimi, *Liaqat Ali Khan*, 317.

[78] Jalal, *State of Martial Rule,* 280. Both *State of Martial Rule* and Jalal's *Democracy and Authoritarianism in South Asia* are necessary readings for understanding how the foundation for authoritarianism was laid in Pakistan. Also important is Allen McGrath's work.

[79] Malik, *Mian Iftikhar-ud-din,* 185–86.

[80] This was an outcome of the CPI's endorsement of the principle of 'self-determination'. See Ali's piece in this volume. Also see Adhikari, *Pakistan and Indian National Unity.*

[81] Despite their efforts, the Left was hardly instrumental in affecting the outcome of the elections. As both David Gilmartin and Ian Talbot show, electoral success largely hinged on the political leanings of Punjab's entrenched power brokers such as landlords and/or *pirs.* See Ian Talbot, 'The

the manifesto of the Punjab Muslim League, which was accused of bearing the 'stamp of Communist ideology', had been co-authored by none other than Daniel Latifi himself.[82] Once in power though, the Punjab League made it a crime for a tenant to read this manifesto in either 'public or private'.[83] That in itself was a profound statement of how far politics had shifted within the space of a few short years. From being erstwhile allies in the 'national struggle', Leftists quickly became political pariahs. By 1948, it was already far too late for the CPI to suggest that:

> The leadership of the Muslim League ... representing the interests of the Muslim capitalists and landlords, had *always* played a disruptive and anti-national role. The Muslim League leadership capitalize(d) the backwardness of the Muslim masses and the failure of the National Reformist leadership (read: the Congress) to draw the Muslim masses into the common struggle.[84]

To this day then, the support to the League is viewed as an egregious mistake by a section of the Left in both India and Pakistan, while in Indian nationalist historiography, this doctrine is viewed as yet another instance when the communist leadership betrayed and damaged the 'national cause'. In the Pakistani narrative, any mention of the Left or the role played by progressive politics in the nation's creation has been deliberately eschewed. After all, mentioning this would only dent the mythical linearity of Pakistan's emergence and

---

Growth of The Muslim League in The Punjab, 1937–1946' and Gilmartin, *Empire and Islam*. Gilmartin also devotes some space in discussing the negligible impact of the Left and the populist tone of the League's manifesto, 196–99.

[82] Lahore, 18 November, No. 47, PPSAI 1944, 637–41.

[83] The punishment for doing was forced eviction from the land. Toor, *The State of Islam,*13.

[84] This was a section of the thesis presented to the CPI's Second Party Congress in 1948. *Despatch from Office of HCUK, Karachi,* CAIP IOR/L/P&J/12/772, 127. The emphasis is mine. This tract was also a telling reflection of how familiar tropes regarding the 'backwardness' of Muslims were also accepted by a section of the Left. This, however, was by no means the only occasion when the Left and its detractors (and in particular the colonial state) shared similar views.

would highlight the inconvenient truth of a nation striking down its former allies immediately after its formation.

So where does that leave us then? It would of course be erroneous to suggest that the Left was in any way instrumental in the creation of Pakistan and the colonial end game. Yet, the Left's political ineffectiveness is also indicative of the limits to radicalism in a political arena that was from the very outset engineered against it. For the most part, this space remained unchanged in the transition from colonialism. This does not merely imply that the colonial state remained unchanged in the transfer of power. Given these formative years and the confusion surrounding the future direction of the nascent polity, it was hardly unexpected that this would be the case. And yet, as far as the Left was concerned, there was virtually no progress to suggest that the post-colonial state was making an effort to rid itself of its repressive legacy. If anything, it reinforced this legacy and introduced further measures to persecute those deemed to be 'subversive'. In line with colonial thinking, 'communism', among others, was also tantamount to 'subversion'. This view was held by state functionaries, who embodied many of the institutional outlooks that were a legacy of the colonial state, as well as the Muslim League and other political actors. The definition of who was considered 'subversive', then, remained by and large consistent. As did the political space, which determined what was considered legitimate in politics. Crucially though, the added element in this space was the rhetorical deployment of Islam. This could perhaps be considered a qualitative, albeit a regressive, change from the colonial era. Yet, the colonial state and the political actors operating within it also regularly invoked religion to delegitimise the Left.[85] Viewed this way, the post-colonial dispensation was different only in the frequent and exclusive use of Islam. In this sense, it was only later that the Pakistani state, with its gradual institutionalisation of Islam, became more removed from its colonial predecessor, though the foundation for that had been firmly laid in the Objectives Resolution of 1949. For their part, the Left could be forgiven for hoping that their politics would have brighter prospects in a post-colonial dispensation.

---

[85] For an insightful analysis into how the colonial state invoked religion, see the second chapter of Shalini Sharma, 'Radical Response to Colonialism'.

This continuity then only questions what 'decolonisation', 'freedom' and 'independence' really meant in the South Asian context. For those on the political fringe, and particularly the Left, the formal transfer of power did not necessarily signal a break with the subcontinent's colonial and repressive past. Rather, independence from the British was part of an unfulfilled political project, which was aimed at the establishment of a democratic republic that was led by and worked for the downtrodden of the subcontinent. If anything, the freedom that many had struggled and yearned for merely brought about a change of 'masters' who willingly inherited the colonial state instead of displacing it. The dream, as Faiz regretfully put it, remained 'unfulfilled'.[86] Thus, at the very least, this perspective encourages a reassessment of what 'independence' meant for those who did not identify themselves with the impulses of nationalist triumphalism.

Additionally, these narratives also provide a glimpse into the formative years of the Pakistani state. At a time of widespread political uncertainty and doubts about the future direction of the polity, actors from all shades of the political spectrum attempted to mould the state and its society in line with their own socio-political visions. Yet, despite this seemingly open playing field, the odds were still stacked against the 'Pakistani' Left. Already weakened by the dislocation of Partition and internal divisions, the Left was dealt a severe blow by a state which, true to its colonial legacy, assumed the sole prerogative of determining what counted as legitimate politics. Thus, as in the colonial period, the Left was compelled to engage with the limitations imposed on it. Despite these serious obstacles though, the Left was successful to some extent in influencing political discourse that was far out of proportion with its actual strength. Indeed, this disproportionate influence only grew in subsequent years. But the key to the Left's success or failure was determined by how it chose to respond to the shifting arena of political legitimacy. Maintaining the balance between the imperatives of pragmatic politics and sacrosanct principles, however, was easier said than done. And it was this balancing act that came to define the future trajectory of progressive politics in Pakistan.

---

[86] Sheema Majeed, *Coming Back Home*, 25.

# References

Adhikari, Gangadhar, *Pakistan and Indian National Unity*, London: Labour Monthly, 1983.

Ali, Anwer M., *The Communist Party of West Pakistan in Action*, Lahore: Criminal Investigation Department, Government of Punjab, Pakistan, 1952.

Ali, Kamran Asdar, 'Communists in a Muslim Land: Cultural Debates in Pakistan's Early Years', *Modern Asian Studies* 45, no. 3 (2011): 501–34.

Ansari, K. H., 'Pan Islam and the Making of the Early Muslim Socialists', *Modern Asian Studies* 20, no. 3 (1986): 509–37.

British Library, *Communist Activities in India and Pakistan, Jan 1947–Oct 1949*. IOR/L/P&J/12/772.

Gardezi, Hasan N., ed., *Chains to Lose: Life and Struggles of a Revolutionary — Memoirs of Dada Amir Haider Khan*, 2 vols, Delhi: Patriot Publishers, 1988.

Gilmartin, David, *Empire and Islam: Punjab and the Making of Pakistan*, London: Tauris, 1988.

Grath, Allen, *The Destruction of Pakistan's Democracy*, Karachi: Oxford University Press, 1996.

Guha, Ranajit, 'The Prose of Counter-Insurgency', in *Selected Subaltern Studies*, Ranajit Guha, and Gayatri Chakravorty Spivak (eds), New York: Oxford University Press, 1988.

Iqtidar, Humeira, 'Jama'at-e-Islami Pakistan: Learning from the Left', in *Beyond Crisis: Re-evaluating Pakistan*, Naveeda Khan (ed.), London: Routledge, 2010.

Jalal, Ayesha, *The State of Martial Rule: The Origins of Pakistan's Political Economy of Defence*, New Delhi: Cambridge University Press, 1992.

———, *Democracy and Authoritarianism in South Asia: A Comparative and Historical Perspective*, Cambridge: Cambridge University Press, 1995.

Kazimi, M. Raza, *Liaqat Ali Khan: His Life and Work*, Karachi: Oxford University Press, 2007.

Majeed, Sheema, ed., *Coming Back Home: Selected Articles, Editorials, and Interviews of Faiz Ahmed Faiz*, Karachi: Oxford University Press, 2008.

Malik, Abdullah, ed., *Selected Speeches and Statements: Mian Iftikhar-ud-Din*, Lahore: Nigarishat, 1971.

National Documentation Centre, Islamabad, *Punjab Police Secret Abstracts of Intelligence (PPSAI) 1946–48*.

Overstreet, Gene D. and Marshall Windmiller, *Communism in India*, Berkeley, CA: University of California Press, 1959.

Raza, M. Ali, 'Interrogating Provincial Politics: The Leftist Movement in Punjab, c. 1914–1950', PhD dissertation, University of Oxford, 2011.

Roy, M. N., 'Historical Role of Islam: An Essay on Islamic Culture', Marxists Internet Archive, 1939. http://marxists.org/archive/roy/1939/historical-role-islam/index.htm, accessed November 2011.

Sharma, Shalini, 'The Radical Response to Colonialism: The Organized Left in Punjab 1920–1947', PhD dissertation, School of Oriental and African Studies (SOAS), 2005.

Singh, Gurharpal, *Communism in Punjab: A Study of the Movement up to 1967*, Delhi: Ajanta Publications, 1994.

Talbot, Ian, 'The Growth of the Muslim League in the Punjab, 1937–1946', PhD dissertation, Royal Holloway College, University of London, 1981.

Toor, Sadia, *The State of Islam: Culture and Cold War Politics in Pakistan*, London: Pluto Press, 2011.

Zaheer, Hasan, *The Times and Trial of the Rawalpindi Conspiracy 1951*, Karachi: Oxford University Press, 1998.

Zaheer, Sajjad, *The Light: A History of the Movement for Progressive Literature in the Indo-Pak Subcontinent*, Karachi: Oxford University Press, 2006.

# ✠ 5

# Alternative Politics and Dominant Narratives: Communists and the Pakistani State in the Early 1950s

*Anushay Malik*

> With political geography cutting against the grain of the ideological protestations of the Islamic state, it has required an improbable array of conjuring tricks, and some somersaults on the tightrope of historical memory as well, to try and nationalize a past contested by enemies within and without. Ayesha Jalal, 'Conjuring Pakistan'.[1]

The composition of nationalist history often involves a re-telling of events that subsumes or just skims over ostensibly contradictory moments, so that instead of revealing alternative political trajectories, they become stepping stones: all leading towards the full realisation of the nation state. As has been pointed out by Kamran Asdar Ali,[2] the history of the Communist Party of Pakistan (CPP) is one of many such histories that needs to be reclaimed out of the enforced inclusion of disparate groups under one national narrative.[3]

Its history is part of the larger story of how the state dealt with opposition and alternatives. In the 1950s, much of what was written on the CPP mentioned the Party and the Left in Pakistan as a footnote to the tale of Pakistan's relationship with the United States in the context of the war against communism.[4] The brief rise of

---

[1] Jalal, 'Conjuring Pakistan', 74.

[2] Ali, 'Communists in a Muslim Land'.

[3] Ibid., 2–3.

[4] Lerski, 'The Pakistan-American Alliance'; McMahon, 'United States Cold War Strategy in South Asia'; and Levi, 'Pakistan, the Soviet Union and China'.

radical politics in Pakistan in the 1960s and the early 1970s saw a smattering of writings that considered the CPP and the Left not as a central focus, but in relation to the rise in radical politics in the country in this period, particularly emphasising politics in what is now Bangladesh and, to a lesser extent, Karachi.[5]

Recent work has significantly deepened our understanding, showing how the cultural politics of the CPP contested nationalist historiography. Kamran Asdar Ali's brilliant account provides an insight into the various historical trajectories that *could* have developed in Pakistan, by looking at how intellectual debates from within the CPP, and the Progressive Writers Association (PWA) in particular, engaged with the state's ideological consensus.[6] Saadia Toor has a more macro-perspective that shows how the CPP and the Left in Pakistan presented an alternative articulation of politics in comparison to that based on religion; hence, the suppression of these groups then represented the marginalisation of 'progressive models for the Pakistani nation-state project'.[7] Similarly, Talat Ahmed discusses the interplay of history and memory in the nationalist project, by recovering the narrative of the role played by the CPP and specifically the PWA in the Rawalpindi Conspiracy Case of 1951, where members of the Party were accused of colluding with army officers to mastermind a coup.[8]

This chapter attempts to contribute to these debates in two ways: first by providing a local case study, centred on the city of Lahore, and second by focusing on state repression. The fact that different regions in Pakistan had variant manifestations of politics underscores the need for a localised study to trace the mechanics, in particular the construction of the CPP as 'troublemakers' and antinational 'traitors', by which state oppression operated. Lahore in the 1950s

---

[5] For work on the political upheavals of this time that contain a discussion of the Left in Pakistan see (amongst others), Ali, *Pakistan: Military Rule or People's Power*; Ali, 'Revolutionary Perspectives for Pakistan'; Rashiduzzaman, 'The National Awami Party of Pakistan'; Franda, 'Communism and Regional Politics'; and Khan, 'A Front for the A.L.'; For localised studies in Karachi see: Shaheed, *The Labour Movement in Pakistan;* and Ali, 'The Strength of the Street'.

[6] Ali, 'Communists in a Muslim Land'.

[7] Toor, *The State of Islam,* 2; for the focus on the PWA see Ch. 3.

[8] Ahmed, 'Writers and Generals'.

is a particularly interesting case because of the changes wrought by the city's insertion into what was then the 'new' Pakistani state. The analysis in this chapter begins with a brief overview of the activities of the CPP and the Left in this 'new' space of an older city. It then goes on to critically assess categories used to describe and restrict the CPP, in three sections. The first of these traces the description of communists as 'godless' versus 'troublemakers'; it studies the method by which the communists, as political trouble-makers for the state, were equated with the problem of them being antithetical to Pakistan's Islamic orientations. The second category is the CPP as political opposition; the focus of this section is on the Punjab Legislative Assembly elections of 1951 to highlight how the communists in opposition were actually part of a political alternative in that their constituency was situated amongst groups of the work-ing poor. By constructing them as troublemakers, the response of the state to the presence of such an opposition was to use a combination of pre-emptive arrests and election fraud to ensure that these groups did not find representation in the assembly. The third section focuses on the title of 'traitors' by looking at the Rawalpindi Conspiracy Case, the discovery of which overlapped with the 1951 elections. It argues that the Conspiracy was part of the same process in that it was used by the state as an excuse to begin a more systematic crackdown on the Left in Pakistan. As it was a conspiracy that was directed against the state, the involvement of communist groups within it meant they could now be deemed traitors against the state itself.

Two main sources have been used in this chapter. One is the *Pakistan Times*, a newspaper that has been referred to as the 'unof-ficial organ of the Communist Party'[9] and in the words of Tariq Ali, 'the newspaper *was* the Left in Pakistan'.[10] Its coverage of the activities of radical movements and communist politics makes it perhaps one of the only sources where an almost daily account of their activities can be studied. The other source was acquired from Ahmad Salim's private archives, the South Asian Research and Resource Centre. This is a two-volume report published by the Criminal Investigation Department (CID), Punjab.[11] It contains

---

[9] Aziz, *The Coffee House of Lahore*, 125.

[10] Ali, *Pakistan: Military Rule or People's Power*, 104.

[11] This source has been used previously by Ahmed, 'Writers and Generals'.

correspondence between CPP members, details of their activities, organisations and affiliations. Other sources used more intermittently include judgements of the Lahore High Court and Cabinet proceedings. Interviews of CPP members and of a student activist at that time have been used (with permission) to supplement this. These allow for the inclusion of anecdotes and personal experiences that contain rich detail about actual political practice that cannot be conveyed through official reports.[12]

## Lahore and the Left

The Communist Party of Pakistan was faced with the daunting task of having to establish itself within a 'new' country struggling to rebuild itself in the aftermath of Partition. Specifically, the city of Lahore found that its status had changed because of its proximity to the border. Before Partition, it was in Lahore that there had flourished the 'coffee house culture' that K.K. Aziz, a well-known Pakistani historian, fondly wrote about,[13] a time when groups such as writers, poets and students would come together for political and literary discussions that lasted for hours. The last remnants of this culture were to fade away slowly as Lahore became a border city. Partially, this was because of the widespread destruction of the urban fabric that attended Partition. The historic walled city for instance, with its small-scale industry and working class neighbourhoods, was almost completely burnt to the ground.[14] Against this background, it is not surprising then, that when the CPP was formulating plans for the now border city, they expressly stated in their correspondence that in Lahore, they should 'not attempt anything big'.[15] Nonetheless, the

---

[12] For example, the Inspector General of Police who compiled the CID volumes reportedly approached Hameed Akhtar while he was in jail after the conspiracy case and asked him to translate one of the documents into English. Hameed Akhtar's daughter told the author that a young CID official was posted outside their house and sometimes when nobody else was home, they would ask him to pick up yoghurt and other necessities from the nearby market. Clearly then, individual actions are not entirely dominated by institutional rules.

[13] Aziz, *The Coffee House of Lahore*.

[14] 'Ancient Walled City a Veritable Sea of Flames' (*Civil & Military Gazette,* 14 August 1947).

[15] Criminal Investigation Department, Vol. I, 240.

Punjab saw various types of popular cultural movements that challenged the national culture and the ruling elite.[16] Lahore's position as the town of traders in the prosperous and politically dominant Punjab as well as its continued administrative importance aided in its recovery in the post-Partition state to a greater extent than cities like Karachi.[17] However, the economic prominence of the province did not mean that the benefits of this were divided equally amongst all classes and regions within the Punjab.[18] The demographic majority of the agricultural areas and the power wielded by the landed classes effectively meant that formal political contests were biased in their favour.[19] Similarly, even while Lahore was the dominant city in the dominant state of Punjab, the city did hold specific *spaces* that presented a potential for radical mobilisation. For instance, the railways and the Mughalpura workshops in the north of the city were the central base for the CPP labour leader Mirza Muhammad Ibrahim and the North Western Railway (NWR) Union that he was the president of. CPP members were also active amongst the workers of the Bata Mazdoor League (BML) in Batapur on the outskirts of what was then Lahore city.

It is important to note that within these spaces, the CPP was allied to, but not coequal with, the Left more broadly. The narrative of the CPP in the early 1950s is intrinsically connected to the more fluid politics of the time.[20] There were groups that were affiliated to the CPP and those that, although not being formally associated with

---

[16] For an analysis of the popular Punjab based 'Punjabiyat' movement against the dominant role of Urdu in national culture see Ayres, *Speaking Like a State*, see: 67–104; Rahman, *Language and Politics in Pakistan*, 191–206; for an overview of women's movements and regional movements within the Punjab see Samad, 'Pakistan or Punjabisation', 35–37.

[17] The dominant position of the Punjab in Pakistan is well established in the literature, see (amongst others): Alavi, 'Pakistan and Islam'; Khan, *Politics of Identity*; Sayeed, 'The Breakdown of Pakistan's Political System'; and for the faster recovery of Lahore and administrative importance see: Talbot, 'A Tale of Two Cities'.

[18] Talbot, 'The Punjabization of Pakistan', 57.

[19] For a historic overview of the continued relationship between landed and political power in the Punjab see: Javid, 'Class, Power and Patronage'.

[20] The existence of fluid identifications that became more rigidified with time is a point that has been made before with regards to ethnic and regional divisions, see: Samad, 'Pakistan or Punjabisation', 24.

it, were sympathetic of its aims. Examples of the former include the Pakistan Trade Union Federation (PTUF), whose president was Mirza Ibrahim, whereas the general secretary was the national poet and PWA member, Faiz Ahmed Faiz; and the Democratic Students Federation (DSF), which, at the time, was more active in Karachi. Although these have been referred to as 'fronts' of the CPP,[21] not all their members were communist. The organisations themselves were formed with the aid of the Party but the affiliated unions of the PTUF and the students who mobilised under the DSF were not all of the same ideology.[22] The latter group of 'progressives' were sympathetic to the CPP but not directly linked to it. One of the prominent organisations that can be classified under this category was the Azad Pakistan Party (APP) of Mian Iftikharuddin.[23]

All these groups were involved in the articulation of an alternative practice of politics. For example, in 1953 Mirza Ibrahim linked the problems faced by NWR workers to Pakistan's foreign policy.[24] Much later, in 1957, while helping the striking workers of the Batala Engineering Company Workers he included 'nationalisation' among their minimum demands.[25] As such, the existence of this alternative within the society allowed for the broadening and politicisation of issues.

Through these organisations, important links and resources could be extended to agitations, which then impacted the chances of a successful movement. This can be seen in the case of the Batapur strikes that took place around the Bata factory in the early 1950s. A deputation of the Bata Mazdoor League linked itself with the Pakistan Trade Union Federation (PTUF) by approaching Faiz Ahmed Faiz and asking for his help in addressing their grievances.[26] As part

---

[21] See: Leghari, 'The Socialist Movement', 47–48.

[22] Naseem, Interview with the author.

[23] 'Formation of Azad Pakistan Party Announced' (*Pakistan Times*, 11 November 1950).

[24] 'Recognition of NWR Trade Union Demanded, Foreign Exploitation Cause of Present Economic Crisis — Mirza Ibrahim' (*Pakistan Times*, 26 January 1953).

[25] 'Government Urged to Take Over BECO' (*Pakistan Times*, 25 April 1957).

[26] 'Bata Shoe Workers Demonstrations Enter Tenth Day' (*Pakistan Times*, 9 July 1950).

of the Progressive Writers Association, Faiz had been involved in pre-Partition discussions that emphasised the need to have a better understanding of the conditions workers had to face.[27] It is then not surprising that Faiz Ahmed Faiz, although never being a formal member of the CPP, was one of the vice presidents of the PTUF in 1951 and an active member campaigning for worker rights. Presumably, his position as an editor of the *Pakistan Times*, in its early years, must have contributed to the intensive coverage the newspaper gave to workers' strikes in the country.

Shortly after this deputation approached Faiz, Mirza Ibrahim began to support the Bata worker strikes openly.[28] Similarly, members of the CPP in their individual capacities were also involved in helping the Bata workers. Tahira Mazhar Ali, one of the founder members of the Democratic Women's Association (connected to the CPP) and an active CPP member herself, went to these strikes to encourage and aid the women who were striking. Indeed the women took part alongside the men in the strikes, often cooking food for them and washing clothes in order to keep the strike going.[29] In addition to their role in the strikes themselves, over 50 women from the workers' colony, clad in burqas, staged a demonstration in front of the offices of the Punjab Muslim League.[30] Although the CPP cannot be given sole credit for the sustained strike actions of the Bata Mazdoor League, their involvement both directly and indirectly, as well as their role in publicising the demands of the League in papers like the *Pakistan Times* and *Imroze*, played an important role in pressurising the state to take action and make negotiations possible. Indeed, in January 1951, the appointment of an adjudicator was deemed to be ' ... the beginning of a new phase in the history of labour disputes in the Punjab because it is for the first time ... that an adjudicator had been appointed and recourse taken to the Industrial Disputes Act.'[31]

---

[27] Malik, 'The Marxist Literary Movement', 653.

[28] 'Bata Workers Strike Enters Second Day, PTUF President Assures Support' (*Pakistan Times*, 25 August 1950).

[29] Ali, Interview with the author.

[30] 'Bata Workers Strike Enters Second Day' (*Pakistan Times*, 25 August 1950); and 'Harassment of Bata Strikers by Police' (*Pakistan Times*, 30 August 1950).

[31] '32 Day Old Bata Workers Strike Ends, Sequel to Appointment of Adjudicator' (*Pakistan Times*, 8 January 1951).

The CPP should then be viewed not as an organisationally strong party but one that helped provide links between individuals and rather diverse groups that broadly referred to themselves as progressive. As the political space in this period allowed for fluidity, many of these groups could (and did) establish linkages to one another that were both political and personal. In some cases, these even included familial inter-organisational links. For example, Mian Iftikharuddin's son, Arif Iftikharuddin, was a prominent member of the DSF.[32] Also in the DSF was Naeem Ashraf Malik who was the younger brother of Shamim Ashraf Malik who was in the CPP District Organising Committee in Lahore and worked with Mirza Ibrahim as the General Secretary of the NWR Workers Union.[33] It was these links that came to the fore when the DSF was involved in the mobilisation of students to launch a movement in 1953 against rising university fees and deplorable conditions in the universities.[34] Although this student movement began in Karachi, the repression it received from the state sparked off wider shows of support amongst students in Lahore.[35]

The CPP may have aided the formation of some alliances, but many of the groups in these organisations did not consider themselves as communist at all and were not even directly connected to the CPP's structure. Nonetheless, they were all repressed in the name of curtailing communism. A student leader arrested after the CPP was banned in 1954 spent seven months in jail and said that while his cellmates included activists, students and journalists who had worked with the CPP, a minority considered themselves as communist.[36] What this serves to illustrate is that there was a porous dividing line between 'communist' and 'the rest' in the everyday politics of Lahore. Thus, the publicly (and loudly) voiced divide based on atheistic communism and Pakistan's religious polity did not necessarily come to the forefront in actual practice; however,

---

[32] Criminal Investigation Department, Vol. II, 390.

[33] Ibid., 387, 391.

[34] Ahmad, 'Flashback: Students Activated'; and Naseem, Interview with the author.

[35] 'Lahore Students Condemn Karachi Firing' (*Pakistan Times*, 9 January 1953); and 'Lahore Students Mourn Slain Comrades' (*Pakistan Times*, 11 January 1953).

[36] Naseem, Interview with the author.

*at particular junctures* this difference was emphasised by the state to serve its own agenda.

## Defining Enemies: 'Godless' Communists or 'Defiant Troublemakers'?

In 1954, Mohammad Ali Bogra announced at a public forum that international powers did not have to be worried about communism spreading in Pakistan because being Muslim automatically protected them from the evils of communism.[37] One also has to keep in mind the audience Bogra was talking to. He was assuring the international arena that while they chased this spectre down in the rest of the world, here, in Pakistan, all was well because communism simply could not compete with the Islamic ideology that was prevalent. In later years, similar assertions stating that 'secularism represents a complete antithesis to Islam'[38] would be made in different contexts. What these statements had in common was a lack of discernment about what precisely this Islam was.

At the time, the state itself could not have provided a coherent answer to this.[39] Indeed, certain views expressed within the upper echelons of the Pakistani state in the early 1950s suggest wariness about the use of an Islamic idiom in politics. The state's secret internal documents from the early 1950s show an aversion to the 'parrot like repetition'[40] that equates Pakistan with an Islamic state without giving any idea of what that entails. This same Ministry of Interior document then goes on to express the fear of intellectuals perceiving the government as 'pandering to orthodoxy'[41] where Islam is concerned, while stressing that the Pakistani state should advocate some strain of 'Islamic democracy and socialism of a modern variety'.[42]

---

[37] *Dawn*, 5 May 1954, cited in Levi, 'Pakistan, the Soviet Union and China', 211.

[38] Gauhar, *The Challenge of Islam*, 300, cited in Hasan, *The Battle of Ideas in Pakistan*, 15.

[39] Discussing the report on the 1953 Anti-Ahmedi agitation, Farzana Shaikh also makes this point about how the '[c]onsensus on the meaning of the "Muslim" remained elusive' see: Shaikh, *Making Sense of Pakistan*, 61.

[40] Ministry of the Interior, 'Internal Situation', 6.

[41] Ibid., 7.

[42] Ibid., 6.

On its own, this statement is interesting because it shows that the combination of Islam and some 'modern variety' of socialism was not viewed as fundamentally incompatible. Although the amalgamation of socialist ideas and Islam is potentially acceptable, a communist polity (also never clearly defined) and orthodox Islam are seen as threatening because one leads to the other:

> ... if the accent on unrestrained religiosity continues to be maintained as at present, there is bound to be a violent reaction and Pakistan would then be, heading straight for communism.[43]

In actual practice as well, the absolute truth of this polarity between religion and the Left was allowed to slide when it suited the ruling elite to do so. The Muslim League was not above the inclusion of particular Leftists within its ranks nor was it against the socialist bent given to its manifesto by Daniyal Latifi in the run up to the 1946 elections.[44]

The issue of defiance and sedition was more important in defining the position of communism in Pakistan's national imagery than its irreligious basis was. In the wake of political unrest in Dacca, the Pakistani Interior Ministry in 1951 discussed the disturbing possibility of the riots spreading to West Pakistan. To prove the imminent possibility of this threat, the report for the cabinet pointed as evidence towards 'incidents involving clear defiance of authority'[45] in Lahore and Peshawar. According to the report, the two evils responsible for this volatile state of affairs were provincialism and communism. Even though the threat of the latter was perceived as being the greatest in East Pakistan, in the rest of the country the threat was real, but invisible:

> The [Communist] Party is biding its time and waiting for an opportunity to reassemble its forces.[46]

This overreaction by the state denotes the level of insecurity that pervaded the Pakistani establishment. Whereas the politics of

---

[43] Ibid., 10.
[44] Leghari, 'The Socialist Movement in Pakistan', 27–28.
[45] Ministry of the Interior, 'Internal Situation', 1.
[46] Ibid., 5.

provincialism and communism represent different demands, made by groups and individuals who were not entirely overlapping, they were seen by the state as being part of the same sort of threat to its authority. The common link between the two was the fact that both were problems seen as provoking political instability, not religious amorality.

That politicians and state officials articulated different opinions on this issue is quite clear. However, this variation also extended to the judiciary. In 1953, Mazhar Ali Khan, who was a CPP member, editor for both *Pakistan Times* and *Imroze* and Tahira Mazhar Ali's husband, was accused of trying to cause disaffection against the government through an article he had written. Although fully aware of Mazhar Ali's political background, the dissenting judgement states that:

> ... knowing the 'iconoclast' and his political associations, the government could ... have relied on the good taste of its people.[47]

In this case, a common elite background sufficed to elide punishment. In contrast, the judicial reaction to an article published in Lyallpur in 1950, which accused the government of creating 'an atmosphere of irreligiousness' thus allowing for the 'flood of communism' and the 'fostering of Qadyaniat', was seen as clearly 'seditious'.[48] What these two examples, persecuted under the same law, highlight is that in some cases, communist affiliations could be regarded as harmless to the national government whereas accusations regarding the lack of religion in the state could be seen as seditious. The point being forwarded here is not that communism and the Islam of the state had a natural affinity but that their clash, as epitomised by the banning of the CPP in 1954, cannot be seen as being based on a primordial ideological dichotomy, but rather on political contingency.

This observation is borne out even on the level of the individual beliefs and strategies of those who associated with the Communist Party in Lahore. For instance, Abdullah Malik, one of the CPP members who joined the Muslim League in the late 1940s, had previously

---

[47] Pakistan Law Reports. 'Mazhar Ali Khan v. The Governor of the Punjab', 268.

[48] Ibid., 416.

flirted with the politics of the *Ahrar* Party.[49] He later became an active and committed member of the CPP and in the later years of his life, prayed and studied the Quran closely.[50]

Similarly, Hameed Akhtar, before joining active politics and becoming a member of both the CPP and the PWA, had learnt the Quran by heart as a boy.[51] Even in discussions within the CPP, some members were keen to link communist regimes with Islam. A fascinating example is that of a CPP member who travelled to Communist China in the early 1950s. On his return, while extolling the virtues of Mao, in addition to commenting on his simple lifestyle, he stated that Mao was, in fact, a Muslim.[52] Even on a more formal, organisational level the fluidity of political practice is borne out by the alliances (albeit sporadic) that the CPP formed with religious groups and vice versa.[53] Clearly then, the divide between Islam and communism was in no way as clearly defined in actual practice as it was in the public statements made by state officials and politicians.

The eventual ban of the CPP was precipitated by international pressure. Discussing the issue of whether the United States could have trusted Pakistan to maintain a distance from communist countries on the international plane, Werner Levi[54] focuses on the apparent conflict between the avowedly secular politics of the Left and of the Islam of the state. He analyses the foreign policy of Pakistan to come to this same conclusion — that the decisions taken by the Pakistani state show not so much an adherence to a particular type of ideology as they do to what was favourable to them at the time.[55] Thus, the conflict between the Left and the state in the early years was not *only* about ideological nuances or about the incompatibility of communism and Islam, it was also about the need of the state to survive and for the status quo to remain untrammelled. It is no surprise then that the crackdown and arrests on communists and labour in Pakistan tended to increase when the state perceived

---

[49] See Tahir Kamran, *Epitome* in this special issue.
[50] Aziz, *The Coffee House of Lahore.*
[51] Ibid., 244.
[52] Criminal Investigation Department, Vol. II, 404.
[53] Iqtidar, *Secularizing Islamists?*, 66.
[54] Levi, 'Pakistan, the Soviet Union and China'.
[55] Ibid.

itself to be under threat, even though this perception was not always reflected in ground realities.

Indeed, the reaction of the state was usually out of proportion to the magnitude of the threat. Although in places like East Pakistan the CPP was very strong, in the city of Lahore it was not a very organised party. Its strength lay more in its support of the working poor in the absence of any other political groups who would do so, as well as its presence as an oppositional political current in the city of Lahore. The construction of the CPP as political 'trouble-makers' adversely affected the advantages that could accrue to labour through involvement with these groups.

In the case of the Bata workers, their association with the PTUF meant that they were labelled as communists by the Management and one of the first issues raised in the court case in their defence was how ' ... it was wrong and quite improper on the part of the Management to dub all respondents as Communists, whereas, in fact, they were plain and honest workers.'[56] The opinion that is being expressed here is quite different from the views given earlier stating that communism is problematic because of its un-Islamic character. It is clearly because of the political activities of the party, and not just its ideological implications, that the term is being used to describe workers who are the antithesis of 'plain and honest'. The term communist perhaps belies what the implications of the term were in this context. It was the overlap in meaning between 'communist' and 'troublemaker' that was of import. Even though the striking workers were not all communist, the Management could emphasise the link between them and the PTUF to term them as such and thus associate their strikes, which were for wages and against victimisation, with the wider aims and perceptions associated with the CPP in order to detract the possibility of a sympathetic response from the wider public or from the government.

## The Left as Political Opposition: The Punjab Elections of 1951

One key technique deployed by the Pakistani state to subsume the political alternatives presented by the Left involved highlighting

---

[56] 'Case Against Bata Mazdoor League Workers Open, Preliminary Objections Raised' (*Pakistan Times*, 22 July 1950).

*conclusions* as opposed to the *process* by which an endpoint was reached. For instance, the Punjab legislative assembly elections of 1951 in nationalist historiography concluded with a resounding electoral win for the Muslim League.[57] Viewing this from a macro-level the undiscriminating observer could conclude that the Muslim League in post-Partition Pakistan remained a popular party with a mass base — a conclusion that misses both the process by which the opposition was marginalised and the advantages offered to the League by its class basis. A breakdown of this electoral victory reveals that 80 per cent of those elected in the Punjab were landlords commanding tenant votes[58] and that no CPP member was ever elected to the West Pakistan legislature, which was taken as an indication of the lack of appeal of the 'cult of communism'.[59] Whereas in Lahore, individual CPP members were elected but were either arrested or made to give up their seat, in direct contradiction to the nationalist narratives of the time.[60]

In the lead up to the elections, it was announced, by the Punjab Provincial Committee of the CPP, that Mirza Ibrahim would be contesting the election for constituency number five of the Lahore City Corporation.[61] Although worker demands and strategies were not enforced or formulated by the CPP alone, its support for people like Mirza Ibrahim was an important part of helping certain individuals emerge as important leaders. Abdul Rauf Malik, who knew Mirza Ibrahim and had spent time with him in prison, said that the CPP saw a lot of potential in Mirza Ibrahim because he was *already* an important worker leader.[62] Although he was not formally educated, he apparently had an impressive grasp of the economic problems

---

[57] Aziz, *Party Politics in Pakistan*, 5.

[58] Maniruzzaman, 'Group Interests in Pakistan Politics', 85.

[59] Aziz, *Party Politics in Pakistan*, 126.

[60] Kaniz Fatima was elected to the women's seat in the outer Lahore constituency and Ali Bux of the APP was elected in Lahore. However, neither of them were part of the Punjab Assembly formed in 1951. Unfortunately, besides Mian Iftikharuddin's statements stating that there were election malpractices in a general sense, the circumstances under which they were excluded is not clear.

[61] 'Mirza Ibrahim to Contest Election' (*Pakistan Times*, 13 January 1951).

[62] Interview with author.

of workers and could list off, by rote, the number of workers in each department and their income.[63] Thus, the CPP did indeed aid particular individuals in terms of providing them with resources and assistance, but it did not solely create movements or leaders.

While the greater politicisation of workers in this period paints a picture of Lahore being a cradle for heightened political awareness amongst the working poor and a centre for the activities of the Left, this heightened activity was actually concentrated in certain pockets of the city. The elections of 1951, for instance, registered a very low voter turnout in most places, averaging at about 30 per cent.[64] In stark contrast, constituency number five, from where Mirza Ibrahim was standing, registered a voter turnout of about 50 per cent, which was the highest registered in any constituency in Lahore.[65] He won the seat at 7030 votes with the Muslim League candidate, Ahmed Saeed Kirmani, following with 4847 votes. This announcement was followed by a procession taken out by the workers of the locality to celebrate his victory.[66] Perhaps the most interesting thing about this election result was that throughout the run-up to the elections, Mirza Ibrahim was in jail.

It was found in court that he had been arrested because his speeches were deemed objectionable. However, nothing could be revealed in court about the exact nature of the objection to the speeches because the orders for the arrest were declared official documents. Revealing their contents was seen as potentially having 'a detrimental effect on law and order'.[67] The basis for the appeal against this decision was that Mirza Ibrahim had been detained to restrict his union-related activities and to prevent him from contesting the elections for the Punjab Assembly.[68] The court had, by this time, already stated that it

---

[63] Abdul Rauf Malik was a CPP member in the early 1950s and head of the People's Publishing House at Lahore: Malik, Interview with the author.

[64] Kamran, 'Early Phase of Electoral Politics', 266.

[65] 'Polling Ends in Punjab, Opposition Gain 43 Seats so Far, Mirza Ibrahim Wins Local Seat in Lahore No. 5' (*Pakistan Times*, 21 March 1951).

[66] Ibid.

[67] 'Mirza Ibrahim's "Habeas Corpus" Petition: Arguments Conclude: Chief Justice Reserves Judgement' (*Pakistan Times*, 24 April 1951).

[68] 'Mirza Ibrahim's Petition Dismissed; Lahore High Court Judgement' (*Pakistan Times*, 26 April 1951).

was 'helpless' to defend Mirza Ibrahim, given that his detention had been ordered under the Punjab Public Safety Act, which prevented the court from investigating the reasons for an arrest made by the executive.[69] Therefore, it was entirely unsurprising that the petition was finally dismissed.

A clearer picture of the context within which arrests were made at this time emerges when it is noted that Mirza Ibrahim was not the only one who had been arrested under this charge. Chaudhry Ataullah Jehanian and Dada Amir Haider were also prominent Leftists who had been detained at the time and all of them had their petitions rejected.[70] It would be stretching coincidence to a breaking point to suggest that these arrests had no connection at all with the fact that both Mirza Ibrahim and Ataullah Jehanian had just previously been announced as Left-wing candidates contesting the elections.[71] In Mirza's case however, his election and subsequent arrest were not enough to quell the matter. Workers, Leftists and CPP members campaigned for the election on behalf of Mirza Ibrahim. Hameed Akhtar, who was a member of both the PWA and the CPP at the time, did not actively take part in worker politics but was involved in this particular election campaign. He and his comrades printed out posters of Mirza Ibrahim in handcuffs, and held meetings and processions to campaign for his election.[72] However, in the case of Mirza Ibrahim's electoral victory, the eventual end point was not a victorious one for the Left in Lahore. It was decided that there was an error in the way the votes had been counted, a 'certain' number of votes were declared bogus and Mr Ahmed Saeed Kirmani was

---

[69] 'M. Ibrahim and Jahanian's Habeas Corpus Petitions, Court Practically Helpless, Says Chief Justice' (*Pakistan Times*, 17 April 1951).

[70] 'Mirza Ibrahim's 'Habeas corpus' Petition: Arguments Conclude: Chief Justice Reserves Judgement' (*Pakistan Times*, 26 April 1951).

[71] 'Left-Wing Candidates for Punjab Elections, 11 Names Announced' (*Pakistan Times*, 16 February 1951).

[72] Akhtar, Interview with the author. The reason that Hameed Akhtar did not usually take an active part in worker politics was that his duties were different; he was assigned to work in the cultural front and, as such, was not involved in the everyday politics of labour. Nonetheless, it does seem that when it came to crucial moments like the elections of 1951, people assigned other work could be called upon to help in the achievement of a common objective.

elected to the Assembly whereas Mirza Ibrahim continued his time in the torture chambers beneath the Lahore Fort.[73]

Commenting on this retrospectively, Craig Baxter writing to the US government from Lahore stated that Kirmani's electoral victory probably involved some 'juggling' of the result.[74] This is highly possible given that within the Punjab complaints of election malpractices abounded.[75] Although the actual electoral success of candidates from the Left was limited, the fact that they could stand at all was made possible through links that existed between these different associations. Although Mirza Ibrahim was a railway worker, he contested and won the seat from constituency number five on behalf of the Communist Party seat. Similarly, Kaniz Fatima, a member of the DWA, contested and won the seat in Outer Lahore constituency number two, for women from the Azad Pakistan Party (APP).[76] The climate was sufficiently open that candidates from the Kisan Committee in the Punjab could also announce their decision to stand for elections as members of the APP.[77]

Thus, the fluidity of politics and connections between these groups could be utilised during elections. The very existence of these groups in the electoral process represents a political opposition that was not overtly Islamist, regionalist or nationalist. The presence of such an opposition is an important part in politicising the working poor and, at the very least, connecting them to some extent to the politics practiced at the level of the state. However, as the rest of this chapter will argue, the Pakistani state's policies subsequently defined, in increasingly narrow terms, what type of politics was acceptable and steadily attempted to obliterate both the diversity of political practices and the older networks that existed.

---

[73] Ibid.

[74] 'Memorandum of Conversation' 31 July 1967 in Khan (ed.) *The American Papers*, 232.

[75] For accusations regarding election malpractices made within the Punjab Assembly see: 'Mamdot Astonished at "Abrupt" Adjournment' (*Pakistan Times*, 8 May 1951).

[76] 'Opposition Captures 38 Seats So Far' (*Pakistan Times*, 28 March 1951).

[77] 'Azad Party Selected No Ex-MLA, Unionist or Rejected Leaguer' (*Pakistan Times*, 16 February 1951).

## From 'Troublemakers' to 'Traitors': The Rawalpindi Conspiracy Case

The events around the Rawalpindi conspiracy case, to this day, are not known in their entirety. What is known is that through informal links, a number of army officers made contact with members of the CPP and then met to discuss the possibility of a coup. However, an attempt at moving the coup out of the meetings and into the realm of actual implementation was never made. This may be because the authorities found out about it beforehand. It is equally possible, as some have stated, that talk of the coup had already been shelved at the time the arrests were made and that these detentions were actually part of the same imperative to quell opposition in the elections.[78] What is relevant for this chapter, however, are the repercussions of the case for the Left and the CPP. In connection with the case itself, important individuals like Faiz Ahmed Faiz, Sajjad Zaheer and Muhammad Hussain Ata were arrested. After these arrests, which were more directly connected to the Conspiracy, the state began a systematic campaign of apprehending members of the Left from all over the country. Although the implications of the case itself had echoes on the national level, there was also a specific crackdown on Leftists in the city of Lahore.

A widespread state of panic was induced by Liaquat Ali Khan's announcement of the unearthing of a plot that was aimed at creating a 'violent commotion', announced in the paper on the same day that polling in the Punjab began.[79] The news of the conspiracy elicited an immediate response from the public. Condolences and messages of support to the government poured in.[80] Even the *Pakistan Times* editorials at this point, although critical of the government employing 'guesswork' about the extent of the plot, nonetheless state that it would be wrong for anyone ' ... to doubt the *bona fides* of government

---

[78] Akhtar, Interview; Faiz, Alys *Over My Shoulder* cited in Genoways, 'Let Them Snuff Out', 94.

[79] 'Brig Latif & Faiz Also Detained, Alleged Plotto Create "Violent Commotion", Minister's Announcement' (*Pakistan Times*, 10 March 1951); and '9 Million Voters Go To Polls in Punjab Today' (*Pakistan Times*, 10 March 1951).

[80] Dryland, 'Faiz Ahmed Faiz', 178.

action'.[81] Discussing public opinion regarding the Conspiracy, Hasan Zaheer[82] asserts that in the minds of most of those who heard of it at the time, the case was seen as 'treason'.[83]

Although the Rawalpindi conspiracy has been described as a grievous error made by the upper echelons of the CPP, not all CPP members were in favour of this involvement.[84] In addition, it seems that discussions of the case tend to forget that its discovery coincided almost exactly with the 1951 elections in the Punjab. At the time of his arrest, Faiz himself thought that he was being arrested so that he could be kept quiet until after the election.[85] Seen from this angle, the announcement of the coup and the association of all Leftists with treason were also part of the process by which the political elite maintained its control over politics in the Punjab. In addition, the repression of *all* Leftists in the aftermath of the conspiracy, especially given that individuals like Mirza Ibrahim and Jehanian had been arrested earlier, suggests that the conspiracy became a reason to crack down on a group that had been, increasingly, making the state uneasy.

The initial impetus for the supposed attempted coup that formed the basis of the case came from the government's decision to cease hostilities in Kashmir, one that was not welcomed by certain groups within the army who disagreed with the civilian administration's judgement.[86] To carry out such a plan the officers approached Faiz Ahmed Faiz in search of political support. Faiz agreed to arrange a meeting for them with Sajjad Zaheer and an informal meeting was accordingly set up.[87] While Talat Ahmed points out that the coup itself was 'not a fabrication' and that several CPP members, including Sajjad Zaheer, did agree to it,[88] whether it would have actually been carried out is by no means clear. Evidence of meetings where

---

[81] Khan, *Pakistan: The First Twelve Years*, 268, 267.

[82] Zaheer, *The Times and Trial.*

[83] Ibid., x.

[84] See: Leghari, 'The Socialist Movement'; and Ahmed 'Writers and Generals'.

[85] Faiz, Alys *Over My Shoulder* cited in Genoways, 'Let Them Snuff Out', 94.

[86] Zaheer, *The Times and Trial*, 29.

[87] Akhtar, Interview with the author.

[88] Ahmed, 'Writers and Generals', 139, 145.

agreements were reached is offset by testimonies stating that the plot did not evolve beyond the initial phase of discussion and it was later shelved.[89] This is supported by the investigation of the tribunal that could not definitively prove the charges against the conspirators even though they were not allowed a defence counsel or witnesses.[90]

Another confusing fact about the timing at which the case emerges is the depth of intelligence available to the Punjab police about 'subversive' activities, particularly with regard to the Communist Party. This is both indicated by Ahmed[91] and visible in the two-volume work on the activities of the Communist Party in West Pakistan published by the Central Investigation Department in 1952. As part of his plea to the CPP to not take part in the coup, Ishaqe Mohammad[92] also pointed out that given the level of monitoring they were subject to, the plans for this coup were definitely not a secret from the authorities.[93] Given this sort of surveillance, it does seem improbable that the state only found out about this attempted plot during the elections in March when it was initially supposed to be carried out in February 1951.[94] While the fact that there was some substance to the conspiracy cannot be denied, these 'grey' areas suggest that the decision of the state to conduct these arrests and widen the purview of whom they arrested was based on more than just security concerns. This approach becomes more convincing when given the background of the elections and the large number of arrests of Leftists that followed.

Even before the official trial into the conspiracy case began, a number of arrests were carried out, with the assurance being given in newspaper headlines that the 'arrests are not connected with the Pindi conspiracy'.[95] There was a total of about 20 arrests made in

---

[89] Dryland, 'Faiz Ahmed Faiz', 182; Interview with Hameed Akhtar; Leghari, 'The Socialist Movement', 65.

[90] Ahmed, 'The Rise and Fall', 254.

[91] Ahmed, 'Writers and Generals', 137.

[92] Besides founding the Mazdoor Kisan Party in Pakistan Ishaq Muhammad was actively involved in the Punjabiyat language movement in Pakistan (see Kalra and Butt this issue).

[93] Leghari, 'The Socialist Movement', 67.

[94] Ibid., 137.

[95] 'Leftist Elements Rounded Up: Arrests Not Connected with Pindi Conspiracy', (*Pakistan Times*, 11 May 1951).

this first round-up in the Punjab. Those arrested in Lahore included Firozuddin Mansur, the secretary of the Punjab Kisan Committee and a veteran CPP member, Mohammad Afzal, the general secretary of the PTUF, Shamim Ashraf Malik and Hameed Akhtar.[96] Hameed Akhtar's book *Kal Kothri*[97] on his prison experiences begins from this exact point. He describes how he heard a loud and persistent banging on his door in the early hours of the morning and saw police standing outside. In an account that is both harrowing and yet tongue-in-cheek, he describes how the police came in a *tonga* — a horse-drawn carriage — because the large number of arrests that had been made meant that all police cars were busy. Although these arrests were new in their intensity as they took place in such a short period of time, the book also reveals how arrests of communist leaders were by no means an infrequent occurrence. While some of his friends in prison were nervous about their plight as they had been roused before dawn and some had just been brought to prison as they were, the veteran communist leader Firozuddin Mansur walked in with all necessities carefully packed, fully prepared and composed because he had been to prison so many times that he knew exactly what to expect.[98]

Even within prison, the 'viral' or polluting threat presented by radicalism was still a consideration. This was reflected in the fact that those arrested were kept in separate compartments from the rest of the prisoners. This is part of the reason why Hameed Akhtar spent several months in solitary confinement whilst in prison in the early 1950s, as the police were afraid that he and his comrades would rouse the sentiments of the prisoners around them. Similar to the case with Mirza Ibrahim and the rest of the group arrested immediately preceding the election, even the basis of the arrest was precautionary:

> I still remember the beginning of my warrant, my name, my father's name, 'whereas the governor of Punjab is satisfied that you are going to act upon in a manner which is prejudicial to the public law and order, the governor is pleased to detain you for six months'.[99]

---

[96] Ibid.

[97] This can be directly translated as 'Black Cell' but that does not capture the implications of the term. It refers to a place that is like a dungeon, dark and calamitous.

[98] Akhtar, *Kal Kothri,* 30–31.

[99] Akhtar, Interview with the author.

In a scathing criticism of the arrests of Leftists outside of those accused in the case, an article in the *Pakistan Times* stated that ' ... it is difficult to avoid the conclusion that the Muslim League governments have misused their special powers in order to weaken their political opponents.'[100] This repression weakened not only opponents but also those whom they worked with. Even though members of the PTUF at the time were active and protesting these arrests under the 'hated' safety act,[101] in the aftermath of this atmosphere worker and peasant unions that had been affiliated with the CPP became fragmented.[102]

On one level, official narratives hide the reality of diverse and often opposing realities. On another level, they can also put a different spin on these same realities. The Rawalpindi Conspiracy Case gave substance to a narrative in which the CPP specifically and the Left more broadly were seen as having betrayed Pakistan. In the conclusion of this case, the CPP's role was viewed as one where it had conspired 'to undermine the existence of Pakistan and to establish an atheist state in Pakistan'.[103] The army officials, by contrast, were absolved of responsibility and considered as passive recipients. This sentiment is quite clearly articulated in the discussion of the conspiracy case in the Constituent Assembly:

> The authors of the present conspiracy had selfish ends to serve; they wanted to grab the reins of Government ... I can never believe that the Pakistan Forces, of whom we are so proud, could have played into their hands.[104]

The new narrative now played with historic memory, selectively erasing things like the fact that, once upon a time, the CPP and Muslim League had been allied and of course denying the realities that would

---

[100] 'Punjab Kisan Leader Arrested Under Safety Act' (*Pakistan Times*, 12 May 1951).

[101] 'Demand for Release of Trade Union Workers' (*Pakistan Times*, 4 July 1951).

[102] Leghari, 'The Socialist Movement', 70.

[103] Ibid., 66.

[104] Sheikh Sadiq Hasan, *Constituent Assembly of Pakistan (Debates)*, 16 April 1951, 88.

later pave the way for Pakistan's multiple military coups. What the Rawalpindi conspiracy case thus actually represents is, to use Jalal's terminology, the manufacturing of 'enemies within'.[105]

## Concluding Remarks

In 1920, after Turkey was defeated in the First World War, a group of refugees left India as a protest against the British bringing an end to the *Khilafat*. These religious and anti-imperialist protestors would go on to become some of the most prominent communists in the early days of Pakistan and particularly the Punjab. Amongst their ranks were names like Fazal Elahi Qurban and Ferozuddin Mansoor.[106] Given this background, the nationalist, religious and communist aspects of their identity overlapped in a way that allowed them to be all these things and yet come to Pakistan. For the Pakistani state however, when Ferozuddin Mansur was arrested in Lahore in 1951 under the Rawalpindi Conspiracy Case, it was because he was a communist. His initial motivations revolving around the *Khilafat* were not of any import — he was arrested as a troublemaker, an atheistic communist and, therefore, a paradox in Pakistan's Islam-oriented nationhood. The multiple realities of individuals who were communist at one point were thus subsumed under the reality of what the Pakistani state said communism was. As this chapter has shown and this example illustrates, this reality did not, however, necessarily conform to varying local strands of communist politics.

The political curtailment of the activities of the Left described above were part of a wider process by which the state restricted political alternatives and defined, increasingly narrowly, what type of political identities were acceptable in the Pakistani state. The ban on the CPP was not lifted till as late as in 1986 and the creation of a category of 'enemy of the state', in this sense, was a political act aimed at not only eliminating political opposition but also narrowly defining the *type* of politics that could be practiced within the ambit of the Pakistani state. In the case of the CPP, their role within the elections of 1951 is an all but forgotten aspect of Pakistani history, partially because of its distance from what is possible in the contemporary

---

[105] Ibid., 82.
[106] Ibid., 23–24.

context, as Hameed Akhtar observed: 'At that time the CPP was the only voice challenging the status quo ... today, could any communist be elected in Lahore?' The combined result of state repression and the conspiracy case was that groups that had connected themselves to other political associations and linked themselves to the articulation of class politics broke off these ties. An example of this was the PWA, which officially separated itself from association with politics and political parties.[107] This signalled the beginning of the process of de-politicisation of such organisations in the Pakistani context.

While the cultural politics of the CPP can be viewed as problematic in the emphasis given to Urdu as a national language,[108] their persistence in pursuing an agenda of linking literary activities to the politics of progress and development meant that individuals like Faiz Ahmed Faiz and Hameed Akhtar played an important role in linking these intellectual circles to the politics of labour in Lahore. These specific political linkages were now to become a thing of the past. Indeed, this phase in Pakistani history also represents the change of an era. While Partition had drawn a geographical boundary line, these events indicate the changes that took place at the interface between an older social and political order and the new imperatives of the nascent state. The culture that allowed the Left to flourish is best represented by the 'coffee house culture' of Lahore. The India Coffee House was one of a number of small establishments that were regularly frequented by individuals like Habib Jalib, (the revolutionary poet who himself was a worker in Lyallpur at one point)[109] and Ferozuddin Mansur. Khursheed Aziz's memoirs, '*The Coffee House of Lahore*', provide a loving and witty portrait of the individuals who visited the Coffee House (as it became known after Partition) between the late 1940s and the early 1950s. This memoir is replete with nostalgia for an age in which Lahore was a cosmopolitan centre of ideas and debates. However, Aziz's memoirs, describing individuals between the late 1940s and the early 1950s, completely skip the break represented by Partition and the effect it had on the public arena within which politics was practiced in Lahore. Indeed, all of the public spaces for meetings, debate and *mushairas* were negatively

---

[107] Ahmed, 'Writers and Generals', 144.
[108] Ali, 'Communists in a Muslim Land', 153–54.
[109] Aziz, *The Coffee House*, 63–65.

impacted by Partition. Bemoaning this same change, an article in the *Pakistan Times* from 1956 discussed the shift in the nature of Lahore from a centre of stormy political and cultural activities to one that was simply attempting to grapple with the consequences of Partition. Now, the article continued, the halls that were so essential to making Lahore so vibrant were either being used to provide shelters or being used as 'godowns' for storing grain.[110] The limited space for the old type of politics in Lahore would go on shrinking in later years as symbolised by the disappearance of the few halls of this sort that were left in the post-Partition city. Abdul Rauf Malik, the head of the People's Publishing House in the 1950s, observed that there were no halls left in the city — the Lajpat Rai hall, the Barkat Ali Muhammadean Hall and the YMCA were all out of use. He bemoaned the fact that now, there are huge five- and three-star hotels where meetings are held with tea, which is expensive and restrictive.[111] Indeed, the decline of the political culture of the city of Lahore paralleled the demise of the Left.

The relationship between the politics of the Left and the mechanics of state repression existed in a very specific context and in a very different kind of public space that existed in Lahore in the early 1950s. Nonetheless, the way that the narrative unfolds provides important insights into the way politics was practiced below the level of the nation state and the manner in which the enemies of the state were identified and marginalised — a process that has been applied time and again to different groups in various periods of Pakistani history. When talking about the popularity of his book *Kal Kothri*, Hameed Akhtar remarked that the book has been published in eight different editions since its original publication in 1953 and is still in demand today because what it describes are the specific arrests that took place in the early 1950s and hence it touches on political circumstances that have been repeatedly created whenever the state has attempted to suppress political opposition. While this has happened all too often in the Pakistani context, if Faiz could retain some tendrils of hope when writing from jail while arrested under the conspiracy case, perhaps it is possible to do the same in contemporary observations of the political future of Pakistan:

---

[110] 'Lahore's Neglected Public Halls' (*Pakistan Times*, 6 May 1956).
[111] Malik, Interview with the author.

Today men of heart go to test their spirits and their faith;
let them bring an army of enemies, we will meet them tomorrow
let them come to the execution yard, we will join the spectacle tomorrow.
No matter how heavy this last hour may seem, my friend:
we will see the light hidden tonight shine brightly tomorrow;
we will see the morning-star sparkle as today edges into tomorrow.[112]

# References

Ahmad, S. Haroon, 'Flashback: Students Activated', *Dawn*, 11 September 2011, http://beta.dawn.com/news/658168/flashback-students-activated (accessed 13 February 2012).

Ahmed, Ishtiaq, 'The Rise and Fall of the Left and the Maoist Movements in Pakistan', *India Quarterly* 66, no. 3 (2010): 251–65.

Ahmed, Talat, 'Writers and Generals: Intellectuals and the First Pakistan Coup', *Indian Economic and Social History Review* 45, no. 1 (2008): 115–49.

Akhtar, Hameed, *Kal Kothri (Black Cell)*, Lahore: Book Home, 2009.

Alavi, Hamza, Pakistan and Islam: Ethnicity and Ideology, in *State and Ideology in the Middle East and Pakistan*, Hamza Alavi and Fred Halliday (eds), New York, NY: Monthly Review Press, 1988.

Ali, Kamran Asdar, 'The Strength of the Street Meets the Strength of the State: The 1972 Labor Struggle in Karachi', *International Journal of Middle East Studies* 37 (2005): 83–107.

———, 'Communists in a Muslim Land: Cultural Debates in Pakistan's Early Years', *Modern Asian Studies* 45, no. 3 (2011): 501–34.

Ali, Tariq, *Pakistan: Military Rule or People's Power*, London: Jonathan Cape, 1970.

———, 'Revolutionary Perspectives for Pakistan', *New Left Review* I/63 (1970): 43–55.

Ayres, Alyssa, *Speaking Like a State: Language and Nationalism in Pakistan*, Cambridge: Cambridge University Press, 2009.

Aziz, Khurshid K., *The Coffee House of Lahore: A Memoir 1942–57*, Lahore: Sang-E-Meel Publications, 2008.

———, *Party Politics in Pakistan, 1947–1958*, Islamabad: National Commission on Historical and Cultural Research, 1976.

Criminal Investigation Department (CID), Punjab, *The Communist Party of West Pakistan in Action*, Volume I and II, by Mian Anwer Ali, Deputy Inspector General of Police, Lahore, Lahore: Superintendent Government Printing, 1952.

---

[112] Faiz Ahmed Faiz, 'The Execution Yard (A Song)' cited in Genoways, 'Let Them Snuff Out', 106.

Dryland, Estelle, 'Faiz Ahmed Faiz and the Rawalpindi Conspiracy Case', *Journal of South Asian Literature* 27, no. 2, Perspectives on Socialist Realism in Asian Literature (1992): 175–85.

Franda, Marcus F., 'Communism and Regional Politics in East Pakistan', *Asian Survey* 10, no. 7 (1970): 588–606.

Gauhar, Altaf, *The Challenge of Islam*, London: Islamic Council of Europe, 1978.

Genoways, Ted, '"Let Them Snuff Out the Moon": Faiz Ahmed Faiz's Prison Lyrics in Dast-e-Saba', *Annual of Urdu Studies* 19 (2004): 94–119.

Habib, Irfan, 'The Left and the National Movement', *Social Scientist* 26, no. 5/6 (1998): 24–25.

Hasan, Sibte, *The Battle of Ideas in Pakistan*, Lahore: Pakistan Publishing House, 1986.

Iqtidar, Humeira, *Secularizing Islamists? Jama'at-e-Islami and Jama'at-ud-Da'wa in Urban Pakistan*, Chicago: The University of Chicago Press, 2011.

Jalal, Ayesha, 'Conjuring Pakistan: History as Official Imagining', *International Journal of Middle East Studies* 27, no. 1 (1995): 73–89.

Javid, Hassan, 'Class, Power and Patronage: Landowners and Politics in Punjab', *History and Anthropology* 22, no. 3 (2011): 337–69.

Kamran, Tahir, 'Early Phase of Electoral Politics in Pakistan: 1950s', *South Asian Studies* 24, no. 2 (2009): 257–82.

Khan, Abdul H., 'A Front for the A.L.', *Pakistan Forum* 2, no. 1 (1971): 13–14.

Khan, Adeel, *Politics of Identity: Ethnic Nationalism and the State in Pakistan*, New Delhi: Sage Publications, 2005.

Khan, Mazhar A., *Pakistan: The First Twelve Years. The Pakistan Times Editorials of Mazhar Ali Khan*, Karachi: Oxford University Press, 1996.

Khan, Roedad, ed., *The American Papers: Secret and Confidential India-Pakistan-Bangladesh Documents 1965–1973*, Karachi: Oxford University Press, 1999.

Leghari, Iqbal, 'The Socialist Movement in Pakistan: An Historical Survey 1940–1974', unpublished PhD thesis, Laval University, Montreal, 1979.

Lerski, George J., 'The Pakistan-American Alliance: A Reevaluation of the Past Decade', *Asian Survey* 8, no. 5 (1968): 400–15.

Levi, Werner, 'Pakistan, the Soviet Union and China', *Pacific Affairs* 35, no. 3 (1962): 211–22.

Malik, Hafeez, 'The Marxist Literary Movement in India and Pakistan', *The Journal of Asian Studies* 26, no. 4 (1967): 649–64.

Maniruzzaman, Talukder, 'Group Interests in Pakistan Politics, 1947–1958', *Pacific Affairs* 39, no. 1/2 (1996): 83–98.

McMahon, Robert J., 'United States Cold War Strategy in South Asia: Making a Military Commitment to Pakistan, 1947–1954', *The Journal of American History* 75, no. 3 (1988): 812–40.

Ministry of the Interior, '*Internal Situation*' *29 February 1952, Reel 2084*, Islamabad: National Documentation Centre, 1952.

Pakistan Law Reports, 'Mazhar Ali Khan v. The Governor of the Punjab', 1953 PLR 253, Lahore: Government Book Depot, 1953.

Rahman, Tariq, *Language and Politics in Pakistan*, New Delhi: Orient Longman, 1996, published in arrangement with Oxford University Press, Karachi.

Rashiduzzaman, M., 'The National Awami Party of Pakistan: Leftist Politics in Crisis', *Pacific Affairs* 43, no. 3 (1970): 394–409.

Samad, Yunas, 'Pakistan or Punjabisation: Crisis of National Identity', *International Journal of Punjab Studies* 2, no. 1 (1995): 23–42.

Sayeed, Khalid Bin. 'The Breakdown of Pakistan's Political System', *International Journal* 27, no. 3 (1972): 381–404.

Shaheed, Zafar, *The Labour Movement in Pakistan: Organization and Leadership in Karachi in the 1970s*, Karachi: Oxford University Press, 2007.

Shaikh, Farzana, *Making Sense of Pakistan*, London: Hurst & Company, 2009.

Talbot, Ian, 'The Punjabization of Pakistan: Myth or Reality', in *Pakistan: Nationalism Without a Nation*, Christophe Jaffrelot (ed.), 51–62, London: Zed Books, 2002.

———, 'A Tale of Two Cities: The Aftermath of Partition for Lahore and Amritsar 1947–1957', *Modern Asian Studies* 41, no. 1 (2007): 178–79.

Toor, Saadia, *The State of Islam: Culture and Cold War Politics in Pakistan*, London: Pluto Press, 2011.

Zaheer, Hasan, *The Times and Trial of the Rawalpindi Conspiracy*, Karachi: Oxford University Press, 1951.

## Newspapers

*Pakistan Times*
*Civil & Military Gazette*

## Interviews Cited

Ali, Tahira Mazhar, 2 February 2008, Interview with the author.
Akhtar, Hameed, 28 May 2011, Interview with the author.
Malik, Abdul Rauf, 2 June 2011 Interview with the author.
Naseem, Syed M., 11 April 2008, Interview with the author.

# ✠ 6

# 'In One Hand a Pen in the Other a Gun': Punjabi Language Radicalism in Punjab, Pakistan

*Virinder S. Kalra* and *Waqas M. Butt*

---

I am the poet of the day, my voice reaches the sky
In one hand a pen, in the other a gun
I am the heir of a martyr, don't hold me back
My shoulders bear the burden of revenge
I salute to those martyred, who sacrificed their life in struggle
Who captured and destroyed the enemies, like a bolt from the blue
I am indebted to that sister who sent her brother to the war.
My head in the cradle of that mother who doesn't have a son anymore.
I am the poet of the day my voice reaches the sky
In one hand a pen in the other a gun.

Mian Salim Jahangir, 'Ballad of the Day'[1]

The relationship between language and politics has been long established, most usually through the lens of nationalism. The model of one nation, one language, one people to some extent was paradigmatic of the ideology of anticolonial struggles. To some extent, the formation of Pakistan was also mobilised around the idea of Urdu as the national language and Islam as the national faith. Indeed, these two slogans ultimately became the rationale for a strongly centralising state.[2] Such equations between nation and language,

---

[1] Jahangir, *Ballad of the Day*, 70–71. This poem is in honour of those who died in Hashtnagar, arguably the most successful Left-wing uprising in Pakistan. See Ahmed, 'The Rise and Fall', for more details. Poem translated by the authors.

[2] See Jalal, *Self and Sovereignty*; and Talbot, *Pakistan*.

however, have done much dis-service to the heterogeneity not only of minority languages but also of hegemonic ones. Thus, there were struggles around the issue of language most prominently in East Pakistan from the very formation of Pakistan. Although there is some debate about how crucial the Bangla language movement was in terms of the final formation of Bangladesh, there is no doubt that the repression of Bengali in favour of Urdu played a significant role in the creation of an independence movement.[3] Less prominent and politically far less successful have been the ethno-national mobilisations around Sindhi, Pashto and Baluchi, which have all at some time made demands on the state in terms of provision for language rights.[4] This chapter discusses the status of Punjabi in Pakistan and its relationship with the Left.

In some senses, the status of Punjabi in Pakistan is an anomaly because on the one hand it is not recognised as an official language of the state and on the other over 80 per cent of residents in Punjab speak the language as a mother tongue and over 60 per cent of the population of Pakistan resides in Punjab.[5] This demographic reality nonetheless does not reflect its status in terms of state provision. There is no provision to teach Punjabi at the school level and it is only offered in a few colleges at the degree level, with only one institution offering postgraduate education in the subject.[6] Indeed, the basic premise of much activism for Punjabi has been for the establishment of primary education in the language. It was only with the formation of the current state of Pakistan in 1971 that an MA in Punjabi was introduced in Punjab University, Lahore. A somewhat bizarre policy, given that there was no formal provision in the subject at any other level of education. The reasons for this neglect by the state will be

---

[3] Talbot, *Pakistan*.

[4] Though Mir (2010) makes the salient point that the state has never in the pre-colonial or colonial project provided support to Punjabi, it is nonetheless the remit of the modern state to make provision for language teaching and development. It could be argued that there is no unifying notion of language without the state providing standardisation over competing claims. The state therefore remains central in terms of Punjabi activism and mobilisation in Pakistan.

[5] Pakistan Census Organisation, *Main Finding of Census on Housing and Population*.

[6] MAs and PhDs in Punjabi are offered at Punjab University, Lahore.

discussed in more detail, but it is important to note at this stage that one of the reasons for Punjabi's marginality is its association with low social status and class. Indeed as the language of the uneducated — of the peasants and the working class, it is shunned by the nationalist elite. Yet it is precisely this status that provides the rationale for its appeal to Left-wing groups and parties.

This chapter begins by placing Punjabi language movements in the general context of South Asian language mobilisations. Then by reviewing the research of Punjabi in West Punjab, two key areas that are not completely addressed are established. First is the lack of an account of the role of the Left in Pakistan in organising around the language issue and second is the neglect of places, other than Lahore, in the description of the various Punjabi movements. Redressing these absences requires a re-reading of the existing material to highlight the connection between activists and various parties, but more particularly with a literary method rooted in Marxist methodologies that language activists deployed. The key figures active in the Mazdoor Kisan Party (Major Ishaque) provide a compelling example of the in-depth relationship between literature and politics in the Punjab. In particular, the work of figures such as Mian Jahangir (one of whose poems opens this chapter) in the 1970s and the influence of these figures on subsequent publications such as Sajjan and Panchim will be used to illustrate the highly politicised perspective on language that emerge in West Punjab of the late 1960s through to the end of the 1980s. Finally, the way in which Punjabi was part of the mobilisation of the National Students Federation will be demonstrated via a case study of the market town of Sahiwal, addressing the overtly Lahore-centred focus of previous studies.[7]

## Language and Politics in South Asia

The politicised nature of language in South Asia has been studied from a number of angles, most prominently in terms of the nexus that emerges in the colonial period between language and religious

---

[7] The research for this chapter is based on both authors' involvement in the Punjabi movement in Pakistan since the 1970s for Butt and since the 1990s for Kalra. Further information was gathered from interviews with MKP activists.

identity, with one result being the consolidation of communal identities. The relationship between Hindi, Urdu and Punjabi becomes synonymous with Hindu, Muslim and Sikh, respectively, and ultimately to ethno-nationalist aspirations.[8] This theme has continued in post-colonial India where language movements came to frame much of the first 20 years of politics in newly independent India.[9] Most prominently the agitation for a Punjabi Suba led by the Sikh party, the Akali Dal follows through the logic of partition with a religious group demanding ethno-linguistic rights, something achieved in 1967 with the formation of a truncated East Punjab.[10] Once the linguistic reorganisation of Indian states was achieved, to a large extent political mobilisations under the rubric of language diminished. Nonetheless, language has played an over-determined role in the political mobilisations and settlements of post-colonial South Asia.

Writings on the Punjabi movement in Pakistan have, to a large extent, remained locked into the political science perspectives on language most well developed by Paul Brass.[11] Language here is an instrument of elites to gain political power or to gain access into the state machinery. It may be motivated by primordial desires, but is nevertheless mobilised for some aspect of political gain or status. More recent work has attempted to move beyond this framework, in particular to offer a view of Punjabi outside of determinative relationship with the state.[12] This perspective focusses on those spaces where Punjabi shows resilience despite neglect and often hostility by the state towards it. The marginal groups and sites in which Punjabi circulates become a site from which the Mazdoor Kisan Party can mobilise.[13] Language in the context of the Left in West Punjab is

---

[8] Oberoi, *The Construction of Religious Boundaries*; King, *Orientalism and Religion*; and Mandair, *Religion and the Specter of the West*.

[9] See Sarangi, *Language and Politics*. It has to be noted that the movements in South India for language were of a different order to those in East Punjab. Nonetheless, these movements are all closely related to the desire of the post-colonial Indian state to reorganise along linguistic lines.

[10] Brass, *Language, Religion*.

[11] Ibid.

[12] Mir, *Social Space*; and Ayres, *Speaking Like a State*.

[13] Rahman, *Language, Power and Ideology*; and Ayres, *Speaking Like a State*.

therefore being used instrumentally, but not for the formation of a linguistic state, but rather for the formation of a communist or socialist state.[14] What underpins this role for Punjabi for the Left is paradoxically the absence of state patronage for the language, as reflected in the pre-colonial and colonial language policy.[15] This situation was rectified in 1967 with the formation of the Punjab state in India but continued in Pakistan.

When Pakistan was formed in 1947 its founding father, Mohammad Ali Jinnah, adopted a quite conservative ideology for the new nation when it came to the issue of language, clearly illustrated by this extract of a speech from 1948:

> Let me restate my views on the question of a state language for Pakistan. For official use in this province, the people of the province can choose any language they wish ... There can, however, be one lingua franca, that is, the language for inter-communication between the various provinces of the state, and that language should be Urdu and cannot be any other. The state language, therefore, must obviously be Urdu, a language that has been nurtured by a hundred million Muslims of this subcontinent, a language understood throughout the length and breadth of Pakistan and, above all, a language which, more than any other provincial language, embodies the best that is in Islamic culture and Muslim tradition and is nearest to the languages used in other Islamic countries ....[16]

To some extent, Jinnah was forging a state in difficult circumstances and hence the necessity of singularity of language intimately linked to Islam is understandable. He did not live to see this vision

---

[14] The perspective offered here is markedly different from Paul Brass, in that his evaluation of the success of a language movement would be in purely political terms, in the extent to which state power was achieved. Breaking the distinction between culture and politics provides an alternative framework for understanding the general conditions under which power relations are changed by political action. Developing this framework is beyond the scope of this chapter but provides an indication of a framework for understanding Punjabi, which can take into account the power of the state without reducing all cultural action to a symptom or reaction.

[15] Mir, *Social Space*.

[16] Mohammad Ali Jinnah, Jinnah, Speech at the Dacca University Convocation, on 21 March 1948, 82.

collapse with the formation of Bangladesh from the province of East Pakistan.[17] Yet for present purposes, it is the provision that any 'province' can choose whatever language it wishes to is of utmost significance for this chapter. Once Bangladesh was created and the modern state of Pakistan formed via the 1973 constitution, Pushto, Sindhi and Baluchi came to be recognised and promoted as provincial languages, whereas in Punjab, Urdu remained the language of primary instruction and governance. After democracy was restored in 2008 to Pakistan, the provincial assembly members in all states other than Punjab took their oaths in the provincial languages. This neglect of Punjabi by the Muslim elite is intimately tied up with British colonialism and has been well covered by Tariq Rahman.[18] The inheritance of this denigration of Punjabi led to the emergence, quite early after the partition of 1947, of a group of literary figures who felt the necessity to promote the language.[19] It is the undertakings of these language activists, based mainly in Lahore, that has attracted academic attention.[20]

## Punjabi Movement in West Punjab

The first study of the Punjabi movement in West Punjab in English begins with Christopher Shackles' article in 1970 and these themes are amplified and illustrated in Tariq Rahman's considerable output and most recently — in 2008 — by Alyssa Ayres.[21] The first issue raised by Shackle is the middle class and urban nature of Punjabi activism derived from his fieldwork in Lahore, the capital city of West Punjab. A simple schema of language use is established where the elite use English, the middle class Urdu and the working class Punjabi.[22] Punjabi language activists are therefore those from the

---

[17] See Kabir, 'Religion, Language'.

[18] Rahman, *Language and Politics*.

[19] Ibid.

[20] See Zaidi, 'A Postcolonial Sociolinguistics' for a comprehensive account of the relationship between Pakistani state ideology and the Pakistani language.

[21] Shackle, 'Punjabi in Lahore'; Rahman, *Language, Ideology and Power*; and Ayres, *Speaking Like a State*.

[22] Shackle, 'Punjabi in Lahore'.

middle class for whom the high Urdu of the migrant literary elite is barred.[23] Their struggle is therefore one to attain a parity with Urdu of the Punjabi language in terms of state resources and thereby to establish themselves securely within the middle class. This point is made explicitly by Rahman, who argues that the activists desire for the Punjabi language are matched by their aspirations to achieve status, the logic being that as the language gains in status, so their own class position will improve.[24] Ayres is critical of this position because she articulates the correct position that Punjabis are already dominant in society; hence, the necessity for the middle class to utilise language to mobilise is a conundrum and indeed this is the thesis of her book, *Speaking Like a State*.[25] However, each of these author's perspectives are found to be limited when the contextual and lived use of Punjabi is analysed.

Shackle's simplistic schema of language use breaks down considerably when looking at context-specific interaction. For example, the feudal elite is still much more likely to use Punjabi when in male company or with their village servants, even in the urban context of Lahore. In the army, to maintain rank hierarchy English and Urdu are used. However, for troops of the same rank Punjabi is the lingua franca, across the regiments from various provinces. In public spaces and with women, even the working class makes an attempt to use some form of Urdu for communication. Perhaps, fundamentally men of all classes find it necessary to be able to communicate in the language as a sign of their masculinity.[26] To be fair to Shackle's descriptions, he is the only author who notes that both the Sufi shrines and Christian churches extensively use Punjabi. In both these cases it is the working class and the lower middle class who

---

[23] The dominance of the Pakistani bureaucracy by Urdu-speaking migrants from UP and Bihar meant that the state machinery was deeply committed to the 'one language' policy. These migrants or *mohajairs* were also relatively more urbanised and educated than their local counterparts (in any of the provinces). It was *mohajairs* who dominated the literary and cultural scene of the new Pakistan.

[24] Rahman, *Language and Politics*.

[25] Ayres, *Speaking Like a State*.

[26] These perspectives are based on fieldwork in Lahore carried out by Lahore University of Management Sciences students 2009–2010.

frequent shrines, and the Christian population of Lahore is mostly engaged in specific menial work areas, reflecting their caste and class composition. It is a lack of an analysis that takes into account class, which misdirects much of the research on the Punjabi movement in West Punjab. Indeed, it is precisely this class composition that makes Punjabi so amenable to the activists of the Mazdoor Kisan Party. It is the affective attachment to Punjabi that is being mobilised and this mobilisation is taking place during the time period over which Shackle is concerned.[27]

Focusing on a later time period in terms of fieldwork (the late 1990s), but nonetheless concerned with the Punjabi movement from the time of partition onward, Alyssa Ayres offers the most comprehensive study to date of the Punjabi language movement and some of its key activists based in Lahore. By including documentation produced by the movement, various manifestos and ephemera such as cartoons, a significant empirical contribution is made to the relatively scarce literature on the Punjabi language movement in Pakistan. The book also includes a brief but nonetheless invaluable documentation of the role of Punjabi films in promoting the image of a masculine, usually rural, heroic figure. Indeed, it is the analysis of films that highlights the strength of Ayres work, in forefronting the popular aspect of Punjabi in West Punjab and its weakness, in that this dimension of the language does not impact the book's theoretical argument. Ayres seeks to understand why Punjabi is the neglected language of the Pakistani state, when the country is dominated by Punjabis in terms of its political economy, specifically in terms of the army and demographically. This conundrum is resolved by resorting to a purely symbolic understanding of the movement: 'the case of Punjab offers compelling real-world data that underscores the importance of symbolic capital as a motivating force in contexts where this force simply cannot be dismissed as epiphenomenal'.[28] This is a reasonable conclusion when focusing on elite discourse, but is significantly flawed for this very reason.[29] The stratification

---

[27] Mir, *Social Space*.

[28] Ayres, *Speaking Like a State*, 101.

[29] It should also be noted that the analysis of most language movements has been to look at the way language has mobilised the elite.

of Punjabi/Pakistani society along the lines of class is not considered in any detail even though recourse to the popular domain and therefore an allusion to the working and peasant classes is made throughout the text. Perhaps more problematic is the way in which this theoretical lens narrows and distorts the vision of key figures in the Punjabi movement itself. For example, Najm Hussain Sayyid is acknowledged as a central pillar of the Punjabi movement and is someone who is clear in his use of a Marxist-inspired dialectical method incorporating historical materialism in his literary criticism.[30] However, this method is re-interpreted by Ayres through the lens of nationalistic revivalism. Indeed, two of the leading characters of Sayyids' historical fiction, Ahmed Khan Kharral and Dullah Bhatti, are rendered as figures symbolically standing for resistance against the undermining of the Punjabi language representing heroic figures of the Punjabi (male) standing in contrast to the image of submissive people.[31] Kharral and Bhatti are, respectively, central characters in Najm's plays *Takht Lahore* and *Ik Raat Raavi Dee* and emerge from a bardic oral tradition of resistance, in these cases British colonialism and Moghal rule, upholding the rights of the peasant of Punjab. Even though Ayres is able to gauge the sense of Najm's works in terms of the formation of a new subject, this is not one that emerges out of a process of dialectical materialism (Najm's own method) but what she calls historical 'revisionism' as if just by stating the act of the formation of the new subject the work is already done, rather than the need for active struggle and resistance.

What is perhaps most startling about Alyssa Ayres' study is the absence of any mention of socialism or communism in her analysis of the Punjabi movement of the 1980s. Indeed, these words are not included in any of the 217 pages of the volume. This is clearly a purposeful exclusion and necessary for the theoretical argument about the symbolic nature of language to be made. However, previous literature alludes to the relationship between Left-wing mobilisation and Punjabi. Rahman makes passing reference to the relationship between the Left and the Punjabi movement in terms of some of

---

[30] This perspective towards literary criticism is made clear for those who attend the weekly Punjabi literary meeting organised in Najm Sayyid's house in Lahore. This meeting (*Sangat*) has taken place for the last 40 years.

[31] Ayres, *Speaking Like a State*, 102.

the key figures involved, for example, Shafqat Tanvir Mirza and Najm Hussain Sayyid. Najm Hussain in particular is said to have a 'secular and Leftist' reputation.[32] Yet this in no way pervades our understanding of this role in the movement. Indeed, it is through the words of a right-wing press statement that we find any notion that Punjabi language activists are adopting a critical perspective towards the language: 'This not serving one's mother tongue. This is only finding ways for the progress of socialist politics under the banner of progressivism.'[33] One can be sympathetic to some extent with Tariq Rahman's perspective as he has always argued that the teaching of mother tongue is a valid and correct demand to be made upon the state.[34] This distancing from the socialist aspect of the movement might be arguably a strategic one to allow for a claim to be made upon the liberal arm of the state, without alienating the religious right, who would be opposed to any socialist politics. What becomes clear from a close reading of the book *Speaking Like a State* is that it overly relies on the perspective of one respondent — Fakhar Zaman — and on one publication — *The Punjabi Language Will Never Die: The Case of Punjabi in Punjab* by Saeed Ahmad Farani. As a lecturer of Punjabi in Jhelum Academy, Farani was not someone actively involved in socialist politics. To some extent, the material that is presented and the version of the movement, particularly the emphasis on the world Punjabi conferences, which were Zaman's initiatives, would also fit into a narrative of elite mobilisation. However, in the case of Zaman, it is only a particular reading of his involvement that is offered, as he was an elected member of the Pakistan People's Party who, in the 1980s, still had a tangible relationship with democratic socialism and whose allegiance to Punjabi would also have come from that political period.[35]

---

[32] Rahman, *Language and Politics*, 80.

[33] Ibid., 83.

[34] It is of course important to note that demands made upon the post-colonial state for language recognition are precisely centred on the idea that, in contrast to the colonial state, the demands of the people were to be met by these new formations.

[35] The most generous reading would be that Ayres' book reflects the way that the Punjabi movement in the 2000s was increasingly shorn of its radical political implications in the wake of attempts to bring East and West Punjab closer, in the context of the overall Indo-Pak peace process. In that sense the

Once there is a recognition that talking about Punjabi necessitates talking about the peasant and the working class, then it is possible to understand its neglect by the state, which for particular reasons had adopted Urdu as the national language.[36] The leading activists of the Punjabi movement at various points in time occupied positions in the Left-wing of political life in Pakistan. To fit these into a nationalist rhetoric and then to reduce that to the symbolic domain at best ignores and at worst misrepresents the history of the Punjabi language movement. All language movements, by their nature, involve the urban educated middle classes, because of their access to the written word. Only when explicit links are made with social and political organisations do they take on the shape of movements, most often nationalist in shape. This utilisation is most prominently seen in the deeds of the Mazdoor Kisan Party (Major Ishaque) and the cadre that subsequently engaged with Punjabi at the cultural level through the newspaper *Sajjan* and the magazine *Panchim*. These figures on the left engage with Punjabi, as the language of the peasant and the working class, rather than in abstract terms divorced from the political economy of Punjab. One could argue that this instrumental use of Punjabi neglects the everyday pervasiveness of the language, yet it is precisely the social conditions of those who show an affective relationship to the language that provide it with its resilience. In that sense the analysis of Punjabi, outside of a state-centred discourse, that is offered here is one that is imbricated with those social conditions and those are ones that the Left has a historic interest in.

## Mazdoor Kisan Party (Major Ishaque) and the Language Question

Despite the almost McCarthy-like purging of the Left in Pakistan in the 1950s, by the mid-1960s the communists had regrouped. In the late 1960s, the Sino–Soviet split divided the Pakistani communist movement into two groups. A further subdivision took place and

---

notion of symbolic recovery, central to Ayres' thesis, reflects the attempts to de-politicise the space that opened up at the cultural level between the two Punjabs during the Musharraf era. See Purewal, 'Borderland', for an overview of this political process.

[36] See Mir, *Social Space*, for a detailed analysis of the way in which Urdu is adopted by the British Punjab state.

two more groups emerged who were pro-Peking, one in favour of the General in charge of Pakistan at the time (1968), Ayub Khan, and the other opposed to him.[37] It was this opposition group that went on to form the Mazdoor Kisan Party (MKP) in 1970, or the Communist Workers-Peasants Party, under the leadership of (ex) Major Ishaque Mohammad. A central figure in communist politics in Pakistan, Ishaque Mohammad, was part of the Rawalpindi Conspiracy case in 1951, which led to his arrest and to the mass clampdown on communist organising in Pakistan.[38] Upon his release from prison, Mohammad continued to play a role in Left politics in Pakistan, the major zenith being the formation of the MKP. The party was based on a theoretical premise that drew from Maoist politics more generally, in Mohammad's own words:

> I abandoned my legal practice and left Lahore for two years. I went and stayed in my village and we picked up two or three districts in the Punjab in order to use the available resources. Similarly, in the Frontier province we confined ourselves to one or two districts; .... The main guideline of the party is the working class ideology of revolution. We use that in analysing situations and in training our cadres. The study of their own people, of the history of Pakistan, of the class structure of Pakistan, of the state of class struggle here is done from that point of view of the proletarian revolutionary theory. That is the guiding thing. But our main stress is on working in the countryside.[39]

It is this relationship to the countryside that explains the parties attitude towards the language question, as it was clear that mobilising in the countryside required a translation of concepts into the language of the people. It was not in the Punjab though that the MKP achieved its most spectacular political success. The guerrilla war waged against feudalism in the valley of Hashtnagar, North West Frontier Province, liberated an area of approximately 200 square miles and inspired similar movements all over Pakistan.[40]

---

[37] For an overview of Maoist politics in Pakistan see Ahmed, 'The Rise and Fall'.

[38] See Talbot, *Pakistan*, for an account of the Rawalpindi conspiracy case.

[39] Mohammad and Ahmed, 'Interview', 7.

[40] See Ahmed, 'The Rise and Fall', for more details of Hashtnagar, though this event has not been sufficiently researched or written about in English.

Major Ishaque Mohammad's rural engagements led him to develop an understanding of the Pakistani society at a level that required engagement with a number of issues that no other political party at the time or subsequently has addressed seriously. The first of these was the caste question; whereas in East Punjab and India more generally the emergence of Dalit politics and a radical relationship between this and other political forms was quite established by the 1970s, in Pakistan no such process had occurred.[41] It was therefore much to Mohammad's credit that while in prison he penned the Punjabi play *Musalli*. This name, which literary means 'man of the prayer mat', is the equivalent of *Harijan* when discussing dalits.[42] The play *Musalli* focuses on rural West Punjab. In the introduction to the play, Mohammad describes the process by which his own awareness of language arose:

> As part of living in a village and interacting with musallis . ... Firstly, I thought they were always speaking in a free poetic form, but when needed they could play with words to maintain the flow. Waves of words flowed whatever the topic, ranging from the plough to love affairs. Secondly, the range of this language surprised me, these people who had been kept away from *patshaalas*, *madrassas* and schools and for whom words were kept out of reach. They had a full command of their own language. Sitting in their school I became convinced about the importance of Punjabi.[43]

This play was radical at many levels but it punctured the national narrative of Pakistan in two very significant ways. First, by giving credibility to the Punjabi language, in terms of literature, the one-nation Urdu nationalism was challenged — something that became especially fraught in the wake of the war of Bangladeshi independence. Second, and perhaps even more of a taboo subject by talking about caste explicitly, the second plank of Pakistani nationalism, Islam was called into question. Armed with an Islamic egalitarian

---

[41] See Ram, 'Untouchability'.

[42] *Harijan* or children of God was the name penned by Gandhi for dalits and was also criticised, as with the term *musalli* for being apolitical and patronising.

[43] Ishaque Mohammad, *Musalli in Ishaque Mohammad de Dramme*, 17–18, translated by the authors.

ideology, one of the distinctions between the new Pakistan and the new India was to be the removal of caste. The treatment of the *Musalli* in Mohammad's play bears witness to the failure of the new state to eradicate caste prejudice or even to acknowledge its continuing salience.

For Ishaque Mohammad, there was little distinction between his literary and political work. Indeed, the role of Punjabi in articulating the desires and needs of the masses was clearly a point of inspiration. *Musalli* was written whilst Mohammad was in prison in 1971. In the book *Punjabi Identity*, Fateh Mohammad Malik notes how Ishaque's 'literary career is organically related to the political struggle of bringing the peasantry into the mainstream of socio-political life in Pakistan.'[44] Indeed, Ishaque Mohammad spent much of his life in prison where he died in 1982. The Punjabi literature of the MKP was usually poetic in form and performed as part of a mobilising strategy throughout rural Punjab. *Musalli* was performed at MKP rallies with party members playing the part of the main protagonists of the play. It was not only at this level that Punjabi was used. There was a party edict that Punjabi would be the language of the MKP in the Punjab. In turn, each of the provincial wings of the MKP in NFWP and Sindh were encouraged to develop party material in their own languages. For the MKP Punjab this meant developing a language of politics that was new for the Pakistani Left in that the dominance of Urdu had to be overcome. Party resolutions and policy documents such as *Lok Raj* began to be published in Punjabi in an attempt to open up the party to peasants and workers. According to Hamza Virk, a central committee member of the MKP, it was the crucial period after the Bangladesh war of independence and the formation of the new state of Pakistan, 1972–1973, that the decision to vernacularise the party took place.[45]

The poem that opens this chapter was performed by Ishaque Mohammed at the First National Congress of the MKP, held on the 12 and 13 May 1973 in Sher Garh, District Mardan (NWFP). Ishaque started his speech by paying tributes to the martyred of the Party during the struggle over the previous five years, particularly in Hashtnagar and recited the poem that opens this chapter. The

---

[44] Malik, *Punjabi*, 33.
[45] In personal correspondence with the authors.

poem's author, Mian Saleem Jahangir, is one of the key figures in the development of MKP's language policy. Whilst the MKP has become associated with the personality of Mohammed Ishaque, Mian Saleem, as he was known, was a senior member in the party hierarchy who gave substance to the vision of engaging with the masses formulated by Ishaque Mohammed. Mian Saleem was central to developing the Punjabi language movement outside of Lahore. His absence from any of the literature looking at the development of the language movement in Pakistan is stark and a clear example of the amnesia about the role of the Left in Punjabi language mobilisation.

A son of a peasant family, Mian Saleem passed his Matriculation examination from Nankana Sahib and went on to study Law in Lahore where he became an advocate. Under the influence of Major Ishaque, he became one of the leading members of the MKP. Integral to the mobilising and educational strategy of the MKP was the use of poetry. In keeping with the oral tradition, which indeed was the main way in which Punjabi as a language had survived in Pakistan, Mian Saleem's poems were recited and remembered by those who attended MKP rallies and meetings. His poems were published in MKP pamphlets and publications, reflecting the close relationship between politics and poetry. It was posthumously in the year of his death that Sibt-ul-Hassan Zegum collated them with additions from his own memory and that of other party workers. The volume, *Aaj Dee Vaar* (Ballad of the Day), was published in 1989 and forms an exemplary cultural work in the service of a party, following a well-worn Marxist tradition. In the introduction to the volume, Zegum offers a narrative of the close ties between Mian Saleem's poetic and political work. It was the Punjab Congress of the MKP in 1972 that, according to Zegum, Mian Saleem displayed his poetic skills for the first time in public, reciting the poem: 'Let's get rid of new dacoits and old thieves from our fields'. In the tradition of resistance poetry, his lyrics were simple and direct, appealing to the masses:

The flute is silent.
Even the songs are scared
People look alive
But their insides are dead[46]

---

[46] Jahangir, Untitled Ghazal, in *Ballad*, 128.

Alongside poems that were concerned with the state of the masses, he also wrote in the heroic tradition about figures in the party such as labour leader Abdul Rahman as well as Major Ishaque. Mian Saleem's style of recitation was integral to the message of his poetry, as Zegum comments: 'He achieved that level of oratory, that those who listened to him were enthralled. Fire spouted out of his mouth when he spoke out against the military dictatorship.'[47] In the introduction to the volume *Aaj Dee Vaar* a number of activists offer commentary on Mian Saleem's life. The President of the MKP, following Ishaque Mohammed's death, Gulam Nabi Kaloo praised Mian Saleem extensively, but also reiterated the parties' perspective on the language question. First, the MKP recognised and gave due importance to all the mother tongues of the people of different nationalities of Pakistan. The role of the Pakistani state in suppressing mother tongues was a source of concern for Mian Saleem and is thus one of the reasons for his use of Punjabi in rallies and in his poetry. Second, Mian Saleem himself demonstrated this commitment by showing pride in his own language and this was an essential part of his political work.

Although the MKP had its own student wing during this period, Mian Saleem was also very close with the larger student organisation, the National Students Federation Pakistan (NSF).[48] The MKP changed the sectarian traditions of Left organisations by developing close ties with other Leftist groups and this was largely due to the efforts of Mian Saleem. The NSF was the best organised and numerically the largest Left-wing student organisation in Pakistan at that time. In the Punjab province, the NSF had active units in all of the major cities and towns where there were college populations. Other than being engaged in college-level politics, the NSF played a wider role in mobilising students towards socialist politics with rallies and

---

[47] Ibid., 17.

[48] The NSF was formed in 1956, ironically with state support as a counter to the banned communist student organisation — the Democratic Students Forum. However, the NSF swiftly also took up the role of the DSF, especially in the counter-Ayub Khan protests in the early 1960s. Even though the DSF made a small comeback in the 1970s, the NSF remained the strongest Left-wing student organisation in Pakistan until the early 1990s. See Butt, *Revisiting.*

speeches on justice and equality.[49] Much of the language of popular protest and interaction, especially at the village level, was in Punjabi, but the NSF also saw 'Urdu as the language of communication' amongst different nationalities within Pakistan. This was a distinct development on the slogan that framed the unity out of the diversity nationalism of Jinnah, which was 'Urdu is our language, Islam is our faith'. By the mid-1970s, the aftershocks of the independence of Bangladesh had a great impact on the way the Left was organising. The NSF itself grew tremendously during the years of Zulfikar Ali Bhutto's regime (1973–1977). In the Punjab, the centres of strength were Multan, Sahiwal, Khanewal, Vihaari, Depalpur, Okara and of course Lahore. The leadership of the NSF was engaged in the question of Punjabi as a suppressed language as well as with the national question itself. Just as Mian Saleem Jahangir fuzzied the borders between his political and language work, so the central President of NSF Pakistan, Latif Choudry and other important office holders of Punjab Province such as Arshad Butt, Masdiq Hussain Asad, Habibulah Shakir, and Saif Allah Saif engaged in revolutionary debate that tied language together with politics.

## Government College Sahiwal

The mutual ideologies of the NSF and MKP when it comes to the language question demonstrate the key role the Left played in the Punjabi language movement and the central necessity of taking into account language when mobilising amongst the peasants and working class. The second issue of the overtly Lahore focus of previous accounts will be addressed in this section by a case study of Sahiwal.[50] Urdu's urban character has long been noted by scholars of the language. In

---

[49] Paracha, 'Student Politics'.

[50] Sahiwal was a small village that, in 1865, was transformed into a market town by the British to accommodate the need for the produce of the expanding canal colonies of the Punjab. The town grew dramatically to take on all the hallmarks of colonial architecture and planning, with markets, a railway junction and central church to mark the British presence on the agricultural landscape. It took until 1966 for the town to shift back from the name Montgomery (named after Lord Montgomery, the Lieutenant-Governor of Punjab at the time) to Sahiwal, though this name was always in circulation amongst the original inhabitants. In contemporary West Punjab, Sahiwal is one of the biggest districts located South of Lahore.

a sense, it is therefore understandable that the Punjabi movements' leading literary figures would have a relationship to Lahore, which was always the de facto capital of the region. By focusing on Sahiwal, the role of Punjabi as the language of articulation of those marginal to the centres of power emerges. Indeed, it is the association of Punjabi with the powerless and in places relatively marginal to the centres of power that makes Sahiwal such an interesting case study. It is necessary, however, to first have an understanding of the relationship between student politics and the MKP, as it was Sahiwal's College[51] that was the main centre of activities. The struggle for language recognition and its impact on student politics could arguably only have taken place in a small town college, as it was relatively marginal to the centres of power in Lahore and Islamabad.[52]

The small village Sahiwal was subsumed during the canal colonies expansion in the 1880s under the name of Montgomery.[53] In independent Pakistan, the now major market town and railway junction reverted to Sahiwal. In the 1970s, the college in the town was a centre of socialist and Punjabi engagement. This was best articulated in the deeds of the National Students Federation, members of who stood for elections and mobilised not just students but local populations. Indeed, the Government College Sahiwal by the mid-1970s had students coming from the rural heartland of West Punjab: although Okara, Depalpur and Pak Pattan were *tehsils* of the district and reasonable sized towns in their own right, students also came from Khaniwal, Vehari, Haroonabad, Chistian, Haveli Lakha, Arif Wala, Hujra Shah Mukeem, Renala Kurd, Cheecha Watni, Noor Shah, and even as far as Faislabad. The total student population was about 3000, with over 700 staying in hostels on the campus. Government College Sahiwal's students politics was essentially a competition

---

[51] Government College Montgomery was set up in 1942 to provide educational facilities to the district at the time. In an attempt to emulate the Government College Lahore, the objective was to set up an elite institution for the landed gentry of the surrounding towns of Okara, Pak Pattan and Gugera.

[52] Indeed, much of the previous research on student politics has focused on Pakistan's main urban centres.

[53] One of the lasting impacts of British colonial rule in the Punjab was the development of an irrigation system and colonisation of common land to agricultural production. See Ali, *The Punjab*, for a comprehensive economic history.

between the NSF and the Jamiaat, the student wing of the Jamaat-i-Islami, what would now be called an Islamist outfit, but in that era would be better categorised as right wing.[54]

The rural College was an important site for the struggle over language, as it was here that state ideology was most coherently represented, in that the official language of instruction was Urdu or English. College lecturers would inevitably be drawn from urban backgrounds, or from the recently migrated Urdu elite of Lucknow and Delhi. The ideology of 'one nation, one language, one faith' was supported not only by the institution of the college but also by the Jamiaat. In that sense the struggle for finding political space in the college system was one that had to work through the politics of culture as well as the principles of equality and justice. The NSF therefore attempted to influence the cultural life of the college as well as support staff, who were attempting to create institutional space. It was during the Bhutto era, in 1972, that the Punjab University in Lahore appointed its first Chair in Punjabi, a job taken up by Najm Hussain Sayyid. Following this, the Punjab government allocated posts in Punjabi to colleges to teach the language at the FA and BA level. The criteria for these posts were the qualification of MA in Punjabi, which could only be obtained from Punjab University. It was Mian Saleem who encouraged one of his relatives — Ghulam Rasool Azad — and another party member — Ali Arshad Mir — to take up MA, with an eye to securing the newly created lecturer jobs in Punjabi. In many ways, this was a mutually beneficial arrangement as the example of Ghulam Rasool Azad illustrates. When the allocation of a Punjabi post came to Government College Sahiwal the progressive college lecturers and the principal at the time were supportive of the idea of having the language taught in Sahiwal. However, it was opposed by the right wing staff members but the principal of

---

[54] There have been a few articles on student politics in Pakistan most comprehensively in terms of scope by Nelson, 'Embracing the Ummah', building on earlier work by Nasr, 'Students, Islam, and Politics'. There is also a chapter on student politics in Iqtidar, *Secularizing Islamists*, Chapter 2. However, the focus of these studies as with much work on Pakistan is an increasing unpacking of the working of the Islamist or right-wing groups rather than the opposition to them. Indeed no comprehensive account of the activities of the NSF and their long-lasting impact on not only student politics but subsequently radical politics in Pakistan and its diaspora.

that time — Agah Amjad Ali — supported the appointment and was aware of the support amongst local students. Therefore, in 1975 Ghulam Rasool Azad was appointed as the first Punjabi Lecturer in Government College Sahiwal. This created a progressive lecturer with good links to the MKP (through Mian Saleem) and a natural ally for the NSF. Indeed, this was a necessary connection for the post to be created in the first place.

The appointment of a college lecturer was the beginning of a series of victories that the NSF managed to wrangle in the name of cultural politics. The existing status quo in the college meant the promotion and support of a college magazine and an annual *mushaira* (poetry recital), which were all in Urdu. The NSF students wanted to establish a section within the college magazine for Punjabi and to open up the *mushaira* for Punjabi poets. This generated a heated debate in the college as the lecturers, who historically helped students organise these literary events, were opposed to the inclusion of Punjabi. Their arguments against Punjabi are worth rehearsing, as they are still prominent when the case is made for the language in contemporary West Punjab. Overall, the inclusion of Punjabi was seen as being against the Pakistani nation: first because Punjabi was cast as 'the language of the Sikhs' and this was therefore a religious language, second and sequentially this meant it was the 'language of the *kaffirs*' (non-believers). Whereas this ideological argument was often quite easily won, by taking recourse in the history of the Sufi poets of Punjab, thereby dismissing the religious and language arguments, further protests arose from the opposition in terms of the lack of standardisation and the huge linguistic diversity of Punjabi. Despite this opposition, after campaigning amongst the rural students in the college, the NSF established the *Punjabi Adabi Sangat* (Punjabi Literary Forum), which penetrated into the college magazine as well as into the poetry readings in the college and Sahiwal town. In the 1976 College elections, the NSF won the key posts of president and secretary, demonstrating the political outcome of the cultural work they had carried out. The impact of the language activism was felt not only in the College but also in the literary and cultural life of Sahiwal town, and it continues to this day.

The decline of the MKP began in the late 1970s, initially with the party factionalising into three camps. Indeed, the general factionalising of Left parties began as the Zulfikar Bhutto period was coming to an end.[55] The splintering of Left groups such as the NSF and MKP meant that their strength in campuses was diminished in the face of the onslaught that was to follow under General Zia. Even though various progressive alliances, against military rule, fought (and often won) against the IJT on campuses across Pakistan, the states' increasing use of violence was reflected in student politics. Weapons, including firearms, became part of the mobilisation of groups and student politics entered a phase of heightened intensity.[56] In this context, the close linkage between language and political mobilisation began to take secondary place to basic demands for restoration of democracy. The death, in 1982, of Major Ishaque effectively saw an end to the direct political support of the language movement by the Left. However, many of the cadres and in particular the ideas of the MKP lived on in a number of publications and the activities of key groups and individuals.

Arguably, the Left as a political force never regained the popular support it had in the 1970s. The legacy in terms of cultural work is therefore all the more significant as this is where the lasting influence of the MKP can still be traced and is why the absence of this role in previous literature is so stark. Perhaps of most note was the brief but effervescent publication of a daily newspaper in Lahore in the period 1989–1990. General Zia died in a plane crash in 1988 and Pakistan breathed a sigh of relief after the harsh years of military rule. In that spirit, a number of socialists and communists came together to produce *Sajjan* (friend/comrade), the first daily Punjabi newspaper of Pakistan. Its first issue appeared on 3 February 1989

---

[55] Nelson's, 'Embracing the Ummah', following the work of Brass, *Language*, makes much play of the factionalising tendency of all student politics in Pakistan. In this way the activities of the right-wing religious parties are equated with those of the Left, a common move amongst contemporary commentators but one that side-lines the extent to which the state was actively involved in breaking up Left-wing groups and aiding (some) right-wing religious parties.

[56] It is only due to the work of journalists such as Nadeem F. Paracha that any narrative of this period exists (in English) and that also on the blogsphere. This information from http://nadeemfparacha.wordpress.com/student-politics-in-pakistan-a-celebration-lament-history/ (accessed 14 September 2011).

and it continued till 30 September 1990. As it was never established as a commercial venture, it is admirable that it lasted for this length of time as it relied almost exclusively on voluntary labour. The most direct link to literary magazines in Punjabi and the MKP is found in the charismatic figure of Saqib Maqsood who was an activist of the MKP in Sheikapura and whose commitment to the language movement is derived directly from the thesis highlighted in this chapter. He was involved in *Ruth Lekha* — a magazine established in 1976 — and then the influential publication *Maboli*. He is indeed still active in the world of Punjabi literature and publishes the magazine *Panchim* in Lahore to this day. At the more general level, Sahiwal still remains the centre of Punjabi language activism, with several Punjabi organisations regularly organising *mushairas* and occasional publications; of particular note in this regard is *Punjab Lok Lehar* under the stewardship of Qaswar Butt. Indeed, the legacy that comes out of the organising of the Left for the continuing salience of Punjabi has a more secure platform in a place like Sahiwal, as a political question in Pakistan, rather than the organising of urban upper middle class activists.

## Conclusion

If the political history of the current geographical territory that is Pakistan is narrowly confined to actual links between constitutional construction and governmental framing, then 1973 would be the birth of that state, not 1947. It would also then be the beginning of a period (which lasts until 1977) of the most active and progressive period of grassroots politics that, that country has seen in its 40-year history. Indeed, this nation state would look much more like many other post-colonial states that emerged with leaders expressing socialism at the ideological level, but carrying out reactionary and authoritarian policies at the level of governance. It is in this environment that the MKP and the NSF were most able to mobilise and exert influence over a number of spheres and where the issue of language linked to socialist politics became most prominent. Punjabi as the language of the marginalised, in a dominant region of the country, becomes entwined through the poetics of mobilisation with groups such as the MKP. This influence is most notable outside of urban centres of power, such as Lahore and in rural towns such as Sahiwal.

The practices of the MKP and NSF provide an example of role of the Punjabi language in relationship to mobilisation for state power. Mir has recently argued that the role of the state is overplayed when it comes to looking at Punjabi, as the pre-colonial and post-colonial state had no role to play in its sustainability and resilience. Not withstanding the general salience of these arguments in terms of noting the resilience of Punjabi, the state (colonial and post-colonial) has, since the 20th century, been subject to petitioning about Punjabi by various groups.[57] Indeed, it is the demand on the state, to provide provision in the mother tongue, that is at the basis of much contemporary West Punjabi language activism. This demand whilst ostensibly about language is also a social demand, given that it is the peasant, working class and poor who speak Punjabi. It is this relationship of language to social status that the mobilisation by the Left most usefully illustrates. Supporting Punjabi is in effect an act of general uplift for those who are socially marginal. Language is therefore an indispensable aspect of the more general aim of social uplift. This may be viewed as an instrumentalist use of language, but that would imply a separation of the symbolic and political.[58] Rather, the Left mobilisations of the MKP demonstrate the irreducibility of language to either the symbolic or political domains when it comes to those who are socially marginal.

Despite the ongoing attempts by Punjabi activists, the language still maintains its neglected status in contemporary Pakistan. Although it remains the spoken language of the majority of the inhabitants, it is still not an official language of the state. Urban Punjab has developed a language that is a mixture of Urdu and Punjabi aided by a relatively new and invigorated satellite media. Much of rural Punjab remains wedded to Punjabi, despite the increasing penetration of Urdu and religiously inspired education. The legacy of the Left in this regard perhaps is most evident in the way that the stigma attached to the language has considerably diminished especially amongst the

---

[57] Singh Sabha activists in the early part of the 20th century petitioned the colonial state for greater recognition of Punjabi and the introduction of the *Gyani* exam was a direct result of this.

[58] This is the fundamental error made by Ayres.

bilingual working class of Lahore, for whom the question of speaking in Urdu in formal situations and Punjabi in the informal seems to have become normalised.[59] Given the perpetual crises that Pakistan has found itself in over the first decade of the 21st century, most of the existing Left-wing groups have also placed the language issue to one side in the face of military rule and ongoing violence.[60] To some extent, this is a repetition of the period under General Zia. Nonetheless, the issue of language in the wider political context remains salient and given the increasing marginalisation of rural Punjab, the potential for political mobilisation remains.

—

# References

Ahmed, Ishtiaq, 'The Rise and Fall of the Left and the Maoist Movements in Pakistan', *India Quarterly* 66 (2010): 251–65.

Ali, Imran, *The Punjab Under Imperialism, 1885–1947*', Karachi: Oxford University Press, 2003.

Ayres, Alyssa, *Speaking Like a State: Language and Nationalism in Pakistan*, Cambridge: Cambridge University Press, 2012.

Brass, Paul, *Language, Religion, and Politics in North India*, Cambridge: Cambridge University Press, 1974.

Butt, Iqbal Haider, *Revisiting Student Politics in Pakistan*, Gujranwala: Bargad, 2009.

Iqtidar, Humeira, *Secularizing Islamists? Jama'at-e-Islami and Jama'at-ud-Da'wa in Urban Pakistan*, Chicago, IL: Chicago University Press, 2011.

Jahangir, Mian Salim, *Ballad of the Day*, Compiled by Silte-ul-Hassan Zaigam, Lahore: Memorial Committee, 1989.

———, *Aaj dee Vaar*, Compiled by, Sibte-ul-Hassan Zaigam, Lahore: Mian Saleem Jahangir Memorial Committee, 1989.

Jalal, Ayesha, *Self and Sovereignty: Individual and Community in South Asian Islam Since 1850*, London: Routledge, 2000.

Kabir, M. G., 'Religion, Language and Nationalism in Bangladesh', *Journal of Contemporary Asia* 17, no. 4 (1987): 473–87.

---

[59] Based on fieldwork carried out in 2007–2009 in Lahore.

[60] Groups such as the *Pakistan Labour Party* and even the remnants of the MKP are more concerned with suicide bombings and US imperialist drone attacks than with the questions of language.

King, Richard, *Orientalism and Religion: Post-Colonial Theory, India and 'The Mystic East'*, London: Routledge, 1999.

Kukreja, Veena and Mahendra Singh, eds, *Pakistan: Democracy, Development, and Security Issues*, New Delhi: Sage, 2005.

Mohammad Ali, Jinnah, *Quaid-i-Azam Mohammad Ali Jinnah: Speeches as Governor-General of Pakistan 1947–1948*, Karachi: Pakistan Publications, 1976.

Malik, Fateh Mohammad, *Punjabi Identity*, Lahore: Sang-e-Meel Publications, 1989.

Mandair, Arvind, *Religion and the Specter of the West: Sikhism, India, Postcoloniality, and the Politics of Translation*, New York: Columbia University Press, 2009.

Mir, Farina, *The Social Space of Language: Vernacular Culture in British Colonial Punjab*, Berkeley: University of California Press, 2010.

Mohammad, Ishaque and Feroz Ahmed, 'Interview Ishaque Mohammad', *Pakistan Forum* 3, no. 1 (Oct, 1972): 5–9.

———, *Five Years of Struggle*, 13–14, Lahore: Pakistan MKP, 1973.

———, *Jadojahid key paanch saal*, Lahore: Pakistan MKP, 1973.

———, *Ishaque Mohammad de Draame*, Compiled by Shabnum Ishaque, Lahore: Sanjh Publications, 2008.

Nasr, S. V. R., 'Students, Islam and Politics: Islami Jamiat-e-Talba in Pakistan', *Middle East Journal* 46 (1992): 59–76.

Nelson, Matthew J., 'Embracing the Ummah: Student Politics Beyond State Power in Pakistan', *Modern Asian Studies* 45, no. 3 (2011): 565–96.

Oberoi, Harjot, *The Construction of Religious Boundaries, Culture, Identity, and Diversity in the Sikh Tradition*, Chicago, IL: University of Chicago Press, 1994.

Pakistan Census Organisation, *Main Finding of Census on Housing and Population*, Pakistan: Statistics Division, 2001.

Paracha, Nadeem, 'Student Politics in Pakistan: A Celebration, Lament and History', http://nadeemfparacha.wordpress.com/student-politics-in-pakistan-a-celebration-lament-history/ (accessed 20 April 2012).

Purewal, Navtej, 'Borderland Punjab', *Seminar* 567 (2006): 27–32.

Rahman, Tariq, *Language and Politics in Pakistan*, Karachi: Oxford University Press, 1998.

———, *Unpleasant Essays: Education and Politics in Pakistan*, Lahore: Vanguard, 2000.

———, *Language, Ideology and Power: Language-Learning Among the Muslims of Pakistan and North India*, Karachi: Oxford University Press, 2002.

———, *Language, Education and Culture*, Karachi: Oxford University Press, 2003.

————, *Language, Power and Ideology in Pakistan*, Karachi: Oxford University Press, 2005.

Ram, Ronki, 'Untouchability, Dalit Consciousness, and the Ad Dharm Movement in Punjab', *Contributions to Indian Sociology* 38, no. 3 (2004): 323–49.

Sarangi, Asha, ed., *Language and Politics in India*, New Delhi: OUP, 2011.

Shackle, Christopher, 'Punjabi in Lahore', *Modern Asian Studies* 4, no. 3 (1970): 239–67.

Talbot, Ian, *Pakistan: A Modern History*, London: Hurst, 2008.

Zaidi, Abbas, 'A Postcolonial Sociolinguistics of Punjabi in Pakistan', *Journal of Postcolonial Cultures Societies* 1, no. 3 & 4 (2010): 22–55. http://www.jpcs.in.

# The Indian Workers' Association Coventry 1938–1990: Political and Social Action

*Talvinder Gill*

---

The Indian Workers' Association's (IWA) political and social action in Britain demonstrated the existence of conventional elements of class agency in the past 60 years, yet they have been sidelined in a general reluctance to write class/social histories. To date, black and Asian citizens and communities have appeared only in the context of their interactions with the state or other official bodies. The recently made available archive of the IWA is significant because it is a rare example of a self-defined South Asian presence in the archives. Upon discovering these archives, I attended a poetry workshop with my father, organised by the Indian Writers Association. Several middle-aged and old Indian men enthusiastically recited literature and poetry and sang Punjabi folk songs, most of whom were all former leaders and members of the IWA in Coventry. Within their chosen artistic medium, each member spoke on a range of diverse topics such as familial relationships, the pastoral beauty of Punjab, working life, Marxism and party politics. Having grown up listening to my father's stories about the transition from the village in Punjab to working life in the Midlands, I learned of the several challenges Indian migrant workers faced, such as racism and poor working conditions. As a rank and file member, he praised the role of these men in helping migrants fight discrimination and assist in matters of civic life. As I was soon to discover, few of these stories were recorded in history books or official mediums, especially from the perspective of the workers and migrants themselves. I became particularly interested in their political ideology and how it affected the culture and identity of Indian migrants and the wider British society in light of contemporary debates surrounding 'multiculturalism'. The Coventry IWA, which was significantly the first to be formed, alongside its sister branches, was at the forefront of antiracist campaigns in the late 20th century and were active creators of their social environments through political action. Not only did they challenge the existing power structures by demanding toleration of ethnic diversity but they also called for public acknowledgement and fair access to resources and representation.[1] Their fight for acceptance as workers and citizens was sustained through a belief in civil rights, Marxism and class struggle. Consequently, the IWA's ideas and use of class interacted with other social registers such as race and ethnicity.

The existing history of the IWA activity in Britain has focused on its role as a class, ethnic or cultural organisation. Instead, I argue that all three of these components are crucial in any understanding of how the IWA operated in British society and made an indelible print on the political landscape of post-war Britain.

## Background

The first IWA was established in Coventry in 1938 to coordinate the efforts of all Indians in Britain in the campaign for Indian independence, which preserves Coventry as a special and unique place in the history of the IWA. During the war years, Indian revolutionaries and political exiles of various backgrounds were attracted to the city. Hence, the early IWA was characterised by a blend of ethnic and political concerns. As soon as British rule in India ended in 1947, the focus of Indian migrants switched to protecting their rights as workers and citizens. Increasing levels of migration from the Punjab saw the number of Indian migrants in Britain's urban and industrial heartlands swell progressively throughout the 1950s and reach its zenith in the early 1960s. This altered the political and ethnic balance of the IWA in favour of a largely communist and Sikh membership. Subsequently, branches of the IWA sprang up in places such as Southall, Wolverhampton, Birmingham, Huddersfield, and Leicester. Following encouragement by Jawaharlal Nehru on a visit to Britain, local associations were brought together to form the Indian Workers' Association Great Britain (IWA GB) in 1958. Increasing

---

[1] Werbner and Modood, *Debating Cultural Hybridity*, 290.

social exclusion and hostility from the state refocused the attention of the IWAs on issues such as immigration laws, housing, racism, education, and policing. Having been frozen out of the Trade Unions, Indian migrants also relied on the IWAs as proxy trade unions in the fight for better working conditions. Naturally, they occupied a crucial community and welfare role for incoming Punjabi migrants in the early years of settlement. However, the radical Left-wing ideology of many of its leaders throughout the country firmly committed the IWA, as a local and national umbrella organisation, to the struggles of all black and minority ethnic groups and working people. However, this was not simply a story of harmony as the group split a number of times for reasons ranging from factional party disputes 'back home' or competing financial interests.

To understand where Coventry's IWA stands in the national picture, it is imperative to look at how the original organisation developed in the city prior to the Second World War. The IWA in Coventry's main political message concentrated on calls for Indian independence and operated mainly as a social and welfare centre for the small group of resident Indians. They raised money for the Amritsar-based Desh Bhagat Parwarik Sahaik Committee, which assisted families and dependants of Punjabis jailed for life because of anticolonial agitation. After independence, the new leaders Joginder Singh, Gurdev Singh Dosanjh and Gurdev Singh Dhami, all communists, signalled the switch to a much more radical political agenda. Following the election in 1953, only Babu Karam Singh Cheema, Anant Ram, Gurbaksh Singh, and Ujagar Singh Randhawa remained from the first Executive Committee.[2] The majority communist wing avoided wearing their communist colours on their sleeves, seeing their primary duty as leading a mass Indian organisation. As the original group, Coventry was central in starting new IWA branches through finance and organisational support.[3] Coventry remained influential due to this early system of patronage even though it was overtaken in size and power by the Southall and Birmingham IWAs. The arrival

---

[2] Coventry, Coventry History Centre, Indian Workers' Association archive, PA2600/9/15/6. Photograph: Executive Committee, Indian Workers' Association, Coventry, includes names of Executive Committee members (1953).

[3] Ibid., 5–6.

of sophisticated political theorists such as Vishnu Dutt Sharma in Southall and Avtar Johal and Jagmohan Joshi in Birmingham provided the leadership required for a large membership. Consequently, the national organisation seems to have been firmly based in London and Birmingham from the late 1950s.

Because of their sizeable membership from which to draw finances, Birmingham and Southall were able to secure independent offices in the form of the Shaheed Udham Singh Welfare Centre and Dominion cinema, respectively. Contrarily, Coventry's IWA had to rely on the homes of individual leaders and limited spaces in community centres to conduct their political and social activities. Coventry could not generate the finances or maintain the unity to own independent offices that would serve as a base for the community and safeguard its future as an important local organisation. Thus, the Coventry IWA was in the second tier of influence within the IWA GB. Nevertheless, Coventry was the third largest city for IWA activity; not least because of its large contingent of political activists. Joginder Singh surmised that there 'were thirty of us who were very active. The number of people who have been active since then has steadily decreased. We had a general membership of approximately five hundred to six hundred'.[4] Membership and finance did not necessarily dictate the strength of individual branches; this was measured more in the strength of the branches' politically active leadership. Since most Indian migrants were uneducated, the public relied on the IWAs for direction and leadership. The more educated and sophisticated leadership would largely formulate the agenda and write reports and articles instructing on certain issues that directed their constituency along a particular line. Consequently, the IWA in Coventry was more of a top-down organisation than a bottom-up movement.

Nevertheless, the battle for control of Coventry's IWA was as intense as any other in the country. The common problems of ideology and competition for financial resources affected unity in Coventry. Mirroring the national trend, there were three local IWA factions in Coventry from 1967, the Rajmal Group, the Joginder Group and the Ajmer Group. The first split in Coventry was a result of Southall's withdrawal from the IWA GB due to the group's

---

[4] Coventry, Coventry History Centre, Gill, IWA Transcripts, Interview Two — Joginder Singh, 2008–2009, 9.

growing communist contingent. Rajmal Singh was a founding member of the IWA in Coventry and wanted to continue the organisation along the ethnic lines of the original group and follow Southall's example. Reflecting on the hybrid character of the early IWA, he was a follower of the Congress Party and did not adopt a militant stand against government actions in India. Nor did he concur with the IWAs' belligerent attitude towards trade union and antiracist campaigns. He accused the Central Committee of the national and Coventry IWA of being explicitly communist and decided to leave the Association in 1964 to form a non-political IWA. His IWA faction adopted a new constitution that prohibited any communist from holding office. However, this branch was especially reliant on Rajmal's leadership and a limited batch of followers, which meant the group did not survive his death in the late 1960s. The biggest branch in Coventry was the group led by Joginder Singh and Gurdev Singh Dhami. Throughout its history, this faction was committed to the radical agenda followed by the IWA GB (Joshi and Johal) and abided by the constitution of 1958. The Coventry IWA GB worked closely with the Birmingham group on a range of local and national issues.

However, Joginder Singh and Gurdev Dhami did not always agree with the Birmingham branch's power within the national movement and were critical of their interference in local branches in Leamington and Bedford. They continued to look for guidance from Indian radicals, in particular, Harkishan Singh Surjeet, and criticised Joshi and Johal for siding with the Naxalites in 1967. Although this group was close to Jagmohan Joshi during this period, it later fell out over his support of the Naxalites. This group, which was the biggest faction in Coventry, later formed a triumvirate with Derby and Leicester to act as a counterweight to the influence of the Birmingham branch in the Midlands. Yet they were undermined when a third IWA faction was set up in Coventry by Ajmer Bains, who broke away to support the stance taken by Joshi and Johal. With an educated background, he was a teacher at a local secondary school. Ajmer was also a sophisticated writer and intellectual who believed in the Marxist-Leninism preached by Chinese communists. Too often it is argued that these difficulties and splits determined the whole story of the IWA in Coventry and elsewhere. Despite factional differences, branches managed to set aside any acrimony and collaborate with each other on the major issues of mutual interest; there was agreement on major issues including class and antiracist struggles. For example, there was often communication between Ajmer's group and Joginder's group in Coventry regarding strikes and public protests. Letters and phone calls would be made to all branches from the IWA GB asking them to attend marches and rallies. Nevertheless, it is clear there was no monolithic IWA organisation, whether at a local or national level. Within 'the IWAs there were groups and quasi groups'; thus, we will always be dealing with a heterogeneous political and social entity.[5]

The Coventry IWA's political activism and constructive social engagement emerged out of the real and imagined politics of the homeland. Most of the members, reflecting migration patterns, were Jat Sikhs. Since their inception, the IWAs constituted an amalgam of class and ethnic concerns and reflected the relationship among the various political groups in India, which was a surprising mosaic. Akalis (Sikh nationalists) and communists could be, and many were, at the same time members of the Indian National Congress.[6] In addition, the IWAs were part of a long tradition of renegotiating and amalgamating religious discourse in their political programmes. Evidence of the IWAs' hybrid character can be seen in their working relationship with Gurdwaras (Sikh temples), where they co-operated on issues such as social work, strikes and cases of racial discrimination.

The IWA's political programme was informed by the collective memory of migrants who had lived through the tumultuous period of the independence struggle and the trauma wrought by partition. Some of those who became radicalised in the industrial landscape of Britain drew on the inspiration of socialists, freedom fighters and communists such as Bhagat Singh to Sohan Singh Josh. IWA members were inspired by an imagined history of pre-partition Punjab. Ties to Leftist radicals in India were discussed because of the sense of identity and purpose they provided to migrants who felt disenfranchised, displaced and threatened. The IWAs played a key role in disseminating this imagery through their cultural events. Here members would celebrate the long revolutionary struggle that tied their organisations to the Ghadar Party and the global communist movement. The Coventry IWA, like most branches, was particularly skilled at invoking claims of a revolutionary inheritance. Pamphlets

---

[5] Ramdin, *Black Working Class in Britain*, 398.
[6] See Engineer, 'Role of Sikhs in India's Freedom Struggle', 158–79.

and posters would often refer to Bhagat Singh, the inspirational leader of the Naujawan Bharat Sabha (NBS). They also memorialised Udham Singh's assassination in London of Sir Michael O'Dwyer on 13 March 1940 for his role of Punjab governor during the Amritsar massacre of 1919. Some had even, mistakenly, credited him as having started the IWA in Coventry in 1938.[7]

Martyrdom pervaded the cultural and social lives of the earliest migrants, something that was also infused by the general martyr tradition prevalent within Sikh heritage. Hence, Bhagat Singh and Udham Singh became venerated heroes, whose lives were an example for those facing problems of state and public racism, unemployment and loss of identity. One IWA leader in Coventry, Ajmer Bains, described how IWA editorials were more than sites for news but had an important function in preserving a distinct culture because they reminded Punjabis of their shared history and traditions:

> To play a good role in the transformation of the world for the life and the world the way you want to where common people can have the same in the wellbeing of the future generation to have that sort of world, one must have the knowledge of the ... Just traditions, take for example, Punjabi, if you don't know who Udham Singh was, who Bhagat Singh was, who his fellows were, why they were hanged, then you miss a very important aspect of life.[8]

By combining foreign influences with local histories, customs and traditions from Punjab, socialism was made relevant and accessible to the growing number of Indian migrant workers. Remembrance of revolutionaries like Bhagat Singh had the practical objective of attracting membership.

Having acknowledged this cultural imaginary, one should not discount the various IWA activists, in particular, the pioneers of the organisation in Coventry, Birmingham and Southall, who emerged as political radicals through the ranks of the Communist Party and, to a lesser extent, the Congress party. Joginder Singh, a leader of the

---

[7] See Clark, 'Recollections of Resistance', 75–77, for a brief discussion of Udham Singh's involvement with Indian political activists in Coventry from 1938 onwards.

[8] Coventry History Centre, Gill, IWA Transcripts, Interview Two — Ajmer Bains, 2008–2009, 29–30.

IWA in Coventry, had been a Communist Party worker alongside Vishnu Dutt Sharma in Punjab before he migrated.[9] Indeed, the communist and socialist groups in India were important political markers for the IWAs because the patronage, ideological instruction and finances available allowed the organisation to survive as a social and political force. The IWAs also shared some genealogical ties with the Ghadar Party. Not only did the IWAs follow the Ghadar tradition of radical alliances and propaganda strategies, there were direct familial links between Ghadar rebels and the founding fathers of the IWA in Coventry. It is claimed that Charan Singh Chima, a founding member of the IWA, was previously an affiliate of the Ghadar Party. In addition, a fellow founding member of the IWA, Karam Singh Cheema's father, Kanega Singh, had been one of the original Ghadar militants based in North America.[10] Thus, patrimonial politics was one important factor in the formation of the IWAs.

## Trade Union Struggle

For the IWAs, the first battleground was the workplace where they actively encouraged the integration of Punjabi migrants into working-class life as part of the general mission of building a class-based movement.[11] Ajmer Bains and Joginder Singh, two leaders of the Coventry IWA, argued that they were strictly focused on integrating migrants through class formation. The defining aspect of the IWA's class politics was the struggle for unionisation. Indian workers led by IWA members were determined to secure better pay and work arrangements. IWA activists had a tangible impact in three areas of industrial relations: the increasing levels of Indian membership of unions, the break-up of the broker system and the campaign against the corrupt practices of local sweat shops. The IWAs in Coventry and elsewhere fought for membership of the Amalgamated Union of Foundry Workers (AUFW) and the Transport and General Workers Union (TGWU). In fact, the general growth in union membership

---

[9] Coventry History Centre, Gill, IWA Transcripts, Interview Two — Joginder Singh, 2008–2009, 17.

[10] Coventry History Centre, Gill, IWA Transcripts, Interview One — Sohan Singh Cheema, 2008–2009, 3.

[11] Singh and Tatla, *Sikhs in Britain*, 213.

in the Midlands during this time can be explained by the increasing commitment of Indians to the labour movement. Disputes at Sterling Metals, Dunlop, Dunn's, and Courthaulds in Coventry during the 1960s were all focused on removing barriers that oppressed black workers, such as segregated washrooms, a block on promotion to better jobs and low wages.[12] A testament to the class politics of the IWAs was their opposition to the creation of black sections in unions, believing that working-class oppression could not be defeated if workers were divided along 'racial' lines.

IWA activists in Coventry, who worked inside and outside of the factory floor, lectured Indian workers on the need for unionisation and self-help. A leading figure in Coventry, Ajmer Bains, argued that 'we published leaflets. There used to be a public house in the Coventry area, Vauxhall Pub it was called or something like that. We went there; people came from the national branches, all over the country, even some white people, to encourage greater participation in the labour movement.[13] Leadership took shape on and beyond the factory floor. Open meetings of the IWA would take place to discuss the potential for strikes and name factories notorious for exploitation of their workers. The IWA offered support to any local strikes, especially where there was a significant group of Indian workers. A prime target of protest was the colour bar practised in certain factories. Joginder commented that 'there were many factories [in Coventry] that would not employ black workers. We would struggle against this discrimination, like on Harnall Street, there was GEC, and they would not employ Indian workers. We struggled hard against them and at first they started to employ the educated workers and later

---

[12] See Coventry History Centre, Indian Workers' Association arhive, PA/2600, for a wide range of documents and materials detailing the organisation's activities from 1938 to 2005. The collection is made up entirely of Manjinder Singh Virk's personal records. He was a senior member of the Coventry IWA. This accompanied a slightly more modest collection housed at the Modern Records Centre, University of Warwick. The archive consists of correspondence, flyers, membership records, pamphlets, photos, reports, statements, and copies of the IWA GB's publications, *Mazdoor*, *Lok Sabha* and *Lalkar*.

[13] Coventry History Centre, Gill, IWA Transcripts, Interview Three — Ajmer Bains, 2008–2009, 3.

the uneducated workers'.[14] The Coventry IWA was successful in publicising the colour bar in employment through the media and by lobbying the local government. IWA activists provided Indians the chance to go beyond kin and village ties and restrictions and instead organise based on working allegiances. They provided a platform for airing grievances and mediating on particular employment disputes but also, crucially, ran lessons on how to be conscious workers.

Trade Union efforts to maintain control during the period of labour and technical change ensured there were many incidents of unions undermining strike attempts by Indian workers. They also actively encouraged white workers to undermine and disrupt strikes centring on the improvement of working conditions for foreign labour. Ajmer spoke of an attempted strike at Mother's Pride bakery in Coventry in 1972 where 85 South Asians, mainly Indians, were ignored by their white counterparts and had to rely on the help of students from Warwick University to create a picket line.[15] The IWA stepped in to lead the strike. As a result of this 'betrayal' of class interests, the IWA provided the basis for struggle and assumed the position of a proxy Trade Union wherever existing unions refused to help. Although not a union itself, for many Indians the IWA performed the role of one. Some of the disputes the IWA supported in the West Midlands included the Coneygre Strike in Tipton in 1967, a strike at the Midland Motor Cylinder factory in Smethwick in 1968 and an industrial action at Dunn's in Nuneaton that carried through from 1972 to 1973. All of the disputes centred on the common issues of segregated toilet and washing facilities, redundancies and low wages. There were also many incidents where the IWA was required to organise legal help and assist workers with other social and welfare services in the event of injury. By intervening in strikes, sometimes at the behest of Indian workers, the IWA encouraged people to become more militant and determined in industrial disputes and valorised the importance of collective bargaining and unionisation. When one wanted to start a union or organise a strike, the Coventry IWA was

---

[14] Coventry History Centre, Gill, IWA Transcripts, Interview Three — Joginder Singh, 2008–2009, 5.

[15] Coventry History Centre, Gill, IWA Transcripts, Interview Two — Ajmer Bains, 2008–2009, 24.

the first port of call. Essentially, they demonstrated the power of Indian workers to resist exploitation and, crucially, be self-reliant. A major factor in finally winning over Indian workers to the need for union membership and collective bargaining was the successful battle waged against the broker system employed by factory foremen. Because of the unskilled jobs and group nature of the work, an English-speaking intermediary was required within the organisation to manage and control the workers. Commonly, these middlemen were former army officers or pedlars who had arrived before the war, together with some ex-seamen.[16] Most middlemen were able to improve their position through better wages and conditions that ensured they remained loyal to their foremen. Brokers retained their own positions through a distribution of patronage in the form of jobs, higher piecework rates and overtime work.[17] The broker system separated Indian workers from the rest of the working class, and this was considered divisive by the IWA. The system had always allowed the existence of racketeering due to the intermediaries' task of finding further recruits. It 'was estimated that of the 17,300 Indians entering Britain between 1955 and 1957 over 70 per cent had invalid documents'.[18] The IWA tackled this problem by lobbying for the issue of passports by the Indian government. When this was granted in 1959, the ability to blackmail workers was massively reduced. However, immigration controls provided new impetus to intermediaries as increasing numbers of immigrants turned to illegal avenues. There were also other areas of corruption and bribery. Identifying the areas where bribes took place was difficult because contacts between 'middlemen' and workers also spread to private spaces such as the public house or during family functions.

There were waves of strikes, assisted by the IWA, attacking the broker system from 1965 onwards. In fact, the first industrial action by Indian workers in the Midlands arose from a case of bribery at Dartmouth Auto Castings Ltd in Smethwick in 1959. A newly elected Indian shop steward for the Amalgamated Union of Engineering

---

[16] Aurora, *The New Frontiersmen*, 81.

[17] Brooks and Singh, 'Pivots and Presents', 97. See Brooks and Singh's essay for an in-depth analysis of how the 'pivotal' system of intermediaries worked to the advantage of employers and the brokers themselves.

[18] Duffield, *Black Radicalism and the Politics of De-Industrialisation*, 42.

Workers was dismissed after protesting that some Indians were offering the foreman money for overtime and other favours.[19] Although levels of unionisation lessened the need for intermediaries, it was the increasing numbers of Indian shop stewards that dealt a lasting blow to the broker system.

The emergence of Indian shop stewards had a very big impact on the mechanics of labour relations in the West Midlands. These shop stewards challenged the foreman on a range of significant issues such as recruitment, promotion, work allocation and the fixing of piece rates. Indian shop stewards of any union had been uncommon in the West Midlands before the mid-1960s. Avtar Johal became the most prominent Indian shop steward in the region and perhaps in the country. He was, of course, a national leader of the IWA and head of the Birmingham branch. However, many other IWA leaders and members also became shop stewards in their respective factories.[20]

In Coventry, Dilbag Gill was fired from various jobs for trying to organise Indian workers into a union. He served as a shop steward at Dunn's and GEC during his long tenure of foundry work. The Indian shop steward played a pivotal role in the troubled relationship between the unions and migrant workers.[21] His was a dual role of workmate and leader. The increasing influence of Indian shop stewards supplanted the previous reliance on middlemen for guidance and instruction. This growing autonomy spread fear amongst the various unions as Indian militancy ignited within factories. Several issues mobilised Indian shop stewards; two of them were the idea of work sharing in the event of redundancies and the implementation of seniority in relation to promotions. In Coventry, there was a strike at Coventry Art Castings centred on the issue of work sharing to save redundancies.[22] Although it is an overstatement to suggest that the IWA was behind every industrial action involving Indians in Coventry during the period, they played a fundamental part in distributing

---

[19] See Singh and Tatla, *Sikhs in Britain*, 145–64.

[20] Ramdin, *Black Working Class in Britain*, 403.

[21] Coventry History Centre, Indian Workers' Association archive, PA2600/1/47/1, *Lok Shakti* article that gives advice on who to vote for in Union elections calling for people to support the broad Left candidates, 13 August 1980.

[22] See Wilson, 'Asian Women and Industrial Restructuring'.

leaflets and displaying posters, spreading awareness, donating to strike funds, offering guidance and joining picket lines. In addition, they were key players in paving the way for Indian employment in the transport sector. In Coventry, Rajmal Singh lobbied for the local council and the local Labour Party secretary regarding the discriminatory practices of the city's transport services throughout 1962.[23] By applying pressure and mobilising through official channels, along with recourse to strikes and marches, they forced local authorities and unions to change the policy and accept Indians into the industry.

A major issue where the IWA in Coventry took a leading role on the national stage was the issue of sweat shops. The Coventry IWA aggressively protested against the exploitation, usually suffered by Indian women, in the plethora of local sweat shops that emerged during the late 1970s and the 1980s. Sasha Josephides estimated that in Coventry alone, 'between 1974 and 1987 the number of clothing firms rose from 22 to 66 ... [and that] these firms ... [were] nearly all owned by Asians with a predominantly Asian workforce'.[24] Ajmer Bains and Joginder Singh claimed that in Coventry in 1977 'there were between forty-five to fifty sweat shops'.[25] Usually, owing to the minimal profit margins of running a small clothing firm, employers would adopt a range of exploitative policies to maximise their profits. This entailed poor working conditions, sub-standard facilities and derisory wages. In 1977, the IWA in Coventry targeted Forward Trading Company and Leofric Shirt Company for strikes and industrial action. Ajmer Bains, who was one of the leaders in the strike against the Forward Trading Company, managed to convince the female workers to join a union. The owner of the factory, Surinder Singh, had to acquiesce to the demands for the TGWU to act as the negotiating body for striking workers. In fact, the Coventry IWA confronted a member of their own branch for exploiting women

---

[23] See Coventry, University of Warwick, Modern Records Centre, Papers relating to Indian Workers' Association, MSS.11/3/37/44, MSS.11/3/37/45, MSS.11/3/15/378, MSS.11/3/18/20, Letters: Rajmal Singh to R. J. Hughes, regarding the policies of the local transport services, 1962.

[24] Josephides, *History of the Indian Workers' Association*, 46.

[25] Coventry History Centre, Gill, IWA Transcripts, Interview Two — Ajmer Bains, 2008–2009, 19.

workers in a factory he owned.[26] Eventually the IWA stepped aside in the dispute to allow the union to represent the workers. What this illustrates was the IWAs willingness to confront exploitation wherever it came, even when it surfaced among its own ranks. Like their role in the large factories, the Coventry IWA helped open up these small businesses to unionisation. Overall, the IWA brought about empowerment to individuals through collective action. Concessions won on the factory floor and the symbolic victory of unionisation encouraged the IWAs to extend their activities to wider issues of social justice. Leaders in Coventry did not countenance the idea that mixing class and cultural claims was contradictory. Rather, they regarded their culture and ethnicity as intertwined with their class position. Simply, their political ideology allowed for a wider conception of class, one that encompassed cultural difference and rights as an ethnic minority. Essentially, they claimed recognition as equal workers and citizens. This was a clear difference from the views in Southall where they chose to focus on Indian politics and narrow ethnic issues.

## Antiracism Movement

The IWA in Coventry alongside its sister branches fought a wide battle for civil rights in the society. From the beginning, the state perceived coloured migration as problematic in terms of integration due to the racial differences between blacks and Asians and western people.[27] Asians were doubly victimised because of their alien culture, language and religious customs. In line with their espousal of working-class solidarity, partnerships with other likeminded organisations, both black and white, were vital to the IWA, thereby making an impact on government policy and changing public attitudes. Ambalavaner Sivanandan surmised that by 1968, blacks and Asians united to fight as a class and as a people, 'the experience of a common racism and a common fight ... united them at the barricades. The mosaic of unities ... resolved itself, before the onslaught of the

---

[26] Coventry History Centre, Gill, IWA Transcripts, Interview Two — Joginder Singh, 2008–2009, 10–11.

[27] See Lawrence, 'Just Plain Common Sense', 45–92.

state, into a black unity and a black struggle'.[28] Strength in numbers was an obvious practical objective for lobbying purposes; however, it also carried an important symbolic message: the struggle against racism was a struggle for the class.[29] Coventry's IWA, alongside its sister branches, aligned with various Left-wing organisations such as the Communist Party of Great Britain (CPGB), Co-ordinating Campaign against Racial Discrimination (CCARD), Anti-Nazi League, Anti-Apartheid Alliance, Black People's Alliance, CND and, at a local level, Coventry Against Racism (CAR).

The question of immigration and the claim to lawful citizenship was an issue that helped unite these various groups and build further alliances. Despite fissures and factions within the IWA GB, most branches coordinated through a sustained and committed campaign against immigration laws. They lobbied the Indian government (through their sister parties in India) to apply pressure on the British government to rethink and ultimately revoke their planned policies for restrictions.[30] The IWA also forwarded policy statements and research carried out by their activists to specific MPs so they could form representation in the parliament.[31] A noteworthy example was the publication of the pamphlet *The Victims Speak* in 1965, a joint venture among the IWAs in Birmingham, Coventry and Wolverhampton, which outlined the potential dangers of control legislation in the wider public sphere. Throughout this period, the IWAs organised several rallies and marches to register their protest to changes in immigration and nationality laws. One particular example was the large-scale march to Downing Street in July 1973,

---

[28] Sivanandan, 'From Resistance to Rebellion', 128.

[29] Ibid., 138.

[30] See Coventry History Centre, Indian Workers' Association archive, PA2600/3/10/2, Letter from Harkishan Singh Surjeet to Shri Misra (Minister for External Affairs, India), 18 November 1979, concerning the announcement of the British government's new immigration rules and discrimination in the United Kingdom. He urges the Indian government to lodge a protest with the British government.

[31] See Birmingham, Birmingham Central Library, Birmingham Archives and Heritage, Indian Workers' Association archive, MS2141/A/3, Policy and administrative papers, 1959–1986 and MS2141/A/4/5, Letters from members of parliament relating to the White Paper on immigration, 1965.

which demonstrated against the 1971 Immigration Act.[32] The Coventry IWA provided over 10 coaches to transport hundreds of people from the city's Pool Meadow bus station to London. These demonstrations illustrate the immense mobilising potential of the IWAs. Crucially, the involvement of the IWAs provided a voice to public anger, which challenged the moral legitimacy and the legality of immigration controls.

A class analysis was provided to change the debate on immigration and question the real motives for changing laws of entry. Moreover, the IWAs' communication practices were vital to the strength of their resistance. Various publications from *Mazdoor* to *Lalkar* notified people of political campaigns and cultural activities and were in wide circulation amongst South Asian groups during the 1960s and the 1970s. All were written from a Marxist-Leninist perspective and were vital in instilling socialist sentiments in the Indian community. Social communication through books, correspondence, handbills, newspapers and other media not only challenged prevailing stereotypes but also sustained the cross-ethnic and political alliance.[33] The Coventry IWA, alongside its sister branches, contributed to an emerging 'counter-public' that was increasingly in operation to challenge the advance of racialist legislation and confront racist politicians. Although the IWAs' campaigns throughout the 1960s and the 1970s against the series of immigration laws failed in the aim of having them overturned or repealed, they were crucial contributors in pressurising for applying for a policy of anti discrimination.[34]

---

[32] Coventry, University of Warwick, Modern Records Centre, Papers relating to Indian Workers' Association, MSS.21/972, Programme: 'Protest at the 1971 Immigration Act — March to Downing Street', 22 July 1973.

[33] See Durrani, *Never Be Silent*, for a study of how publishing and communication networks shaped the anti-imperial and anticolonial struggle in Kenya. This also explores the links between the Mau Mau rebellion and Left groups around the world such as the Movement for Colonial Freedom in the United Kingdom and Liberation Support Movement in Canada.

[34] The government responded by starting a process of improving 'race relations' at the time of the 1962 Commonwealth Immigrants Act. They set up multi-racial bodies such as the campaign against racial discrimination in 1964 (CARD) and the Commission for Racial Equality (CRE) in 1976 as part of the Race Relations Act provisions. See 'Race Relations Policies and the Political Process', in Solomos, *Race and Racism in Britain*, 76–94. The

In terms of direct action, the campaign against the 'colour bar' was a marked success in terms of opening up access to previously restricted social areas and public places. IWA members in Coventry came together with local people, often students from Coventry and Warwick Universities, to challenge the 'colour bar' in public houses and other social centres.[35] Bold steps to confront and overcome explicit forms of discrimination were vitally important in creating a multicultural space but also because long-term alliances were formed with liberal and radical white people.[36] Coventry against Racism (CAR) was formed by the local IWA branch alongside the local Communist Party, some Trade Union associations and other progressive groups. Through the mobilisation of these alliances, colour bars were overturned in places like the General Wolfe pub and the Royal Court Hotel. By opening up social spaces to Indians and other immigrant groups, the IWA helped redefine the spatial and legal boundaries of the public sphere.

The Coventry IWA was also part of a 'black power' movement that increasingly became more militant and proactive in terms of self-defence in the face of racist attacks. For the IWA, 'black workers, because of their particular history and class position, are the group destined to lead the fight against racism' and by consequence, lead the class struggle.[37] As Sivanandan argued, IWAs in the West Midlands were at the very centre of the 'black power' movement, which gained a great deal of prominence and influence during the 1960s and the 1970s. Indeed, the 'black power' alliance had a major impact in politicising and radicalising ethnic minorities behind an antiracist and socialist message. Most leaders of the IWA in Coventry viewed racism and class oppression as a universal phenomenon rooted in Western imperialism; hence, anti-imperialist and minority struggles around the world also attracted their attention and support. The

---

CRE was created by joining the Race Relations Board (which had been set up in 1965) and the Community Relations Commission and its three main duties were to eliminate discrimination, promote equality and keep under review the workings of the Race Relations Act.

[35] Coventry History Centre, Gill, IWA Transcripts, Interview Three — Ajmer Bains, 2008–2009, 9.

[36] John, *Indian Workers' Associations in Britain*, 175.

[37] Josephides, *History of the Indian Workers' Association*, 29–30.

Coventry IWA campaigned against the Vietnam War, apartheid rule in South Africa and forged links with Left-wing organisations around the world. The main lesson drawn from the American experience of 'black power' and nationalist struggles from around the world was that it was acceptable and in fact necessary to fight racist forces aggressively and uncompromisingly. Certainly, this was a powerful view espoused by the charismatic and influential IWA Birmingham leader, Jagmohan Joshi. Between 1976 and 1981, it was estimated that 31 black people had been murdered by racists throughout the country, such as Gurdip Singh Chaggar, Akhtar Ali Baig, Sewa Singh and in Coventry, Satnam Singh Gill.[38] As with the 'colour bar', the IWAs organised numerous protests and marches against these racist attacks.Indian migrants stood up and gave a clear message, that they would not be intimidated in the face of racial violence; the community opted for a path of self-reliance in meeting the threat of fascist groups such as the National Front.[39] In this way, the Coventry IWA became a major part of the local system of self-defence that was developed by black and South Asian communities against racial violence.

Collective action during the 1960s and the 1970s also encompassed a fight against the discrimination in welfare provision and the racism of politicians. IWA activists fought against Powell sympathisers in the local and general elections by utilising the increasing power of black voters.[40] The government had no choice but to recognise

---

[38] See Chandan, *Indians in Britain*, 54–58.

[39] In '*The House That Made Me*', a television programme for Channel Four, Sanjeev Bhaskar recounts his experiences dealing with racism and the National Front while growing up in Southall during the 1970s. He discussed the polarisation of communities and the pervading fear of violence that gripped local minority groups. See Jackson, 'Sanjeev Bhaskar'.

[40] Contemporary interest in the work of the IWA was further boosted by the depositing of Birmingham's two most influential IWA leaders, Avtar Johal and Jagmohan Joshi's personal collections at the Birmingham Central Library. This formed part of the 'Connecting Histories' initiative, of which the University of Warwick was a leading sponsor, and aimed to stimulate research into the history of ethnic minorities in the post-war period. These records form part of a massive collection and are a valuable resource to study the organisation, administration and functions of IWA. See MS2141/A for Joshi's papers and MS2142/A for Johal's records. These collections contain correspondence, flyers, membership records, pamphlets, photos,

Indians and other coloured migrants as part of a new public arena. Their commitment to a civil rights and antiracist agenda contributed to the socio-political space of 'multiculturalism'. The IWA's ability to lobby successfully on particular issues also contributed to changes in the national curriculum and local housing policy. For example, the IWA lobbied banks and building societies to start lending fairly to Indian migrants. They also conducted housing surveys and used questionnaires to understand the housing needs of migrant workers better.[41] By lobbying local MPs and the housing minister, the government was made aware not only of the housing requirements of Indian workers but also of their unwillingness to accept discriminatory housing policy. Most IWA branches including Coventry agreed on a policy of multicultural education as a way out of the exclusion and low achievement suffered by Indian children. A joint project between the Coventry and Wolverhampton branches, represented by Naranjhan Singh Noor and Ajmer Bains, argued that the assimilation model would perpetuate the disadvantaged position of ethnic minority children.[42] Local Education Authorities (LEAs) were pressurised

---

reports, statements and magazines relating to the IWA in Birmingham but also branch records of IWAs around the country such as Wolverhampton, Bedford, Derby, Leicester, Southall, and Bradford. Both collections also contain records of the Shaheed Udham Singh centre (IWA community centre and office on Soho Road), which includes case work papers from 1981 to 2000 relating to immigration and deportation cases and other communal activities. Both collections also hold documents from sister organisations and partners from the anti-racist alliance such as Trade Union groups, the Anti-Nazi league, Anti-Apartheid Alliance, Black People's Alliance, Co-ordinating Campaign against Racial Discrimination and Campaign against Racial Laws and CND.

[41] Coventry History Centre, Indian Workers' Association archive, PA2600/3/2/10, Housing Research and Surveys Report: IWA — Community Development and Welfare Project, undated.

[42] Coventry History Centre, Indian Workers' Association archive, PA2600/3/1/2, Pamphlet: 'Education Needs of Asian Children in the context of Multi-Ethnic racial Education in Wolverhampton', N. S. Noor, IWA GB, 1977–1978. Noor conducted a survey of parents' views and attitudes on education policy in Wolverhampton in 1977 and the results were published and circulated to all the local branches under the banner of the IWA GB. The survey was conducted through door-to-door contact with Asian people and IWA members through branch meetings. Noor stated that 80 per cent

to set up mixed advisory boards to develop multicultural educational policies, especially ones related to lesson content, organisation and counselling needs. From the 1970s onwards, the government became increasingly aware of the need to modify the education system and a raft of proposals was introduced to address the needs of Asian and Afro-Caribbean parents, but also to change attitudes and raise awareness.[43] For example, syllabuses for Punjabi and Urdu were issued by various education boards. This represented a degree of success for the IWAs since their political lobbying and analyses of the problems in education played a part in forcing LEAs and the government to account for Indian children.

One must also recognise the important role the local and national IWA played in winning the right for Sikhs to wear turbans and carry *kirpans* in public places and areas of work. However, the issue developed into a bigger question about the recognition of separate religions and ethnic minority customs by the state through which issues of citizenship and national identity were brought into play. The turban dispute, which had sprung up in Wolverhampton and Birmingham, was a major precursor to changes in public policy and the advent of political multiculturalism.[44] At this point, Sikh organisations such as the Shiromoni Akali Dal UK and local temples joined forces with the IWAs to oppose government policies towards ethnic minorities. The IWA GB claimed they had spent around 60,000 pounds on the turban campaign following donations from all the branches.[45] The

---

categorically expressed their views that the local schools were not doing justice in the education of their children. Only 50 parents (5 per cent) were found to be satisfied with their children's achievement. An overall majority of 95 per cent wanted the language barrier between their children and the other children and teachers to be alleviated.

[43] Sivanandan, 'RAT and Degradation of Black Struggle', 21–22.

[44] The first major incident regarding the right to wear a turban at work was the case of Tarsem Singh Sandhu in August 1967. He had been sacked as a bus driver for wearing a turban; this led to a national, local and, indeed, transnational political campaign opposing the local transport authority. See Singh and Tatla, *Sikhs in Britain*, 128.

[45] Birmingham Archives and Heritage, Indian Workers' Association archive, MS2142/A/1/4/17, Celebration papers: Indian Workers' Association 50th Anniversary, 1988, 13.

most significant individual case was Mandla v. Dowell Lee because it led to a change in the law regarding the recognition of Sikhs as a separate ethnic group.[46]

Naranjan Singh Noor, a leader of Wolverhampton's IWA, was again at the forefront of the movement for ethnic rights through his 'Turban Action Committee'.[47] However, by 1983, he was criticised by the majority of the IWA GB's leadership for taking the movement too far. It was felt that IWA as a secular organisation should not promote the turban case too overtly because it infringed on its dominant class agenda. Leaders such as Avtar Johal and Prem Singh argued that the campaign should be led by religious-based organisations; Noor disagreed and believed the IWAs should take a central role. As a result, Noor was expelled from the IWA GB in November 1983 and he set up his own organisation.[48] A tension between acting as a class or ethnic organisation was at the heart of the IWAs from their inception and ruptured at moments of crisis, namely the split with Southall's IWA and later the emergence of Sikh nationalism in Punjab. Nevertheless, the Coventry IWA, like the majority of their sister branches, adopted a nuanced and contextual approach to ethnic politics. At the core of their class and ethnic agenda was the concept of equality; fair access to employment and public spaces was tied to the recognition of cultural and religious rights: not having to deny one's origins, family or community, but expecting others to respect

---

[46] A Birmingham schoolboy, Gurdev Singh Mandla, was refused entry into Park Grove School by his headmaster Dowell-Lee because he was wearing a turban. The matter ended up in the High Court following a legal challenge by the boy's father. Demonstrations were held in London and the Midlands over the decision of the Court of Appeal to support the position of Dowell Lee. On a further appeal to the House of Lords in March 1983, the decision of the courts was overturned to grant Sikhs the same position as Jews, that of a separate ethnic group under the Race Relations Act of 1976.

[47] See Coventry History Centre, Indian Workers' Association archive, PA2600/4/1/52, Leaflets and letters: Wolverhampton Turban Action Committee, N. S. Noor, 1979–1999.

[48] See Coventry History Centre, Indian Workers' Association archive, PA2600/3/2/1–24, Correspondence between N. S. Noor and Sarwan Bhart (undated) who discuss the dispute between his faction and the rest of the IWA GB, in particular, Prem Singh and Gurdev Dhami who opposed his stance. Noor accused Prem Singh and Dhami of taking an anti-Sikh position.

them, and to adapt public attitudes and arrangements. Essentially, they called for integration through class solidarity but with some considered clauses of ethnic rights that were vital for community cohesion. This position helped negotiate and renegotiate the spatial, cultural and political boundaries of multi-racial Britain.

## Community and Welfare

In terms of day-to-day activity, the IWA functioned as a social and welfare centre for the Indian community in Coventry. They performed tasks such as filling forms for those who could not speak English, informed migrants of their civil rights including welfare provision and assisted people with their passport applications. Even tasks we take for granted, like going to the hairdressers or to the doctors, often required the assistance of an IWA member. The early Indian community in Coventry grew around the service of men such as Babu Karam Singh Cheema, Charan Singh Cheema, Anant Ram, and others. The Coventry IWA worked across the Midlands during the late 1940s and the early 1950s, until branches were set up in Birmingham, Leicester and Wolverhampton. In this regard, the Coventry IWA had all the hallmarks of an ethnic association that acted on behalf of Indians as a separate and specific community within the local population.[49] Without community organisations such as the IWA, the process of acclimatisation, especially for those who did not have access to a large kin network, would have proven a lot more difficult. Alan James described the IWA as part of the self-sufficient social organisation of the Indian community.[50] Indeed, their role as translators provided the organisation a great deal of power to influence the political direction of the emerging local Indian population. Even today, the few IWA activists who remain in Coventry still offer help on various tasks for the Indian community and particularly for newly arrived immigrants. Birmingham's IWA have maintained a much bigger social welfare role. The Shaheed Udham Singh centre remains in operation and is an enduring symbol of IWA's legacy of social work.

---

[49] Josephides, *History of the Indian Workers' Association*, 52.

[50] James, *Sikh Children in Britain*, 94.

Alongside their social work, the IWA was also vital to the social lives of Indian migrants. The social and cultural events organised by the IWA consolidated a sense of community and they were an important way of bringing people together and celebrating aspects of their identity and culture. In fact, sociability was central to the function of the IWAs, especially the way meetings were conducted, which commonly took place in town halls, pubs and even at the homes of individual leaders. The public house was perhaps the most significant hub of social life for Indian migrants, particularly in the early years when they lived as single men. Not only did the liaisons in the pub forge a sense of belonging at a time of great uncertainty, but drinking alcohol amongst friends was also an important safety valve against the intense pressures of foundry work and providing for the whole family. The IWAs were part of the drinking culture that emerged amongst Indian migrants in Coventry: they would often hold their meetings in local public houses and organise pub runs. The Railway Club, Barras Club and General Wolfe were all favoured haunts for IWA members in Coventry. Visiting luminaries from India such as Harkishan Singh Surjeet or dignitaries from these shores regularly adorned IWA gatherings and entertainment came in the form of films, dance and music.

In fact, cinema played a crucial part in sustaining local Indian culture and was the definitive social experience for many Indian migrants during the 1960s and the 1970s. The Coventry IWA was central to the Indian scene due to its relationship with the Ritz cinema. Bollywood films were usually imported from India or rented from the Indian High Commission. The space around the Ritz cinema on Longford Road 'would have been teeming. It was a visual spectacle; the women sported beehive haircuts, polka-dot saris, and platform shoes and the men bell-bottom trousers, wide collars and bomber jackets'.[51] Films were also shown at the Savoy on Radford Road, the Coventry Theatre, later renamed the Hippodrome, The Palladium

---

[51] Two projects in the last decade have done much to bring the Indian cinema scene to public consciousness and to the historical record. First, Puwar and Powar, 'Khabi Ritz, Khabie Palladium', documented the Asian cinema culture in Coventry between 1940 and 1980. This was followed by an oral history study by Virdee, *Coming to Coventry*, which focused on the social life of local migrants.

in Hillfields and the Tree Tops cinema on Foleshill Road. Since Coventry was the first to offer these film showings, it briefly became the home of Asian cinema in Britain with migrants from other towns and cities such as Leamington, Wolverhampton and Leicester travelling to the city for a night of entertainment. The popularity of cinema lay in the fusion of art, food, fashion, entertainment, politics and social networking. It really was a celebration of everything Indian.

The IWA wanted to maintain interest in Indian matters, which meant a commitment to their indigenous languages, social and cultural customs. Hence, many activists wrote poems and novels, and performed songs and plays that reflected their views, feelings and desires. Within the Coventry IWA, Ajmer Bains was one of the more esteemed poets and regularly wrote collections of poems on a typewriter. These collections were often distributed to colleagues and members personally, or added to the list of IWA publications. He also regularly contributed to the diasporic Punjabi press and established a partnership with a small publisher in Jullundhar, Punjab, to publish his works.[52] Like many within the IWA and the Punjabi poetry tradition, Ajmer commonly wrote in the *Ghazal* style and within the *qisse* tradition. *Ghazal* was a poetic form that consisted of rhyming couplets, with each line sharing the same metre. Usually, this medium would express feelings of love, loss, pain and separation.[53] Crucially, IWA activists believed that art was an important weapon in the ideological struggle between the classes but also as a way of bringing people together. Art could reveal the reality behind racism and therefore promote more harmonious relations between different racial groups. What the artistic and social activities of the Coventry

---

[52] See Coventry History Centre, Gill, IWA Transcripts, Interview Three — Ajmer Bains, 2008–2009, 16–17.

[53] *Ghazals* originated in Persia and became popular in Punjab through Sufi mystics and spread to people from all backgrounds, including Sikhs and Hindus. This poetic medium has also been used in the West, especially by German poets in the 19th century. Ghazals were part of the larger tradition of Punjabi *qisse*, which became a popular form of oral story telling as it focused on the themes of love, valour, morality, gender relationships and connection musically. Although these traditions of story telling derived from a Persian origin, they were situated in the local landscape and rooted in Punjabi social relations when used by poets and writers.

IWA highlighted was that the folk tradition was not alien to South Asian immigrants but was actually something rooted in Punjabi culture. Storytelling through speeches, dance and plays along with music forms a large part of Punjabi cultural life. Hence, articulating their politics through these media is entirely natural and effective. Importantly, most IWAs used cultural performance and artistic expression as an organising and mobilising tool. The values of everyday life and experience located and understood in vernacular traditions and speech but most notably through folk song were venerated by post-war Marxist historians as central to developing a socialist movement.[54] Consequently, the engagement of IWA activists in artistic expression placed their organisation within the wider 'New Left' cultural movement of the post-war period. This legacy of artistic endeavour was highly influential on second- and third-generation political and cultural activity most potently carried by Asian Youth Movements (AYMs). In the 1980s and the 1990s, Asian musicians drew inspiration from the organisational traditions of the IWA, where politics and art were mixed in a calculated political-cultural programme.[55] Virinder Kalra, John Hutnyk and Sanjay Sharma argued that this period of combining art and politics influenced Asian musicians long after both AYMs and IWAs had declined, citing the example of Asian Dub Foundation and Fun^Da^Mental. They also point out that the early British Bhangra scene was running parallel to the IWA's mobilisation against state and popular racism.[56] Bhangra

---

[54] See Long, *Only in the Common People*. He provides a series of case studies including CEMA — the forerunner of the Arts Council, the broadcasting and the radio work of Charles Parker and Arnold Wesker's Centre 42 project to investigate how these projects and practices were formulated to describe, confirm, rejuvenate or generate 'authentic' working-class culture as part of the re-imagining of 'Britishness' in the post-war context. The likes of Raymond Williams and Richard Hoggart (amongst other cultural historians) had also done much to demystify art and reclaim the aesthetic for the working class but had neglected the role of immigrants in the development of a distinct proletarian culture. As keen proponents of the folk song, novels and theatre, the IWAs were part of the wider post-war working-class culture in Britain.

[55] See Kalra, Hutnyk, and Sharma, 'Re-Sounding (Anti) Racism, or Concordant Politics?', 127–55.

[56] Ibid., 145.

represented a dual function of identity for Asian youth. First, AYMs used bhangra to display pride at their distinct ethnic identity, but it also carried connotations of a secular struggle due to the songs regularly invoking nationalist heroes like Udham Singh and Bhagat Singh. Bhangra, like sport, showcased Indian youth as capable of embracing multiple identities. However, the AYMs also signalled a socio-political agency that marked some sense of generational change because they favoured a more independent militant stand, whereas the IWAs stressed the need for cross-party alliances with groups like the ANL.[57] Groups like the 'Bradford Twelve' took an active and belligerent stand against the National Front and disrupted many of their activities in the area. Nevertheless, IWA messages of active resistance remained a powerful message to disaffected Indian youth during the late 1970s and the 1980s.

Despite the continuous battles against racism and discrimination, the IWAs recognised the value of fostering positive community relations with the host society. When Indian immigrants first arrived, friendship and social networks typically followed regional and ethnic lines. It can be argued that the strong presence of the IWA in Coventry was one factor that helped bring communities together. The local populations were invited to partake in cultural events and festivals alongside the Indian community to cultivate greater understanding between ethnic groups. Through their vibrant social and cultural activities, IWA activists helped ordinary people and local officials understand the values and customs of the Indian community in Coventry. Leaders of the IWA also encouraged participation in proletarian British cultural pursuits such as football and hockey despite the experience of racism. This was a powerful mechanism in bringing white Coventrians and Indian migrants together. By stressing mutual social exchange and encouraging multifarious modes of cultural production and expression, the IWA promoted community cohesion and contributed to the possibility of cultural navigation. Moreover, multiculturalism became a daily fact of life in the city. This reworking of the public arena had profound effects on the socio-cultural landscape of British cities and impacted the internal dynamic of Indian communities.

---

[57] Ibid., 136–37.

Two important areas of potential identity change were the positions of gender and caste. Ostensibly, the IWAs were a male-dominated association but they were concerned with gender issues, particularly in the workplace. The IWA in Coventry assisted strikes led by Indian women against mainstream employers and Indian-owned textile factories that exploited women as cheap labour. Although I do not make the claim that the Coventry IWA completely empowered local women to overcome patriarchal attitudes, they certainly helped women fight for equal rights and fostered the possibility of renegotiating gendered roles outside of the factory floor. However, the IWAs' record on dealing with issues of gender outside the area of work was largely a failure and it was left to independent women's organisations like the Southall Black Sisters and the Sahil Project to represent South Asian women on political and, mainly, private matters such as domestic violence.[58] Likewise, the IWAs' efforts on tackling caste discrimination were a mixed bag. The Coventry IWA was eager to include all members of the Indian community and took explicit steps to champion a secular character; many members did indeed come from other castes. From a series of oral history interviews I conducted as part of doctorial research into the local organisation, I was introduced to leaders from the Ramgharia and Ravidasi castes. In addition, the foremost national figure of the IWA, Jagmohan Joshi, was a Hindu Brahman from Birmingham. This goes against the established Jat-centric explanations of IWA activity. They

---

[58] Independent women's organisations like the Southall Black Sisters (SBS) and the Sahil Project represented South Asian women in Britain on sensitive matters such as domestic violence. Both demonstrated alternate ways of dealing with the issue, the former taking a much more militant stand than the latter. These organisations believed it was up to women themselves to defeat patriarchy and that the reliance of male organisations would be a contradiction and ultimately self-defeating. South Asian women's projects have become more visible in challenging racist and sexist stereotypes, structures and expectations, found both inside and out of South Asian communities. The Southall Black Sisters was founded in Southall in November 1979 during the high point in racial tension in Britain and they followed the antiracist stand adopted by the IWAs and similarly championed a discourse of 'black unity'. However, they attacked the patriarchal attitudes of the IWA, whom they accused of suppressing their militancy within the South Asian community. Refer to Southall Black Sisters, *Against the Grain*.

created an environment for friendship and collaboration amongst various castes that was not always possible in India. However, ethnic concerns and communalist tension transferred from the sub-continent derailed the efforts for meaningful and long-lasting transformation. Caste prejudices remained and were, in fact, rearticulated in the diaspora setting, especially amongst second- and third-generation South Asians. A major split in the association occurred during the late 1970s and the 1980s at the height of Sikh nationalism. There was also a growing trend for caste-specific Gurudwaras and community centres in Coventry; the perception and the reality is that caste still exists as a 'class within a class' in the Indian diaspora.

## Decline of the IWAs

The decreasing role and influence of the IWA in Coventry and elsewhere coincided with the gradual decimation of the motor and other manufacturing industries in Britain. Consequently, first- and second-generation Indians moved away from manufacturing jobs in favour of self-employment and more professional occupations as early as in the 1970s. Second- and third-generation Indians continued to diversify their occupations and aspirations, which naturally led to a diversification of identities; class formation no longer seemed relevant or desirable to a group that developed new consumption patterns and relations to the British society. Many have blamed the demise of organisations like the IWA on the co-option of the state. First, numerous leaders and members of the IWA turned to affiliation and representation from the mainstream political parties. In Coventry, several members of the IWA including Raj K. Malhotra stood for Labour in council elections. Second, the Commission for Racial Equality (CRE) and other state bodies handed massive sums of money from its 'Urban Aid' programme to key black self-help groups, which had the impact of dulling radicalism. In the process, the fight against racism was transformed into a fight for culture and a fight for the individual.[59] The Sikh community, for example, switched from class to identity politics, a change that was hastened by the rise of the Khalistan movement in Britain from 1984. The new post-colonial realities, along with the regular current of political

---

[59] Sivanandan, 'Reclaiming the Struggle', 72.

splits emanating from India, stripped organisations like the IWA of the collective agency that had powered their political and social programmes.

## Conclusion

A history of the Coventry IWA engages with a broader social history of post-war Britain because it involves the key issues of class, race and community relations. It also addresses the complicated relationship between the political and the social in modern historical scholarship, given that class is reconsidered to be a discourse that can involve all other categories of culture and identity. For the Coventry IWA, class politics was a collaborative category that reacted with other social 'registers' such as race and religion. Thus, the IWA's politics and sociology formed a dialectical relationship that first manifested on the factory floor but then spread to other social spaces and the wider public sphere. Consequently, their political and social action formed part of multiple struggles, which were at times coalescent and at others appeared contradictory. Nevertheless, they were crucial to the formation of community and individual identities during the early years of Indian settlement. Moreover, they were determined 'actors' in protecting the rights of Indian workers and their marrying of class and ethnic politics contributed to the 'multicultural' society of Britain, especially where it can be deemed a success in the integration of Indian migrants.

## References

### Manuscript Sources

*Birmingham, Birmingham Central Library, Birmingham Archives and Heritage, Indian Workers' Association archive*

MS2141/A/3, Policy and administrative papers, 1959–1986 and MS2141/ A/4/5, Letters from members of parliament relating to the White Paper on Immigration, 1965.
MS2142/A/1/4/17, Celebration papers: Indian Workers' Association 50th Anniversary, 1988.

*Coventry, The Herbert Art Gallery, Coventry History Centre, Indian Workers' Association archive*

PA2600/9/15/6, Photograph: Executive Committee, Indian Workers' Association, Coventry, includes names of Executive Committee members, 1953.

PA2600/3/10/2, Letter from Harkishan Singh Surjeet to Shri Misra (Minister for External Affairs, India), 18 November 1979.

PA2600/4/1/52, Leaflets and letters: Wolverhampton Turban Action Committee, N. S. Noor, 1979–1999.

PA2600/3/2/1–24, Correspondence between N. S. Noor and Sarwan Bhart, undated. PA2600/3/2/10, Housing Research and Surveys Report: IWA — Community Development and Welfare Project, undated.

PA2600/3/1/2, Pamphlet: 'Education Needs of Asian Children in the context of Multi-Ethnic racial Education in Wolverhampton', N. S. Noor, IWA GB, 1977–1978. PA2600/1/47/1, *Lok Shakti*, August 1980.

Talvinder Gill, IWA Transcripts, Interview Two — Ajmer Bains, 2008–2009.

Talvinder Gill, IWA Transcripts, Interview Three — Ajmer Bains, 2008–2009.

Talvinder Gill, IWA Transcripts, Interview Two — Joginder Singh 2008–2009.

Talvinder Gill, IWA Transcripts, Interview Three — Joginder Singh, 2008–2009.

Talvinder Gill, IWA Transcripts, Interview One — Sohan Singh Cheema, 2008–2009.

*Coventry, University of Warwick, Modern Records Centre, Papers relating to Indian Workers' Association*

MSS.11/3/37/44, MSS.11/3/37/45, MSS.11/3/15/378, MSS.11/3/18/20, Letters: Rajmal Singh to R. J. Hughes, 1962.

MSS.21/972, Programme: 'Protest at the 1971 Immigration Act — March to Downing Street', 22 July 1973.

## Primary Sources

Indian Workers' Association GB. Souvenir to Celebrate Shaheed-E-Azam Bhagat Singh's Birth Centenary, Leicester, 2007.

## Secondary Sources

Aurora, G. S., *The New Frontiersmen: A Sociological Study of Indian Immigrants in the United Kingdom*, Bombay: Popular Prakashan, 1967.

Brooks, Dennis and Karamjit Singh, 'Pivots and Presents — Asian Brokers in British Foundries', in *Ethnicity at Work*, S. Wallman (ed.), 93–114, London: Macmillan, 1979.

Chandan, Amerjit, *Indians in Britain*, London: Oxford University Press, 1986.

Clark, David, 'Recollections of Resistance: Udham Singh and the IWA', *Race & Class* 17, no. 1 (1975): 75–77.

Duffield, Mark, 'Rationalisation and the Politics of Segregation: Indian Workers in Britain's Foundry Industry, 1945–1962', in *Race and Labour in Twentieth-Century Britain*, K. Lunn (ed.), 142–72, London: F. Cass, 1985.

——, *Black Radicalism and the Politics of De-Industrialisation: The Hidden History of Indian Foundry Workers*, Avebury: Aldershot, 1988.

Durrani, Shiraz, *Never Be Silent: Publishing & Imperialism in Kenya, 1884–1963*, London: Vita Books, 2006.

Eley, Geoff and Keith Nield, *The Future of Class in History: What's Left of the Social?* Ann Arbor: University of Michigan Press, 2007.

Engineer, Asghar Ali, 'The Role of Sikhs in India's Freedom Struggle: Some Points for Consideration', in *They Too Fought for India's Freedom: The Role of Minorities*, Asghar Ali Engineer (ed.), 158–79, Haryana: Hope India Publications, 2006.

James, Alan, *Sikh Children in Britain*, London: Oxford University Press, 1974.

John, DeWitt, *Indian Workers' Associations in Britain*, London: Oxford University Press, 1969.

Josephides, Sasha, *Towards a History of the Indian Workers' Association*, Coventry: University of Warwick, 1991.

Kalra, Virinder S., John Hutnyk and Sanjay Sharma, 'Re-Sounding (Anti) Racism, or Concordant Politics? Revolutionary Antecedents', in *Dis-Orienting Rhythms: The Politics of the New Asian Dance Music*, Sanjay Sharma, John Hutnyk, and Ashwani Sharma (eds), 127–55, London: Zed Books, 1996.

Lawrence, Errol, 'Just Plain Common Sense: The "Roots" of Racism', in *The Empire Strikes Back Race and Racism in 70s Britain*, Centre for Contemporary Cultural Studies (Birmingham) (ed.), 45–92, London: Routledge, 1994.

Long, Paul, *Only in the Common People. The Aesthetics of Class in Post-War Britain*, Newcastle: Cambridge Scholars Press, 2008.

Puwar, Nirmal and Kuldip Powar, 'Khabi Ritz, Khabie Palladium: South Asian Cinema in Coventry: 1940–1980', *Wasafiri* 43 (2004): 41–44.

Ramdin, Ron, *The Making of the Black Working Class in Britain*, Aldershot: Gower, 1987.

Sharma, Shalini, *Radical Politics in Colonial Punjab: Governance and Sedition*, Abingdon: Routledge, 2010.

Singh, Gurharpal, *Communism in Punjab: A Study of the Movement Up to 1967*, Delhi: Ajanta Publications, 1994.

Singh, Gurharpal and Darshan Singh Tatla, *Sikhs in Britain: The Making of a Community*, London: Zed Books, 2006.

Sivanandan, Ambalavaner, 'From Resistance to Rebellion: Asian and Afro-Caribbean Struggles in Britain', *Race & Class* 23 (1981): 111–52.

———, 'RAT and the Degradation of Black Struggle', *Race & Class* 26, no. 1 (1981): 1–33.

———, 'Reclaiming the Struggle', *Race & Class* 42 (2000): 67–73.

Solomos, John, *Race and Racism in Britain*, Basingstoke: Palgrave Macmillan, 2003.

Southall Black Sisters, *Against the Grain: A Celebration of Survival and Struggle*, London: Southall Black Sisters, 1999.

Tatla, Darshan Singh, *The Sikh Diaspora: The Search for Statehood*, London: UCL Press, 1999.

Virdee, Pippa, *Coming to Coventry: Stories from the South Asian Pioneers*, Coventry: Coventry Teaching PCT & The Herbert, 2006.

Werbner, Pnina and Tariq Modood, *Debating Cultural Hybridity: Multi-Cultural Identities and the Politics of Anti-Racism*, London: Zed Books, 1997.

Wilson, Amrit, 'Asian Women and Industrial Restructuring — New Struggles, New Strategies', Paper presented at the 8th International Conference of the Gender and Science and Technology Association, Ahmedabad, January 1996.

## World Wide Web Sources

Jackson, Tina. "Sanjeev Bhaskar: Goodness, I'm home!" (*The Guardian*, 4 December 2010). http://www.guardian.co.uk/lifeandstyle/2010/dec/04/sanjeev-bhaskar-childhood-channel-4 (accessed 5 January 2011).

# ✠ 8

# A Long, Strange Trip:
# The Lives in Exile of Har Dayal

*Benjamin Zachariah*

---

For a historian of ideas, the lives of the Indian political exiles who travelled the world between the wars is of particular interest. They attest to Pierre Bourdieu's warnings about 'the biographical illusion' most eloquently: the structural teleologies of writing the life stories of persons as if there was a consistent line from start to finish, the child is the father of the man, the man the father of the hero, and the hero develops to his full (and somewhat gigantic) stature in the course of the story. Bourdieu suggests that the continuities of lives are illusions created by the biographer.[1] Har Dayal (1884–1939) might well have been Bourdieu's prototype for not writing such a history of continuity.

Despite complaints from admirers that Har Dayal has been unfairly neglected in the history of the 'national movement', legends of Har Dayal have been written several times: the most academic of biographies of Har Dayal, from 1975, repeats some of these legends, defuses some others and contributes to a few more.[2] 'It goes without saying that Har Dayal was a genius', declares another biography, by a man who knew him.[3]

Its Foreword, by the eminent historian and Hindu right-winger, Dr R.C. Majumdar, draws attention to the possibility that Har Dayal did not die a natural death but was 'assassinated' and criticises the

---

[1] Bourdieu, 'L'illusion biographique', 69–72.
[2] Brown, *Har Dayal*.
[3] Dharmavira, *Lala Har Dayal*, (iii).

book's author for not exploring this possibility in depth.[4] Another biography, by members of his family, concludes that the best biography remains the academic one of 1975, but decides to add a few tales of its own.[5] Har Dayal appears, of course, as a major player in other plots: in writings on the *Ghadar* movement, in biographies of other central figures associated with revolutionaries in exile and of course in narratives of the 'German-Indian Plot' during the Great War.[6]

The several Har Dayals that emerge from this body of writing are eminently fascinating figures, from many perspectives. The point of the present chapter, however, is not so much to reconcile these Har Dayals with one another as to use them to track the multiple engagements and encounters of an Indian student and political exile abroad and to attempt to contextualise them against the backdrop of wider contemporaneous histories of which such persons found themselves a part. For too long, the paradigm of the heroic revolutionary exile has dominated writings on such figures; this framework is extremely reductionist and can erase all but the 'national' engagements of these eminently international figures. At the same time, the apparent ease and 'cosmopolitanism' of these international encounters must not necessarily be taken for an internationalism that abandons the narrowly national, parochial or sectarian.

Har Dayal's association with the Punjab is an indication of how important networks formed in exile were to the conduct of agitational activity against British imperial rule in India. Although Har Dayal completed his MA at Lahore University, he grew up not in the Punjab but in Delhi and after leaving for Oxford in 1905 was only briefly in the Punjab again in 1908 (he was in India from January to September 1908);[7] this Punjab association is largely based on his

---

[4] Majumdar, 'Foreword', in Dharmavira, *Lala Har Dayal*, (ii).

[5] Paul and Paul, *Har Dayal*.

[6] Bose, *Indian Revolutionaries Abroad, 1905–1922*; Sareen, *Indian Revolutionary Movement Abroad (1905–1920)*; Barooah, *India and Official Germany 1886–1914*, 157–228; Barooah, *Chatto*; Ramnath, *The Haj to Utopia*; Oesterheld, *'Der Feind meines Feindes ist mein Freund'*; Krüger, 'Har Dayal in Deutschland', 141–69; Liebau, 'German Foreign Office', 96–129.

[7] Brown, *Har Dayal*, 46–61.

years in the United States, where he became something of a spokes-man for an Indian community of mainly Punjabi migrants, and one of the central figures in the *Ghadar* movement, and thereafter on his activities in Germany among Indian prisoners of war, many of whom were from the Punjab.[8] It was therefore as a Punjabi that he was classified and tracked by the colonial authorities for the rest of his life; he was the concern of the Punjab Police, and his periodic pleas after the First World War to be allowed to return to India were assessed and rejected by the Punjab Government.[9] We might defer further reflections on the nature of such political exile and the retrospective or contemporaneous (re)claiming of the exile by various 'homes' while we consider the trajectories of Har Dayal's lives. What follows does not consist in unearthing new biographical details;[10] it is more concerned with unearthing the complexities and contradictions of an anti-British movement that is usually condensed into the word 'nationalism' and to track these 'inconsistencies' in a life that can serve as a stalking horse for an analysis of wider trends.

---

[8] The only properly critical account of the *Ghadar* movement so far is Ramnath, *The Haj to Utopia*. Ramnath points out that *Ghadar* has retro-spectively been claimed as a 'nationalist' and a 'Sikh' movement, whereas it was in fact significantly wider than that.

[9] Sedition Committee, *Report*, 143–46; National Archives of India (hereafter NAI): Foreign & Political, War B (Secret), Progs. Feb. 1916, Nos. 32–34; NAI: Home (Political), Progs., Nov. 1919, Nos. 23–24; NAI: Home (Political) 192 Part B, 1924; NAI: Home (Political): KW to 9/V-32, 1932; NAI: External Affairs (External), 1939, 234-X (Secret).

[10] This chapter uses published biographical material, Har Dayal's own writings, and archival material to be found in Calcutta (West Bengal State Archives, Intelligence Bureau files) (WBSA); Bombay (Maharashtra State Archives) (MSA); Delhi (NAI); London (the India Office Records) (IOR) and Berlin (the Foreign Office files, *Politisches Archiv des Auswärtigen Amtes*, *PA-AA*; and the Horst Krüger papers at the Zentrum Moderner Orient, much of the latter being archival material meticulously gathered and photocopied—in an age where this meant taking photographs—from archives across the world, most usefully containing much material from the USA including proceedings and newspaper reports of the San Fransisco Conspiracy Case, and from Sweden). For reasons of space, this rich material remains under-utilised in the chapter.

# The Lives of Har Dayal

A brilliant student, from a Kayastha family in Delhi, Har Dayal studied at St Stephen's College, Delhi.[11] Despite his middle-class and upper-caste Hindu background, he had a strong background in Persian and Urdu, as had his father, Gauri Dayal Mathur (if we were to step briefly into a framework of 'the father-is-the-father-of-the-man')[12] — unsurprisingly, for a man born in 1884, when these were the languages of elite educational aspiration. Thence, he proceeded to change to: Punjab University in Lahore and thereafter to Oxford, studying history and Sanskrit on a government scholarship. This scholarship he resigned in strange circumstances in his third year at Oxford, in 1907, and after a brief return to India in 1908, he journeyed once again to England. As a student in England, he had already become a part of the India House circle around Shyamji Krishnavarma, the former Arya Samaj preacher, Sanskritist and later propagandist for Indian independence, a circle that included Vinayak Damodar Savarkar, the future ideologue of Hindu *völkisch* nationalism, Madanlal Dhingra, the celebrated and successful assassin of the imperial official Sir William Curzon Wylie, and Virendranath Chattopadhyay, the future communist and once-again-to-be colleague of Har Dayal's in the 'Hindu–German plot' during the First World War.[13]

Har Dayal had also become a convinced indigenist during his sojourn at Oxford, and even before he returned to India, he was seen wearing *dhoti* and *kurta* and denouncing all things foreign and all things Muslim.[14] He also proclaimed the need for celibacy in the service of the nation, an idea he expounded in a letter to the *Indian Sociologist*, Shyamji Krishnavarma's journal: although not

---

[11] The account in this section is mainly based on Brown, *Har Dayal*, and supplemented by Dharmavira, *Lala Har Dayal*, unless otherwise stated; the latter has been used sparingly, as its contents appear in many instances to be less than reliable.

[12] Dharmavira, *Lala Har Dayal*, 10.

[13] Brown, *Har Dayal*, 167–206; Barooah, *Chatto*, 7–33; Fischer-Tine, 'Indian nationalism and the "World Forces"', 325–44.

[14] Brown, *Har Dayal*, 41; Dharmavira, *Lala Har Dayal*, 51.

[15] Brown, *Har Dayal*, 31.

'indispensable', celibacy should be the highest ideal.[15] (This was a strange change of mind; only a few years before, he had kidnapped his own wife and taken her back to Oxford with him rather than have her await his return at home in India, as was the usual custom for Indian students abroad.)[16] He wrote from Oxford, to which city he returned, of the need to set up cow protection societies in every city, because 'the cow is the flag of the Hindu nation'.[17] It is probable that this is why he was an advocate of physical self-strengthening, because it takes some strength to hoist such a flag.

An article he published in the *Modern Review* of Calcutta in 1909 spoke of the 'social conquest of the Hindu race'. His causal chain was simple: 'The decay of the moral calibre of a nation paves the way for foreign domination which, in turn accelerates the process of decline by its very existence'. How did one resurrect a 'fallen race'? (The question of whether 'Hindus' were a 'race' is not raised). It was 'the leaders and thinkers of a fallen race' that had to achieve this:

> Sooner or later, the unsubdued heart and mind of the sturdy race will seek its outward sign and symbol, its embodiment in the world of fact, *viz*, a national state. The great duty of a subject people consists in guarding the Promethean spark of national pride and self-respect, lest it should be extinguished by the demoralising influences that emanate from foreign rule.[18]

This cannot be achieved by foreigners like Annie Besant, Theosophist and founder of the Central Hindu College of Benares; even if they are genuine and sincere, they become a part of the social conquest in denying the Hindus their self-strengthening.[19] Without this

---

[16] Ibid., 20–1. When he left India for the second time after his brief return in 1908–1909, he left his wife behind. He never saw her again, nor did he see his daughter, who was born after his departure. Dharmavira, *Lala Har Dayal*, 55, claims that he 'decided, with the permission of his wife, to become a friar', and the index to the same book politely indigenises this as 'Takes to Sannyasa' (352). The attribution of celibacy is of course completely inaccurate, and probably deliberately so, for no Indian who dabbles in or is claimed for nationalist heroism is ever permitted a sex life of any description by his worshippers.

[17] Brown, *Har Dayal*, 64.

[18] Har Dyal [sic], 'Social Conquest of the Hindu Race and Meaning of Equality' (quotes from p. 239).

[19] Har Dyal, 'Social Conquest', 241.

self-strengthening, the Hindu race accepts its subordinate position without the need for force of arms or law, as the Pariah in South India accepts Brahmanical authority without question, despite that authority being forced upon them neither by arms nor by legislation.[20] It follows that 'the Hindus of today' must learn the meaning of equality, internally as well as externally, or they will remain prisoners of 'the hateful antitheses of Aryan and dasyu, dvija and sudra, landlord and tenant, raja and praja' and therefore cannot achieve 'social progress and efficiency'.[21] A present-day reader might suggest that the author anticipates Frantz Fanon, Steve Biko or post-colonial theory in its argument about national self-respect as the route to equality; s/he might equally suggest that he mixes up class and caste categories.

From England Har Dayal went to Paris, where he edited a short-lived journal called *Bande Mataram* (named after the one started by Bipin Chandra Pal in 1905 and later edited by Aurobindo Ghosh), and relied on the networks of Madame Bhikhaji Cama, fellow Indian exile and political agitator. Thence he went to Algiers and thereafter to Martinique, where his old acquaintance from his Lahore, University days, the Arya Samaji Bhai Parmanand, found him considering the founding of a religion on a Buddhist model, while he subsisted mainly on boiled grain and potatoes, slept on the floor and spent long hours in meditation. By the time he appeared in the United States in 1911, however, he seems to have abandoned these ideas, as he passed swiftly through the universities of Harvard, Berkeley and Stanford, proclaiming himself an atheist to his friends, acknowledging the greatness of Hindu philosophical systems, but extolling the practical civilisations of the 'west'. He also became an advocate of what was then quaintly called 'free love' — a number of sources mention this obsession, but are all strangely reticent about providing further details.[22]

## *'Free Love' and 'Anarchism'*

'Free love' meant, at least, that sexual liaisons before or outside formal marriage were not taboo. The irregularities, from the perspective of the conventional morality of the time, in the lives of Indian males

---

[20] Ibid., 240.
[21] Ibid., 245.
[22] Brown, *Har Dayal*, 104, 114, 162.

in the United States have been written about elsewhere and fictionalised in the American radical Agnes Smedley's novel, *Daughter of Earth*, which dwells in some length on the double standards of the Indian male exiles who claimed a sexual freedom they had great trouble in accepting among female (mostly non-Indian) colleagues.[23] To what extent this aspect of the exiles' lives were based on principles held firmly and/or made up in retrospect is difficult to tell. But it did cause unease among supporters of their politics. A *Ghadar* suspect, interviewed by the police, admitted to having been attracted to the idea of liberating India from the British, but reports a certain nervousness among Har Dayal's potential political recruits for fear that they might have to share his lifestyle.[24] In his years in Germany, complaints that 'free love' was widespread among the Indian community in Berlin were made to the German Foreign Office by their Indian informants. Later, during the Great War, Har Dayal suddenly vanished from Istanbul, where he had been assigned to work with other Indian exiles and the Turkish government to organise an expedition of deserted Indian troops via Afghanistan to India, and reappeared in Geneva; he was living with one Mansur Rifat, an Egyptian nationalist and the German Foreign Office, who wanted him to return to his political work for them, implied a relationship of some intimacy between the two men when they suggested that the route to persuading Har Dayal of anything was through Rifat, even to the extent of suggesting that although Rifat was not required in Berlin, if Har Dayal refused to travel without him, they would accept the condition.[25]

Har Dayal also began to be regarded as an anarchist, not in a loose sense of the word, but more ideologically. He was associated with and lectured to the Industrial Workers of the World (IWW), popularly known as the 'Wobblies', and his political statements and writings moved sharply away from the 'eastern spiritualism' theme

---

[23] Smedley, *Daughter of Earth*, esp. 171–270.

[24] Bombay Abstract, dated 24 July 1915, Para.706, S.B. Bombay, 24 July 1915. Statement of WAMAN SAKHARAM SANT-AKOLEKAR, b.1886. WBSA, Calcutta, IB Records, IB Sl No 12/1915, File No. 102/1915, 106–97.

[25] *PA-AA*, WK 11f series; on Rifat and his relationship with Har Dayal, see PA-AA, WK 11f, File R21073, 84, 103, and especially 113, cypher telegram 24 October 1914: 'Falls Har Dayal verlangt Rifat mitzubringen hiermit einverstanden'.

that he had adopted not too long ago, although some of the rhetoric made spiritual references, even Christian ones: men like Kropotkin were, he said, 'the St Francises and St Bernards of labour'; terrorism only provided an opportunity for the state to respond with greater violence, whereas a labour movement's 'martyr' would be martyred nevertheless, 'killed not for killing, but for his greater love'.[26] Gradually, he blew his cover as a professor of Indian philosophy at Stanford and was eased out of his post, jumping before he was pushed. He was co-founder of the Radical Club, whose full title was the 'International-Radical-Communist Anarchist Club', and continued to lecture on 'free love'.[27]

Although Har Dayal was among the first Indians to take Karl Marx seriously, publishing 'Karl Marx — a Modern Rishi' in the *Modern Review* of March 1912,[28] he was on shaky ground in his reading. As the title indicates, he was not an atheist in his rhetoric. The article opens with a quotation from St Matthew and is written throughout in a religious-spiritual mode, explaining that 'saintliness does not consist only in repeating religious formulae and singing hymns';[29] he is less efficient at explaining Marx than at evoking outrage at the poverty that co-exists with affluence in Europe as well as in India. In its allusions and its tone, the piece is Biblical. In its description of Marx's ideas, three ideas are dealt with. First, the 'materialistic conception of history', which is dismissed as a 'half-truth', compared with Herbert Spencer's idea of social evolution, both being treated as mechanical and dismissed in favour of Thomas Carlyle's 'theory of civilisation as a product of personal influence'. Second, the 'theory of class struggle', which Har Dayal also sees as only a partial truth, pointing away from class struggle to 'social cooperation based on the appreciation of a higher ideal' as evident in bourgeois (and Marx's own) participation in the International. And third, the 'analysis of surplus value', 'which seems to be the soundest part of his work in the province of pure theory', but which Har Dayal says he is not

---

[26] Quoted in Brown, *Har Dayal*, 110–11. Brown does not spot the spirituality and Christian rhetoric, seeing it merely as a move away from 'the East' towards 'the West'.

[27] Brown, *Har Dayal*, 113–14.

[28] Har Dayal, 'Karl Marx', 273–86.

[29] Ibid., 273.

interested in fully understanding.[30] He then proceeds to see money itself as 'treason to the race' of men, with the obligatory quote from St Paul about the love of money being the root of all evil and paraphrasing it deliberately to 'money is the root of all evil'. The editors of the *Modern Review* added a footnote: 'we cannot conceive how civilised existence would be possible without some sort of money'.[31]

In Har Dayal's attempt to find a 'Fraternity of the Red Flag' and a 'monastery' for that order, which was for '[t]he service of the Radical ideal of life', he included in its Radical principles those of '[p]ersonal moral development through love and self-discipline', '[p]ersonal intellectual development through education and self-culture' and 'personal physical development through hygiene and eugenics'. As one of the goals for 'Institutional Revolution', he included '[t]he establishment of the complete economic, moral, intellectual and sexual freedom of woman, and the abolition of prostitution, marriage, and other institutions based on the enslavement of woman'.[32]

## Ghadar

The best-known phase of Har Dayal's life is of course his association with the *Ghadar* movement, initially San Francisco and Vancouver-based, but quickly to spread to global proportions, to be associated with the 'German plot' against the British Indian Empire during the First World War. It is clear from a number of accounts that Har Dayal was a major source of much of the *Ghadar* agitational material and a major inspiration behind its early years of organisation. Har Dayal's activities among students and among the agricultural workforce that made up the bulk of the *Ghadar* rank and file were known to British intelligence through their foresight in having seconded W.C. Hopkinson, formerly of the Calcutta Police, to Canadian intelligence, and Hopkinson worked closely with US immigration authorities to try and find a way to stop these activities (Hopkinson was later assassinated).[33] One of Hopkinson's informers was an Indian Christian

[30] Ibid., 282–83.
[31] Ibid., 284.
[32] Manifesto reprinted in Brown, *Har Dayal*, 114–15.
[33] File on Hopkinson's secondment to North America, IOR: L/P&J/12/1.

student called Pandion, whose scholarship to Berkeley, the Guru Govind Singh Scholarship, had been created through the joint efforts of a potato farmer, Jawala Singh, and Har Dayal, but the failure of the potato crop in the year of the scholarship's inception had placed all the students on a financially unstable footing.[34]

A few contemporaneous accounts might be interesting from the perspective of the reach of the *Ghadar* movement and the reputation of Har Dayal as its leader. The first is from Manila, Philippines, where an anti-British party had been set up among the East Indians, also called the Hindustan Association, as it was in the United States.[35] At the end of 1912, 90 'East Indians', as they were called to distinguish them from 'West Indians', attended a meeting where one G.D. Kumar asked that 'all East Indians should help each other and follow the ideas of Mr L. Har Dayal MA[,] whose idea was Anti-British and who founded a seditious party at San Fransisco'.[36] G.D. Kumar left Manila in mid-1914, after which Bhagwan Singh came from the United States and became Secretary. He left mid-1915, and Kundar Lall of Manila became Secretary and Dost Mohamed also of Manila became President. This information is not from a suspect but from an informer, one P.N. Sharma, who claimed to know, from having translated their writings into English for the British Consulate and the Philippines Constabulary, the names of Har Dayal himself, Pandit Ram Chand, the editor of the *Ghadar* newspaper of the same name, and Mehar Singh and Badri Posard, workers. 'The Hindustani Association is still receiving seditious papers from San Fransisco and distributing them among East Indians and the Turks.'

This Association was receiving a monthly paper by the name of Jaoanul Islam from Constantinople through him [it is not clear from context who 'him' is — probably Har Dayal]. Har Dayal who was forwarding the paper from Switzerland to the Head Office at San Fransisco from where all the branches of the association were receiving the said paper and were distributing among the sympathisers. But since the date Ottoman Empire declared War on Russia the paper was discontinued.

---

[34] Brown, *Har Dayal*, 127–28; Dharmavira, *Lala Har Dayal*, 148–52.

[35] WBSA, Calcutta, IB Records, IBSl No. 12/1915, File No. 102/1915, 145–53: Statement extract of one P.N. Sharma from Manila, Philippines.

[36] WBSA, Calcutta, IB Records, IB Sl No 12/1915, File No. 102/1915, 145–46.

The said paper was Edited by Moulvi Abdul Jamid who is an intimate friend of the Editor of the 'Zemindar Akbar' of Lahore.[37]

Another statement, this time from Bombay Presidency, of one Waman Sakharam Sant-Akolekar could provide something of an autobiography of a political radical of the times, if taken as a whole. What we are interested in here is his account of Har Dayal: 'I knew practically nothing of this gentleman when I was in India. When I went to the United States, I heard his name very often. Almost every student of India residing in America knew about Mr Har Dayal.'[38] Har Dayal administered the Guru Govind scholarship for students, given by Mr Jwala Singh of Holt. Har Dayal allegedly said that Indian students of all ranks were to be given a scholarship; six were on offer, and one Professor Tej Singh said only Sikhs should be offered them. Har Dayal won the argument, and Tej Singh 'left California for good'. Har Dayal selected the students.[39]

Mr Har Dayal hired a house in Berkely [sic] for the maintenance of those students. Mr Har Dayal was somewhat eccentric in his ways. He never observed American ways and customs. He used to live like a beggar. When he was a professor in Standford [sic] University he acted like a mad man. He professed to be a philosopher. The Hindi students in America at that time thought that the scholarship holders would have to live according to the wishes of Mr Har Dayal. This is one of the reasons why the scholarship holders did not care to live in the house constructed by Mr Har Dayal.[40]

Sant-Akolekar names the scholarship holders as Nand Singh, G.B. Lall, B.S. Sharma, Pandya (the same person as the informer, Pandion)[41] and Khokatnur.

I heard of one Muhammadan student, but I did not get a chance of seeing him, when I had been to Berkeley in September 1912. I remember

---

[37] Ibid., 144–53.
[38] Bombay Abstract, dated 24 July 1915, Para.706, S.B. Bombay, 24 July 1915. Statement of WAMAN SAKHARAM SANT-AKOLEKAR, b.1886. WBSA, Calcutta, IB Records, IB Sl No 12/1915, File No. 102/1915, 106–97.
[39] Ibid.
[40] Ibid.
[41] Brown, *Har Dayal*, 131, 135.

that I had warned Mr Khokatnur about Mr Jwala Singh and Mr Har Dayal. I even suggested that the house could not last long as Mr Jwala Singh was not known to be a rich man. Afterwards I learned from Mr GP Uplap that the house was broken up. Mr Jwala Singh failed to pay and Mr Har Dayal tried the experiment of turning these scholars into sages, but he too failed. Mr Har Dayal was known to every Hindi student as a scholar and practical philosopher. Nobody ever knew his political ideas till he started his revolutionary campaign. Many of the Hindi students loved him for his vast knowledge, but hated him at the same time for not observing the ways and customs of the American people. When he showed his disloyal nature, the members of the Hindustani Association condemned him. Mr Har Dayal was a famous socialist and avowed anarchist. Some of his lectures on socialism were nothing but sermons on anarchism. The attention of every student in America was drawn towards Mr Har Dayal when he was arrested in San Francisco. Some time in the month of February 1914 they (the students) watched closely the action of the Government of the United States. I do not know the source of the news that Mr Har Dayal was arrested at the request of the English Government and that an arrangement had been made between the Governments to hand over Mr Har Dayal to the English Government. This news created a sensation among his admirers — Americans as well as Hindus. Finally, nobody knew how Mr Har Dayal left the USA. For good. It must be mentioned that though he left America, still he exercised the same influence over the *asram* which he started in San Francisco. He bought the *Ghadar* Press. I believe he managed the *Ghadar* paper for more than two or three months. His influence among socialists in America was undoubtedly immense. Even in his absence his admirers (Americans) helped the *Ghadar* Press financially. He was the cause of upsetting the minds of the poor labourers. Any body of common sense will admit that the existence of such a dangerous personage was the source of constant trouble to the British Raj, and also the cause of misfortune to his country.[42]

The necessary tone that is acquired in being asked to testify to the police is obvious; they must hear what they want to hear, in the

---

[42] Bombay Abstract, dated 24 July 1915, Para.706, S.B. Bombay, 24 July 1915. Statement of WAMAN SAKHARAM SANT-AKOLEKAR, b.1886. WBSA, Calcutta, IB Records, IB Sl No 12/1915, File No. 102/1915, 106–97. Quote from f. 101.

'prose of counter-insurgency'[43] that also becomes the language of 'approver's testimony'.[44]

Har Dayal left the United States in March 1914 'voluntarily' (having been charged with being in the United States illegally as the US Government came under considerable pressure from Britain to deport him, he claimed that his departure satisfied 'the exigencies of the law').[45] He reappeared in Geneva. There, and in Berlin and Constantinople, he was a central figure in what was to be known, somewhat sensationally, as the 'Hindu–German Conspiracy'.

## Har Dayal and the 'Hindu–German Conspiracy'

Optimism that a strong Germany successfully challenging Britain in a war might lead to a weakening of Britain's hold on India predated the outbreak of the Great War and had of course been encouraged by German official circles. Har Dayal's US speeches in 1913 had already drawn attention to the fact 'that Germany was preparing to go to war with England, and that it was time to get ready to go to India for the coming revolution'.[46] Har Dayal was among many others who, upon the outbreak of the war, sought to assist this process, gravitating towards Germany (and Switzerland, which remained a base for pro-German activities) along with other fellow Indians in American exile (notably Tarak Nath Das, the Bengali activist from the Swadeshi era who had acquired US citizenship, and Bhupendranath Datta, the younger brother of the Hindu missionary, Swami Vivekananda) to join those already there (for instance, Viren Chattopadhyay, who had been studying at Halle University) or those who arrived in Germany from elsewhere in Europe (Champakaran Pillai from Switzerland), forming the Indian Independence Committee (IIC) in Berlin.[47] The

---

[43] Guha, 'The Prose of Counter-Insurgency', 45–88.

[44] Amin, 'Approver's Testimony, Judicial Discourse', 166–202.

[45] Letter to Commissioner-General of Immigration, from Geneva, 22 July 1914, reprinted in Brown, *Har Dayal*, 166.

[46] Sedition Committee, *Report*, 146. Speech by Har Dayal at meeting held at Sacramento, 31 December 1913.

[47] The literature on this subject is relatively large, but not particularly analytically rich: see for instance, Bose, *Indian Revolutionaries Abroad, 1905–1922*; Sareen, *Indian Revolutionary Movement Abroad (1905–1920)*; Barooah, *Chatto*; Oesterheld, *'Der Feind meines Feindes ist mein Freund.'*

Committee itself was the brainchild of the *Nachrichtenstelle für den Orient* and its director, the Orientalist Max Freiherr von Oppenheim, who tended to refer to the IIC as *Meine Inder* ('my Indians').[48] The Indians on the Committee were expected to assist with propaganda material to induce desertions and surrenders among British Indian troops in Europe; expected to conduct propaganda among the Indian prisoners of war in German prison camps, inducing them to desert to the German side and volunteer for a military expedition to free India from foreign rule; and expected to assist in a move to bring Indian troops into India via Afghanistan, where a Turkish government would use the authority of the Sultan as supreme Commander of the Faithful to incite at least the Indian Muslims to rebellion against the British. Har Dayal had his part in the devising of this strategy: although it played well with some German Orientalists' (and Oppenheim's own) views of the 'warlike' and temperamental Mohammedans',[49] the *Auswärtiges Amt* records credit Har Dayal with suggesting in September 1914 to Geissler, the German Consul in Geneva, that once a force had entered India from Afghanistan and joined by 'young men ready for any sacrifice'[50] who would undertake terrorist strikes in the rest of India, the country would rise in rebellion against the British.[51] Har Dayal also agreed to coordinate the activities of Ghadar supporters in East Asia, East Africa and the United States, as well as to go to Constantinople or Mecca himself in the pursuit of this cause.[52] In the end, he was sent to Constantinople,

---

[48] *PA-AA:* file series WK 11s and WK 11f series; on 'Meine Inder', see for instance PA-AA: WK11f, R20173, 137–38.

[49] Manjapra, 'The Mirrored World', 90.

[50] Quoted in Barooah, *India and Official Germany*, 194.

[51] This also coincided with the views of other volunteers to the German cause: the former missionary Paul Walter, in volunteering his services and expertise from his India years to the cause of the German Foreign Office, wrote a quasi-historical note speculating *inter alia* what would have happened if the 1857 Revolt had instead happened in 1855, during the Crimean War, and noting in conclusion, 'Der Zündstoff ist da, es kann von unermesslicher Bedeutung werden, wenn wir die Brandfackel hineinwerfen'. *PA-AA*: WK 11f, file R21070, 2–5.

[52] Barooah, *India and Official Germany*, 194–95; *PA-AA:* WK 11f, R21070, 79–80, cipher telegram to *Auswärtiges Amt*, Berlin, from German *GeneralKonsul* Geißler, Geneva, 3 September 1914.

travelling on a German imperial passport as Ramalingamdass, a trader born in Dar es Salaam.[53] Har Dayal was in Constantinople in September and early October 1914 and then vanished from Constantinople and reappeared in Geneva, complaining of the arrogance of the Germans in Constantinople.[54] He was persuaded to come to Germany by his old comrade from his India House days, Virendranath Chattopadhyay, and his San Fransisco comrade, Maulvi Barkatullah, both already active in Berlin.[55] While still in Constantinople, he began writing propaganda leaflets to distribute to soldiers at the front to persuade them to desert, which his German superiors considered far too intellectual (although, given that they filed them upside down, it is unclear whether they knew what he was writing).[56] He then went to Constantinople again to coordinate matters related to a proposed delegation to Kabul and was quickly at odds with his colleagues, in particular the Kheiri brothers, who had moved from being Boy Scout masters in Beirut to language teachers in Constantinople to Islamic revolutionaries during the War, but reckoned that Har Dayal, despite his current mission, was anti-Muslim, as was the Berlin India Committee; in summer 1915, Har Dayal left for Berlin via Budapest.[57]

---

[53] PA-AA: WK 11f, R21070, 108–9, cipher telegram to *Auswärtiges Amt* from Geißler, 5 September 1914.

[54] PA-AA: WK 11f, R21073, 25–26, cypher telegram to *Auswärtiges Amt* from the German *Botschafter*, Therapia, 15 October 1914, reporting Har Dayal's departure without his German imperial passport and with a Turkish one bearing the name of Ismael Hakki Hassan of Basra and speculating on possible bad blood between Indian Hindus and Muslims in Turkey; PA-AA: WK 11f, R21073, 84–85, cipher telegram from Geißler to *Auswärtiges Amt*, 20 October 1914, quoting Mansur Rifat as saying Har Dayal was upset at German and especially Oppenheim's, arrogance.

[55] PA-AA: WK 11f, R21073, 46–50, 66–68, 84, 103–4, 106–7, 113, 118. Krüger, 'Har Dayal in Deutschland'; Brown, *Har Dayal*, 183–89.

[56] The text in Devanagari script is on file upside down, with the pages mixed up: PA-AA: WK 11f, R21072, 177–79. Given that it contains simple slogans: '*Maro Angrez Ko! Germany ki Jai ho! Hindustan ki jai ho!*' [Kill the English! Victory to Germany! Victory to Hindustan!] or [the English] '*apne labh ke liye tumhara khun bahana chahte hai*' [are shedding your blood for their own gain], it does not seem too intellectual to grasp.

[57] Siddiqi, 'Bluff, doubt and fear'.

The much-told tale of the 'Hindu–German plot' has had many takers: the romantic secret-service treatment, popular[58] or histori-cal,[59] the ironic (and simplistic) Hindu- agitators-failing-to-mobilise-Muslim-soldiers troop,[60] as well as more descriptive treatments, from various perspectives.[61] The details are not quite as sensational. The 'plot' was highlighted and sensationalised in the press during the famous San Francisco Conspiracy Case of 1917–1918, when the United States joined the war and proceeded to take action against Indians and their sympathisers operating from within the United States.[62] In reality, its military goals were very far from being met, which included using deserted British Indian troops to enter India and link up with internal rebellions (the largest attempt of which failed in 1915), although a government-in-exile was set up in Kabul by early 1916, with Maulvi Barkatullah, formerly Urdu lecturer at Tokyo University and latterly a member of the Ghadra in San Francisco, as Prime Minister, and Raja Mahendra Pratap, maverick traveller and activist for Indian independence, its President.[63] Meanwhile,

---

[58] Hopkirk, *On Secret Service East of Constantinople*, is not much less sensationalist than Buchan, *Greenmantle*. Hopkirk (b. 1930), who has dabbled in intelligence work himself and remains an Empire loyalist, at least in retrospect, continues to write 'true' spy stories, following the exploits of the British Empire in the East, untroubled by historiographical conventions or the inconvenience of footnotes. Hopkirk's predecessor, the Scotsman John Buchan (1875–1940), was also, apart from being a published writer, an official propagandist as well as a diplomat working for the British Foreign Office during the First World War. He ended his career as Governor-General of Canada (1935–1940).

[59] Popplewell, *Intelligence and Imperial Defence.*

[60] Manjapra, 'The Illusions of Encounter', 363–82.

[61] A sample would include Brown, 'The Hindu Conspiracy, 1914–1917', 299–310; Dignan, 'Hindu Conspiracy in Anglo-American Relations', 57–76; Jensen, 'The "Hindu Conspiracy"', 65–83; Hoover, 'The Hindu Conspiracy in California, 1913–1918', 245–61 (all focused on the United States); Fraser, 'Germany and Indian Revolution, 1914–1918', 255–72; Hughes, 'The German Mission to Afghanistan, 1915–1916', 447–76; and we are leaving out, for now, a number of biographical sources, autobiographical writings, and contemporaneous reports, governmental or otherwise.

[62] See Ramnath, *The Haj to Utopia*, 91–94; Brown, *Har Dayal*, 185, 204.

[63] Pratap, *Reflections of an Exile*, 11–19, 63–70; *My Life Story of Fiftyfive [sic] Years*, 39–60.

Har Dayal continued attempting to organise volunteers for the cause of Indian independence — independently of the Germans — during the course of the war, utilising IWW and anarchist connections.[64] Less than successful in these attempts, he spent much of the rest of the war in various German spa towns at governmental expense;[65] then, he was allowed to follow Viren Chattopadhyay to Sweden, where a strategic branch office of Indian nationalists had been set up and from where Chatto and his colleagues had begun communicating with the Bolsheviks in the run-up to the October Revolution.[66] He managed to get to Stockholm in October 1918, 11 months after the Revolution, during which time he had offered his services to the Berlin India Committee as a 'socialist', who could communicate in a socialist language and would be able to start a journal addressing Indian grievances in the newly legitimate socialist language. He himself would be suitable for the purpose, he said, because 'I can write in the regular socialistic style, with quotations from Marx, etc., etc'.[67] After the Armistice, he stayed on in Sweden, in common with a number of members of the India Committee, but unlike them, this was the end of his radical political career.

## Recantation and Attempted Return

From Sweden, after the Great War, Har Dayal tried to prepare a return to India, communicating with Professor Arnold of University College, London, declaring that he had broken all ties with Berlin and returned his German passport and requesting a British one and 'some financial aid' while he was looking for a publisher for his booklet, entitled *44 Months in Germany and Turkey*.[68]

My real purpose is to show that the Indians and Egyptians will not find disinterested friends among other nations, which may set themselves

---

[64] Brown, *Har Dayal*, 208–9.

[65] Krüger, 'Har Dayal in Deutschland'.

[66] Barooah, *Chatto*, 100–56.

[67] Brown, *Har Dayal*, 215.

[68] Letter from Har Dayal, Stockholm, to Professor TW Arnold, 23 February 1919, reprinted in NAI: Home (Political), Proceedings, November 1919, Nos. 23–24, 17–18.

up as rivals of England. It is, therefore, best to accept the principle of Imperial unity, and work for the establishment of democratic institutions with the help of Englishmen.[69]

This book is a strange document in the history of Har Dayal's life. It contains various attacks on Germany and Germans, Turkey and Turks, in an undifferentiated and crude manner quite unbecoming of the intellectual that its author undoubtedly was and, alongside this, praise of British rule, civilisation and values, rejecting his previous goal of Indian independence in favour of a longer British connection for India and Dominion status within the Empire.[70] In its crudity, the booklet appears definitely to have overstated its case. The Government duly noted its publication, ordered several copies to distribute in India as propaganda material in favour of British rule and had it translated into Indian languages, but refused to allow Har Dayal back into India, deeming him dangerous and regarding the book as a strategic lie on the part of its author.[71] It is not difficult to see why. For instance, in the course of his repetition of the by-now standard and widespread convention of argument that declared middle and upper class Indians to be 'unrepresentative' of their country (and one that British colonial officials were known to use regularly), Har Dayal denounced this 'demoralised and denationalised', 'effete' class who 'do not know much about their national literature or history' and 'belong to no organised Church'. 'A healthy and moral society is organised as a Church and a State'.[72] These are strange views for one who was so recently considered an anarchist.

Har Dayal's 10 years in Sweden marked a return to the life of a scholar-Orientalist, now living a precarious life of lecturing and writing on matters Indian. He studied Greek and Latin, read Chinese philosophy, wrote on 'Buddhism' and on education, and occasionally intervened in Indian political debates. A much-cited article, originally appearing in the *Pratap* of Lahore in 1925, contained this gem:

---

[69] Letter from Har Dayal, Stockholm, to Professor TW Arnold, 31 March 1919, reprinted in NAI: Home (Political), Proceedings, November 1919, Nos. 23–24, 20–21: quote on p. 20.

[70] Dayal, *44 Months*.

[71] NAI: Foreign & Political, General, Proceedings, January 1922, Nos: 870–886 B.

[72] Dayal, *44 Months*, 71.

I declare that the future of the Hindu race, of Hindusthan and of the Punjab rests on these four pillars: (i) Hindu Sanghatan; (ii) Hindu Raj; (iii) Shuddhi of Moslems; and (iv) Conquest and shuddhi of Afghanistan and the Frontiers. So long as the Hindu Nation does not accomplish these four things, the safety of our children and great grandchildren will be ever in danger, and the safety of the Hindu race will be impossible. The Hindu race has but one history and its institutions are homogeneous. But the Mussulmans and Christians are far removed from the confines of Hinduism, for their religions are alien and they love Persian, Arab and European institutions.[73]

Afghanistan and the frontier regions, 'formerly part of India', had to be retaken for the safety of Hindustan, both cultural and military.[74]

Har Dayal's apparent transformation into a somewhat eccentric scholar-Orientalist, though of course always a possibility given his background in history and Sanskrit, was a surprising coda to a rather passionate political life. This was interspersed with repeated attempts to be allowed to return to India.[75] The Punjab Government in particular was not keen on this, and Har Dayal himself did not risk, for a time, entering British imperial territory without an assurance of amnesty for his wartime activities. From late 1926, Har Dayal began a relationship with one Agda Erikson, whom he acknowledged as his wife from 1932, although he was still married to his wife in India. He did not tell Agda of this, nor his Indian family, friends or acquaintances of her (and it was only after his death that Agda was to find out that he had a wife in India and had left all but 200 pounds to his Indian widow).[76] In 1927, he moved to England with her, and he continued to write communications for the Hindu communal press in India. He completed a PhD from the School of Oriental and African Studies in London in 1930, and it

---

[73] Har Dayal's message, quoted in Prakash, *A Review of the History*, 49, and reprinted in Baxter, *The Jana Sangh*, 16. A longer quote from the article appears in Brown, *Har Dayal*, 233–34, from which the last sentence quoted here appears (233); the quote from Baxter is shorter.

[74] Brown, *Har Dayal*, 233.

[75] NAI: Home (Political) 192 Part B, 1924.

[76] Brown, *Har Dayal*, 270. Dharmavira, *Lala Har Dayal*, leaves out Agda Erikson from his story altogether, referring instead to 'one Mrs Ericsson' founding her Folk High School of Viskadelen in 1926 with Har Dayal's help (249).

was published as *The Bodhisattva Doctrine in Buddhist Sanskrit Literature* in 1932.[77] In 1934, he published *Hints for Self-Culture*, containing advice on physical culture, intellectual culture, aesthetics, 'cosmopolitan clubs' and an ideal of the World-State; much of this, addressed 'To A Young Fellow Rationalist', rambles on in a pedantic tone about various ways in which 'the young men and women of all countries', and of course Indians as well by implication, should improve themselves for coming challenges.[78]

The anti-capitalist remarks in the book are out of joint with his continued Hindu communalist remarks in the Indian press. Still, for some reason in 1938, he was able to become Secretary of the Left Book Club.[79]

## The End

Permission to return to India was finally granted in a letter of 25 October 1938. Har Dayal was living at the time in Edgware in Middlesex, England. The India Office wrote that:

> neither the Government of India nor the Punjab Government will prosecute you or take other action against you in respect of past events so long as you faithfully observe your assurance not to participate directly or indirectly in any unconstitutional movement. But in the event of a breach of your undertaking the Punjab will not hesitate to take action. They also hold themselves at liberty at any time to publish the fact that you gave this undertaking.

He would have to surrender his passport on return to India, and the Government 'would not be prepared' to have him go abroad again.[80]

Har Dayal in reply, writing from Philadelphia, thanked the Secretary of State for India, the Government of India and the Punjab Government for their 'kindness and magnanimity' and accepted

---

[77] Dayal, *The Bodhisattva Doctrine*.

[78] Dayal, *Hints for Self-culture*; the book is summarised in Brown, *Har Dayal*, 244–47. Quotes taken from Preface and 'To A Young Fellow Rationalist', no page numbers.

[79] NAI: External Affairs (External), 1939, 234-X (Secret), 21–22.

[80] Letter, A Dibdin, for the India Office, to Har Dayal, 34 Churchill Road, Edgware, 25 October 1938. NAI: External Affairs (External), 1939, 234-X (Secret), 2–3.

their offer but said he was unable to state exactly when he could return, listing his many forthcoming engagements: he would return to England from the United States in April 1939, had promised to preside at the Summer School of the Peace Academy in Switzerland in August and had been invited for a lecture tour in America by the World Fellowship of Faiths in 1939–1940. He said he should like to return to India via Ceylon, Siam and Burma, where he wished to study some Buddhist manuscripts before proceeding to India and requested that the passport he be given be endorsed accordingly.[81] The process of securing the necessary permissions was underway — Ceylon and Burma refused to admit him[82] — when on 4 March 1939, Har Dayal died of a heart attack in Philadelphia. He was not yet 55. Among the last letters he wrote was one from Philadelphia to S.R. Rana on 27 January 1939:

> Thanks for your kind letter, which I have received here in America. I came here in October for a lecture tour, & shall stay here until April. I hope to see you in the summer. I have now obtained amnesty, but I don't know when I shall go back to India. I have promised to complete some literary work in Europe & America, and that will take time. But I am glad that the way is clear now, and I can return whenever I like. I may be able to do some good work there, for my health is quite all right, and I have many ideas and plans in my head. I don't feel old at all.
>
> I met some of the old-timers in New York, like Basanta Kumar Roy.
>
> I am planning a comprehensive book on 'New India'. It may be useful, as it can be circulated in the country without any difficulty.
>
> I hope that Europe can maintain peace this year ...[83]

## In Conclusions: Trajectories or Fragments?

Har Dayal is remembered now mostly by those who appropriate his ideas to the Hindu right, and clearly, this is not without reason.

---

[81] Har Dayal to Under-Secretary of State for India, 10 November 1938. NAI: External Affairs (External), 1939, 234-X (Secret), 3–4.

[82] NAI: External Affairs (External), 1939, 234-X (Secret), 20–21.

[83] Har Dayal to SR Rana, from 701 Park Manor Apartments, Parkside Avenue, Philadelphia, dated 27 January 1939, copy in Krüger papers, Box 7, File 49, No. 2, ZMO, Berlin.

Vinayak Damodar Savarkar, the anointed prophet of the Hindu right, used the occasion of Har Dayal's death to highlight the story of the continuing struggle that had begun in London, when Savarkar, Har Dayal and the communist Viren Chattopadhyay, who had recently vanished in the Soviet Union, had been colleagues and co-revolutionaries in the India House group, on the editorial board of the *Talwar*, the India House group's journal, and in the leadership of the *Abhinav Bharat*, the revolutionary network created by the group.[84]

Perhaps it is worthwhile using this story to problematise the linear intellectual histories (to the extent that there are any intellectual histories) that we might be tempted towards, of a left and right wing of a nationalism. We could here raise the question of what exactly a 'radical' intellectual or political position might have been in the contexts of the fluid movements of ideas and people that characterised the early 20th century as well as the world of anti-imperialist engagements. The conventional categories of our classificatory systems seem to break down in the face of the bewildering variety of Har Dayal's multiple engagements as an exile. Benedict Anderson suggests that after Marx's death in 1883, anarchism became 'the dominant element in the self-consciously internationalist radical left'.[85] Har Dayal had his anarchist phase, but 'radical' is a term that can be employed and mobilised in a variety of ways, and Har Dayal's 'radicalism', which is difficult to pin down as left or right, is interspersed with periods of straightforward conservatism.

Men make history, but not in circumstances of their own choosing, and one suggestion that could problematise this narrative is that a historical actor might choose from available languages of legitimation to build an argument with likely resonances in a social context in which s/he must speak. This of course does not explain choices that were strange and disconsonant with many of the contexts in which Har Dayal operated; it might explain the 'approver's testimony' or

---

[84] Transcript of Vinayak Damodar Savarkar's speech in Poona on 14 May 1939, MSA: Home (Special) 60-D (h), 1939–41, S157–61; see also police transcript of Savarkar's speech in Poona, also on 14 May 1939, DIG (CID) Bombay, copy in Krüger papers, Box 6, File 24, No. 1, ZMO, Berlin; these are meetings at different times on the same day, where Savarkar delivered substantially the same speech.

[85] Anderson, *Under Three Flags*, 2.

the disavowals and denunciations of previous selves in some, but not all contexts. Many of the ideological frameworks of the early 20th century appear to share certain eugenic or bio-moral assumptions (physical fitness, self-strengthening, national discipline) that cut across political differences[86] but there is no indication that Har Dayal found this to be the key to reconciling his political shifts — indeed, there is no particular indication that he saw them as uncomfortable or unusual or that he sought to reconcile them. The search for consistency, then, is the biographer's search, and bearing in mind that biography is more a genre than a methodology, the rules of the biographical genre push us gently towards establishing motive and connection, where the conventions of historiography would pull us in another direction and urge prudence. The temptations of ascribing consistency are, therefore, worth resisting.

In lieu of a conclusion, this chapter is thus left with a series of disavowals. Can we say anything of the motives and intentions of historical actors? These often remain opaque, even to the individuals concerned; instead, we might have an indication in a source of *proclaimed* motive and *proclaimed* intention, which is obviously framed by them in terms of existing idioms of legitimacy, and perhaps we can therefore learn much about the idioms of legitimacy in which individuals operated from the language and arguments they use. Biography must operate in historical contexts; that is obvious. But when do we as historians resort to personal, political or conjunctural explanations of events in the lives of individuals? And while we follow the life of a person, we can also see the individual as non-agent, as subject to and victim of the circumstances of his times, the individual as stalking horse across contexts. We can push this analogy towards another one: we know of the Vedic practice of the *aswamedha yajna*, in which the emperor's army stalks a horse until it is resisted by another army at which point there is a battle, after which the horse is sacrificed. Obviously, the expectation of the emperor who lets the army stalk the horse is that the horse will not be challenged, or if it is, that his army is powerful enough to defeat the challenger and impose the route. The end-point is known to the king, as it is to the historian, but not to the horse or the individual,

---

[86] Franziska Roy, 'International Utopia and National Discipline'; Zachariah, *Developing India*, 242–52.

and the horse-individual is sacrificed to the larger plan. This is the danger of the biographical temptation: the individual becomes a metonymy for community, nation, social movement, ideology or something far larger, and it is awkward when the same individual is inconsistent, for he cannot be too many metonymies at once.

Har Dayal, then, drifted through various intellectual moments on his way elsewhere. Do we regard his life as a journey? Towards what? Do we reduce what is too easily rendered as a 'transnational intellectual biography' to a moment of origin or a moment of destiny (in a recent study of M.N. Roy, the man is allowed by the biographer's pen to emerge as a world traveller, a 'cosmopolitan' and a 'transnational intellectual', but is in the end reduced to his Bengali 'swadeshi' origins; in another one of Subhas Chandra Bose, the leader-who-almost-was becomes the guiding theme)?[87] I have expressed discomfort with the frameworks of transnationalism and cosmopolitanism elsewhere;[88] it might be worth mentioning here that focusing on the 'transnational' reifies the national by marking every border-crossing as special, and a 'cosmopolitan', at 'home' for various periods in various places, might still be parochial, ethnocentric or racist — the last three adjectives relating in one way or another to nationalisms of various description. 'Cosmopolitan' is thus in danger of becoming a non-concept, making sense only in a hyphenated relationship with something else.[89] We could chase our man with nets marked 'diaspora' or 'exile' with similarly dissatisfying results; fragments would still slip out of the mesh.[90] Any of these frameworks

---

[87] Manjapra, *M.N. Roy*; Bose, *His Majesty's Opponent*.

[88] Zachariah, *Playing the Nation Game*, 262–65.

[89] Harvey, 'Cosmopolitanism and the Banality of Geographical Evils', 529–64. The phrase 'all manner of hyphenated versions of cosmopolitanism', which I find useful, appears on p. 530. As far as list-making on 'cosmopolitanism' goes, we should at least add Vertovec and Cohen, *Conceiving Cosmopolitanism*; Cheah and Robbins, *Cosmopolitics*; Archibugi, Breckenridge et al., *Cosmopolitanism*.

[90] One could start by citing Benedict Anderson on the international contexts of nationalism, 'bureaucratic pilgrimages' to the metropolis, and models 'available for piracy' to illustrate this 'transnational' nature of nationalism (and note that the word in favour is no longer *inter*national, which Anderson himself used): Anderson, *Imagined Communities*. Anderson, in a published lecture entitled *Long-Distance Nationalism: World Capitalism and the Rise*

can be invoked to satisfy those intent on multiplying examples to meet current historiographical trends; but this would be all too easy. We might instead make the observation that Indian nationalists had a particular problem with coming up with a consistent and stable idea of what ought to constitute the Indian nation or the future Indian state and that Har Dayal's inconsistencies are somehow symptomatic of this. But that would not be something peculiar to the Indians, and the importance of being Har Dayal would then be marginalised in the quest of the typologies — the sacrificing of the stalking horse. On the other hand, the biographical exercise of a historian's sharing of the long, strange trip does at least illuminate a great number of contexts, spaces and ideologies, all of which impinged upon the life

---

*of Identity Politics*, observes, following Lord Acton, that 'exile is the nursery of nationality' (the phrase is a quotation from Acton, on p. 2), and later on comments that the modern-day long-distance nationalists who supported the Khalistan movement or the Liberation Tigers of Tamil Eelam from their safety in Canada or Britain, were '[n]ot, like Kossuth and Mazzini, true exiles awaiting the circumstances of their triumphal return to the heimat [sic], but emigres who have no serious intention of going back to a home' (12). The distinction, I think, based on judging intentions, which I have already said remain more or less opaque to historians, and not on circumstances, is difficult to sustain (how safe was a Tamil Sri Lankan in Sri Lanka?). Whether these framing devices are appropriate to Har Dayal's life or not is difficult to decide; they are certainly not adequate. We could then go on to longer sets of observations about the national framework, diasporas, homeland national-isms and exiles, often in the context of understanding past and present issues relating to migration—but we would be quibbling about the meanings of terminologies, trying hard to fix our character in a grid that makes retro-spective sense to academics today, and in addition imposing anachronistic modes of thinking on our subject: see, for a representative sample of a vast literature, Basch, Schiller and Szanton Blanc, *Nations Unbound*; Schiller, Basch and Szanton Blanc, 'From Immigrant to Transmigrant', 48–63; Wimmer and Schiller, 'Methodological Nationalism and Beyond', 301–34; Vertovec, *Transnationalism*; Ong, *Flexible Citizenship*; Tölölyan, 'Beyond the Homeland', 27–45 (the distinction between exilic and diasporic national-isms I find slightly forced). This rather long footnote, and the previous one, is dedicated to the anonymous referee who wanted me to respond to the writers and theories cited above, and it could have been much longer; in short, the theorising does not work for Har Dayal's life and times. For a survey and a critique of this field, see Brubaker, 'The "Diaspora" Diaspora', 1–19.

of an individual who is usually rendered as a Punjabi and possibly as an Indian and a nationalist. To avoid such reductionism is, at least, revisionist.

## Acknowledgements

The title of this chapter is inspired by: 'Sometimes the light's all shining on me/Other times I can barely see/Lately it appears to me/What a long, strange trip it's been.' Robert Hunter, Bob Weir, Phil Lesh, Jerry Garcia, 'Truckin', from the Grateful Dead album *American Beauty* (1970). The Grateful Dead were from San Francisco, where Har Dayal spent a number of crucial years; the lyrics quoted above might well belong to a set of autobiographical reflections of Har Dayal. I am grateful to Franziska Roy, Ali Raza and Shalini Sharma for their comments on this chapter.

## References

Amin, Shahid, 'Approver's Testimony, Judicial Discourse: The Case of Chauri Chaura', in *Subaltern Studies V*, Ranajit Guha (ed.), 166–202, New Delhi: Oxford University Press, 1987.

Anderson, Benedict, *Imagined Communities: Reflections on the Origins and Spread of Nationalism*, London: Verso, 1983.

———, *Long-Distance Nationalism: World Capitalism and the Rise of Identity Politics*, The Wertheim Lecture. Amsterdam: Centre for Asian Studies, 1992.

———, *Under Three Flags: Anarchism and the Anti-Colonial Imagination*, London: Verso, 2005.

Appiah, Kwame Anthony, *Cosmopolitanism: Ethics in a World of Strangers*, New York: WW Norton, 2005.

Archibugi, Daniele, ed., *Debating Cosmopolitics*, London: Verso, 2003.

Barooah, Nirode K., *India and Official Germany 1886–1914*, Frankfurt: Lang, 1977.

———. *Chatto: The Life and Times of an Indian Anti-Imperialist in Europe*, New Delhi: Oxford University Press, 2004.

Basch, Linda, Nina Glick Schiller, and Cristina Szanton Blanc, *Nations Unbound: Transnational Projects, Postcolonial Predicaments and Deterritorialised Nation-States*, London: Routledge, 2003 [1994].

Baxter, Craig, *The Jana Sangh: A Biography of an Indian Political Party*, Bombay: Oxford University Press, 1971 [1969].

Bose, Arun Coomer, *Indian Revolutionaries Abroad, 1905–1922: In the Background of International Developments*, Patna: Bharati Bhawan, 1971.

Bose, Sugata, *His Majesty's Opponent: Subhas Chandra Bose and India's Struggle Against Empire*, Cambridge, MA: The Belknap Press of Harvard University Press, 2011.

Bourdieu, Pierre, 'L'illusion biographique', *Actes de la Recherche en Sciences Sociales* 62–63 (1986): 69–72; translated as 'The Biographical Illusion', by Yves Winkin and Wendy Leeds-Hurwitz, in *Identity: A Reader*, London: Sage Publications, 2004.

Breckenridge, Carol A., Sheldon Pollock, Homi K. Bhabha, and Dipesh Chakrabarty, eds, *Cosmopolitanism*, Durham: Duke University Press, 2002.

Brown, Emily, *Har Dayal: Hindu Revolutionary and Rationalist*, Tucson: University of Arizona Press, 1975.

Brown, Giles T., 'The Hindu Conspiracy, 1914–1917', *Pacific Historical Review* 17, no. 3 (August 1948): 299–310.

Brubaker, Rogers, 'The "Diaspora" Diaspora', *Ethnic and Racial Studies* 28, no. 1 (January 2005): 1–19.

Buchan, John, *Greenmantle*, London: Hodder and Stoughton, 1916.

Cheah, Pheng and Bruce Robbins, eds., *Cosmopolitics: Thinking and Feeling Beyond the Nation*, Minneapolis: University of Minnesota Press, 1998.

Dayal, Har, 'Social Conquest of the Hindu Race and Meaning of Equality', *Modern Review* (July–December 1909): 239–48.

———, 'Karl Marx — a Modern Rishi', *Modern Review* (March 1912): 273–86.

———, *44 Months in Germany and Turkey*, London: PS King, 1920.

———, *The Bodhisattva Doctrine in Buddhist Sanskrit Literature*, London: Routledge & Kegan Paul, 1932.

———, *Hints for Self-culture*, London: CA Watts, 1934, Reprint: Ferozpore Cantonment: English Book Depot, 1960.

Dharmavira, *Lala Har Dayal and Revolutionary Movements of His Times*, New Delhi: Indian Book Company, 1970.

Dignan, Don, 'The Hindu Conspiracy in Anglo-American Relations During World War I', *Pacific Historical Review* 40, no. 1 (February 1970): 57–76.

Fischer-Tine, Harald, 'Indian Nationalism and the "World Forces": Transnational and Diasporic Dimensions of the Indian Freedom Movement on the Eve of the First World War', *Journal of Global History* 2 (2007): 325–44.

Fraser, Thomas G., 'Germany and Indian Revolution, 1914–18', *Journal of Contemporary History* 12 (April 1977): 255–72.

Guha, Ranajit, 'The Prose of Counter-Insurgency', in *Subaltern Studies II*, Ranajit Guha (ed.), 45–88, Delhi: Oxford University Press, 1983.

Harvey, David, 'Cosmopolitanism and the Banality of Geographical Evils', *Public Culture* 12, no. 2 (2000): 529–64.

Hoover, Karl, 'The Hindu Conspiracy in California, 1913–1918', *German Studies Review* 8 (May 1985): 245–61.

Hopkirk, Peter, *On Secret Service East of Constantinople*, London: John Murray, 1994.

Hughes, Thomas L., 'The German Mission to Afghanistan, 1915–1916', *German Studies Review* 25 (October 2002): 447–76.

Jensen, Joan M., 'The "Hindu Conspiracy": A Reassesment', *Pacific Historical Review* 48, no. 1 (February 1979): 65–83.

Krüger, Horst, 'Har Dayal in Deutschland', *Mitteilungen des Instituts für Orientforschung* X, no. 1 (1964): 141–69.

Liebau, Heike, 'The German Foreign Office, Indian Emigrants and Propaganda Efforts Among the Sepoys', in *When the War Began We Heard of Several Kings': South Asian Prisoners in World War I Germany*, Franziska Roy, Heike Liebau, and Ravi Ahuja (eds), 96–129, New Delhi: Social Sciences Press, 2011.

Manjapra, Kris, 'The Illusions of Encounter: Muslim "Minds" and Hindu Revolutionaries in First World War Germany and After', *Journal of Global History* 1 (2006): 363–82.

———, 'The Mirrored World: Cosmopolitan Encounter between Indian Anti-Colonial Intellectuals and German Radicals, 1905–1939', unpublished PhD thesis, Harvard University, 2007.

———, *M.N. Roy: Marxism and Colonial Cosmopolitanism*, New Delhi: Routledge, 2010.

Oesterheld, Frank, *'Der Feind meines Feindes ist mein Freund': Zur Tätigkeit des* Indian Independence Committee (IIC) *während des Ersten Weltkrieges in Berlin*, unpublished *Magisterarbeit*, Humboldt-Universität zu Berlin, 2004.

Ong, Aihwa, *Flexible Citizenship: The Cultural Logics of Transnationality*, Durham: Duke University Press, 1999.

Paul, E. Jaiwant and Shubh Paul, *Har Dayal: The Great Revolutionary*, New Delhi: Roli Books, 2003.

Popplewell, Richard J, *Intelligence and Imperial Defence: British Intelligence and the Defence of the Indian Empire 1904–1924*, London: Frank Cass, 1995.

Prakash, Indra, *A Review of the History and Work of the Hindu Mahasabha and the Hindu Sangathan Movement*, 2nd ed., Delhi: Akhil Bharatiya Hindu Mahasabha, 1952.

Pratap, Raja Mahendra, *Reflections of an Exile*, Lahore: Indian Book Co, 1946.

———, *My Life Story of Fifty five [sic] Years (December 1886–December 1941)*, Dehradun: World Federation, 1947.

Puri, Harish K., *Ghadar Movement: Ideology, Organisation and Strategy*, Rev. edn., Amritsar: Guru Nanak Dev University, 1993 [1983].

Puri, Harish K., *Ghadar Movement: A Short History*, New Delhi: National Book Trust, 2011.

Ramnath, Maia, *The Haj to Utopia: How the Ghadar Movement Charted Global Radicalism and Attempted to Overthrow the British Empire*, Berkeley: University of California Press, 2011.

Roy, Franziska, 'International Utopia and National Discipline: Youth and Volunteer Movements in Interwar South Asia', in *The Internationalist Moment: South Asia, Worlds, and World Views, 1917–39*, Ali Raza, Franziska Roy and Benjamin Zachariah (ed.), 150–87. New Delhi: Sage, 2014.

Sareen, Tilak Raj, *Indian Revolutionary Movement Abroad (1905–1920)*, New Delhi: Sterling, 1979.

Schiller, Nina Glick, Linda Basch, and Cristina Szanton Blanc, 'From Immigrant to Transmigrant: Theorizing Transnational Migration', *Anthropological Quarterly* 68, no. 1 (January 1995): 48–63.

Sedition Committee *Report*, Calcutta: Superintendent, Government Printing, 1918.

Smedley, Agnes. *Daughter of Earth*, London: Virago, 1979 [1927].

Siddiqi, Majid Hayat, 'Bluff, Doubt and Fear: The Kheiri Brothers and the Colonial State, 1904–1945', *Indian Economic Social History Review* 24 (1987): 233–63.

Tölölyan, Khachig, 'Beyond the Homeland: From Exilic Nationalism to Diasporic Nationalism', in *The Call of the Homeland: Diaspora Nationalisms Past and Present*, Allon Gal, Athena S. Leoussi and Anthony D. Smith (eds), 27–45, Leiden: Brill, 2010.

Vertovec, Stephen, *Transnationalism*, New York: Routledge, 2009.

Vertovec, Stephen and Robin Cohen, eds, *Conceiving Cosmopolitanism: Theory, Context and Practice*, Oxford: Oxford University Press, 2002.

Wimmer, Andreas and Nina Glick Schiller, 'Methodological Nationalism and Beyond: Nation-State Building, Migration and the Social Sciences', *Global Networks* 2, no. 4 (2002): 301–34.

Zachariah, Benjamin, *Developing India: An Intellectual and Social History, c. 1930–1950*, New Delhi: Oxford University Press, 2005.

———, *Playing the Nation Game: The Ambiguities of Nationalism in India*, New Delhi: Yoda Press, 2011.

## Archival Material Cited

*Auswärtiges Amt,* Berlin
*Politisches Archiv des Auswärtigen Amtes*
File series WK 11s and WK 11f

## British Library, London

India Office Records: Indian Political Intelligence file L/P&J/12/1.

## Maharashtra State Archives, Bombay

MSA: Home (Special) 60-D (h), 1939–41

## National Archives of India, New Delhi (NAI)

NAI: External Affairs (External), 1939, 234-X (Secret)
NAI: Foreign & Political, General, Proceedings, January 1922, Nos: 870–886 B
NAI: Foreign & Political, War B (Secret), Progs. February 1916, Nos. 32–34
NAI: Home (Political) 192 Part B, 1924
NAI: Home (Political), Proceedings, November 1919, Nos. 23–24
NAI: Home (Political): KW to 9/V-32, 1932

## West Bengal State Archives, Calcutta

Intelligence Bureau Records, IB Sl No 12/1915, File No. 102/1915

### *Zentrum Moderner Orient*, Berlin
Krüger papers, Box 7, File 49, No. 2
Krüger papers, Box 6, File 24, No. 1

# ✠ 9

# Communism and 'Democracy': Punjab Radicals and Representative Politics in the 1930s

*Shalini Sharma*

Indians inherited much of their version of democracy from their colonial rulers. This is not to agree with apologists of empire who celebrate the British attempts to democratise the areas under their rule. Neither can it be said that British administrators were overly concerned at spreading the virtues of the Westminster system up and down the Indian subcontinent while they dealt with wars, and taxation, political resistance and ungrateful princes on a daily basis. However, it is difficult to see how independent India would have developed into the largest functioning democracy in the world without the representative structures set up by the British. In addition, it follows that these structures, blatantly undemocratic as they were, created arenas where politics was officially played out in the years before independence. Politicians changed their policies and direction to fit the structures set up by the British. However, this was not a one-way street as the clamour of different interest groups in each provincial government of British India itself transformed the political structures in which they were trying to be heard. The story of the radical Left in the 'politically backward' Punjab during and after the election in 1937 illustrates this point. This chapter will suggest that their example also presages the workings of democracy in independent India.

Colonial Punjab offers a worthy template of independent India because of its dominant agricultural power bases and its celebrated cross-communal linkages. Within this arena a small group of communists and socialists, 13 of a total of 175, was elected into the Legislative Assembly in 1937. Despite their size, they succeeded in carving out a niche for themselves in a very hostile field and they were able to articulate their political demands effectively, which in turn influenced the ideological foundations of the newly independent Indian state.

The fact that they took part in the election was not altogether consistent with their previous actions however. Indeed in the late 1920s, the organised Left, under the aegis of the Naujawan Bharat Sabha, the Communist Party and the Kirti Kisan movement, had a very clear and definite vision of democracy. In the columns of *Kirti,* the government of the Punjab and its legislative assembly was regularly denounced. In its place,

> Communists wish to establish a real democracy, but we think that a real democracy cannot be attained under the capitalistic social system, nay, both these things are contradictory to each other. What equal right can a poor man have as compared with a rich man at present?[1]

'Real' democracy was not to be based upon the Westminster model. Nor was it simply to be a replica of the Soviet system. Actually, the New World, quite as much as Russia, influenced and inspired many of these young radical socialists. Some young Punjabis had made America their home, and they had been influenced by living in a country where liberty, rights and freedom were written into the constitution.[2] Of course, some of them, particularly the Ghadars, had left the United States, disillusioned that they had not been given the rights of citizenship in full measure because of their race. Nevertheless, even the Ghadars understood and valued the rights that the people of the United States possessed under the constitution.

---

[1] Copy of *Kirti* (Urdu), August 1928, translated by Morid Husain, Government of India, *Meerut Conspiracy Case, Prosecution Exhibits*, 84, NMML.

[2] Home Political File 375/25, NAI. This respect was also illustrated by the proclamation that 'The object of the association shall be to establish a Federated Republic of the United States of India by an organised and armed revolution ... the final form of the constitution of the Republic shall be framed and declared by the representatives of the people at the time when they will be in a position to enforce their decisions'.

Speeches by the radicals warned the people of the Punjab of nationalist politicians who claimed to speak for the people. Their own emphasis was on the emancipation of the masses. Calling upon Punjab to question the accepted notions of deference and representation, they questioned the standing of nationalist leaders and instead urged a variant of communism tailored to the needs of the Punjabi peasantry, which eschewed communal politics, got rid of caste inequalities and above all would win India freedom from colonial oppression.

By the late 1930s, these very same people were appealing to different religious communities in a very specific religious idiom, comprehensively aligned with the Indian National Congress and fully participating in the legislative proceedings imposed by the British Raj. It would be too easy to explain these actions by referring to a particular bent in the communist personality as has been done by many Cold War historians.[3] Rather it may be more beneficial to examine, first, the constraints and opportunities through which they operated and, second, how their political choices then determined local understandings of communism and, in this case, democratic practice.

The 1930s marked a new phase in Indian politics. The national movement, Congress, had now to make friends capable of winning at the ballot box and find ways of influencing a much enlarged electorate. These developments had an impact on communists and socialists, who for their part also had to devise new tactics to protect and consolidate their political position, both locally and nationally. Underlying this sea change were two major developments: the Communal Award of 1932 and the Government of India Act of 1935. By enshrining the principle of Muslim separatism in the constitutional arguments by which India was given a much greater measure of provincial autonomy, the Award and the Act that followed it changed the rules of the game, and this led, in the Punjab as elsewhere in India, to a realignment of the major political groupings.

It is well known that the 1935 Act was a strategy for the British to stay on in India and to retain hold over the key determinants of

---

[3] The epitome of this genre was Overstreet and Windmiller, *Communism in India*.

power and sovereignty by a retreat to the centre, and not (as some Whig interpretations would have it) a significant milestone in a planned and staged withdrawal from the empire. What are less well known are the ways in which the small print of the electoral arrangements introduced in 1935 was designed, as in the reforms of 1920, to fortify the hands of those perceived to be Britain's collaborators and friends and to weaken its critics and enemies. By recasting the electoral balance between town and countryside in favour of the latter, the Legislative Assembly in the Punjab, in which, under the Montagu and Chelmsford reforms, the rural constituencies outnumbered urban constituencies by four to one, the towns now had only 19 seats, whereas the countryside had 130, or a ratio of seven to one between secure rural localities and the hotspots of urban unrest. Urban representation in effect had been halved.[4] The plan was that urban 'dissent' and militancy were to be redressed in the new arrangements by fortifying the hand of loyal peasants and landed interests. These moves were carefully calculated with political canniness, indeed cunning, in a province regarded as strategically vital, and they were further afforced by provisions at the centre to prevent any combined assault by provinces upon central citadels.

The party that had been nurtured by the British to represent these dominant agricultural interests was the Unionist Party. The influence of the Unionist Party and its leadership upon the making of the 1935 Government of India Act can hardly be exaggerated. In some respects, the Act, and the Award that preceded it, was written to a Unionist brief: Muslims got 86 of the 175 seats in the new Assembly, guaranteeing the Muslims majority of *c.* 55 per cent of the population almost half the seats (49 per cent), thereby assuring their continued dominance over the politics of the Punjab.[5] Since the very considerable measure of provincial autonomy that the Act gave them largely insulated the Punjab and its politicians from the all-India stage, the Unionists could continue, in a Punjab ring-fenced, to an extent, from what was going on in the rest of India, to plough their regional furrows despite major changes taking place beyond their provincial boundaries.

---

[4] Report of the Committee in connection with the Delimitation of Constituencies, *Parliamentary Papers 1935–36*, Volume IV, 55.

[5] Mitra, *Indian Annual Register, 1932, Volume II* , 236.

The 1935 Act weakened, and almost destroyed, the fledgling Congress movement in the Punjab, a development that in its turn changed its relationship with the radical Left. Since the 1920s, Congress in the Punjab had divided into two warring factions, with rather different spheres of influence, different sources of local support and a different focus to their efforts at political mobilisation.[6] However, they had much in common as well. Congress was already so weak in the Punjab, indeed on the verge of extinction, that its divided leadership realised that their internecine strife might be the end of both houses. Hence, both factions of this much-weakened Congress in the Punjab had reason to bury the hatchet and join in resisting the government to win a share of representation under the new electoral arrangements. Both factions spoke with one voice on the Poona Pact, by which the 'depressed classes' were denied separate electorates under the provision of the Communal Award. The all-India imperatives that made Congress so keen to keep the depressed classes within the Hindu fold are self-evident. However, in the Punjab, the provisions of the Poona Pact led to severe cuts in the already exiguous representation of Hindus in the General seats. Because of the Poona Pact, eight of 43 Hindu or General seats were henceforth reserved for members of the depressed classes.

---

[6] Since Lala Lajpat Rai's death in 1928, Congress in the Punjab had divided into two warring factions, that of Dr Satyapal on the one hand and on the other that of his rival Dr Gopichand Bhargava, who captured Lajpat Rai's Servants of the People Society. By claiming to be Lajpat Rai's political legatee, Bhargava and his faction, moreover, had joined with the Congress High Command to claim to be spokespersons and protectors of trading and non-agricultural Hindu interests in the province. The other faction of the Congress in the Punjab was also predominantly Hindu. It too had its roots in similar Arya Samaj soil. However, Satyapal's faction played down its specifically Hindu identity, hoping instead to gain influence by capturing existing networks of Congress workers in the towns. Satyapal, in the 1920s the man behind the Naujawan Bharat Sabha, which had done so much to radicalise students in the Punjab, had a record of working on the ground in the Punjab's urban constituencies. Yet the rift between Bhargava and Satyapal and their factions was to dominate and distract Congress politics in the province for years to come.

One attempted resolution to what was in fact an impossible dilemma was to try and re-brand the Punjab Congress to appeal to the much larger rural electorate and to forge alliances with parties that had already shown that they were more in tune than Congress with the aspirations of the new voters. One such group was the radical socialists and communists in the Punjab. From uncertain beginnings, they had become a force that had made inroads into the Punjabi hinterland. The context of Punjab politics had changed, and with it, the political trajectory of the radicals. Both factions of the Punjab Congress forged alliances with comrades, 'atheistic' and 'doctrinaire' though they were, and despite their having been previously shunned by Congressmen. In other arenas of Indian politics, the strategy of Gandhi and the Congress High Command is well known. That strategy looked to Congress cadres, recruited primarily from dominant agricultural castes, mainly from central and western India, who were urged to direct their energies to constructive work, 'harijan uplift' and spinning the yarn. However, there were other leaders in Congress, disillusioned by the stop–start tactics of civil disobedience, who wanted to attack its inherently conservative and capitalist leadership and transform it into a socialist body. In 1934, these leaders set up the Congress Socialist Party, which held its first conference on 17 May 1934 in Patna,[7] just when the government was about to outlaw the Communist Party of India under powers it had arrogated to itself under the Criminal Law Amendment Act.

The big question for our present purposes, however, is how the radical Left responded to these challenges within a rapidly changing political environment.

In July 1934, the Punjab government outlawed five communist and socialist organisations[8] and soon after one more.[9] In taking these draconian measures, Lahore was the first provincial government in India to act, reflecting its particular sensitivities to the perceived

---

[7] Mitra, *Indian Annual Register, 1934, Volume 1*, 341–42; Lakhanpal, *History of the Congress Socialist Party*, 12.

[8] Home Political File 7/20/1934, Reports from Local Governments regarding action taken under the Criminal Law Amendment Act, 1908, to declare local Communist Associations or Organisations to be Unlawful, NAI.

[9] Action taken against Communists under the Criminal Law Amendment Act, 1908, 1935–1937, IOR/L/PJ/12/474, OIOC.

threat from the Left. After communism was once again outlawed, the party's political choices became significantly narrower.

Parroting their master's voice in Moscow, Indian communists were required to condemn the Congress, its Central Committee denouncing Congress as its real enemy and mocking fellow travellers such as Nehru.[10] However, within a year, things had changed dramatically. The world was in flux, whether in the Far East or in Europe. For the first time, Lenin's doctrine that there could be circumstances when the priorities of national liberation took precedence over those of the class struggle made sense in a substantial setting. In India, the recently organised Congress Socialist Party began to win a measure of support among militant youth within the Congress ranks. To leverage the radical trends in Congress, the Indian Communist Party's manifesto urged its cadres to accept the Congress for what it was: a mass movement despite being led by Gandhi, a leader who was usually described in communist parlance as a 'reactionary'. Hence, its members were urged to join the mass movement headed by Congress but to try and give it a new leadership.[11]

Earlier in 1934, Sohan Singh Josh, the leading communist of Punjab, had tried and failed to unite all the groups on the Left in the Punjab. The main reason for his failure was that each faction still had its own distinct source of money, whether Ghadar links in the US, or the Comintern or more local providers of funds such as the Congress Socialist Party or the Naujawan Bharat Sabha. If they had united to form one official party, it was likely that they would have

---

[10] 'Draft Political Theses of the Communist Party of India' adopted by the Provincial Central Committee in December 1933. Published in 'The Communist', Central Organ of the Communist Party of India. In Basu, *Documents of the Communist Party of India, Volume III*, 143–63. Also see Verma, *From Marxism to Democratic Socialism*.

[11] 'In order to survive the crisis it has got involved in, under the inspired guidance of Mahatma, the Congress must be a militant mass organisation. To undergo such a transformation it must have a clearly defined programme of National democratic revolution, and a new leadership that can guide it in the struggle for the realisation of the programme. Nationalism that is the striving of the oppressed and exploited masses to be free from imperialism is a revolutionary movement'. Home Political File 24/1/1935, Communist Party of India Manifesto, NAI.

lost some of these inflows of funds and certainly quarrelled over the division of the spoils.[12]

However, Josh did manage to set up a Karza (or debt) Committee, which contained representatives of all these factions, to push for debt relief for the Punjab peasantry, demonstrating that on particular issues the left could sometimes work together, while remaining separate and divided institutionally.[13] From time to time, the Congress Socialists and Kisan Sabhas joined to organise strikes against rents or water rates; in these campaigns, they had a measure of success in matters that concerned the people. However, the communists could exploit popular discontents only if they were prepared to adopt flexible tactics and eschew the Bolshevik dogma. This is what the Communist Party of Great Britain, in particular Rajani Palme Dutt and Ben Bradley, advised them to do, stressing how important it was to achieve 'Unity of all the anti-imperialist forces in the common struggle'.[14] In fact, this policy suited the Punjab conditions quite well, and markedly better than those of some other provinces. In the Punjab, the Congress was weak and hence there was not such a gulf between its position and that of communists and socialists as elsewhere in India. In the Punjab, the Communist Party's line of depicting Gandhi as a betrayer of the nationalist cause, particularly by his failure to prevent the hanging of the young revolutionary Bhagat Singh in March 1931, echoed what everyone to the left of centre already thought. 'The Mahatma sits on the shoulders of the forces of the national revolution like the old man of the sea, paralysing their power to think by blind faith, dampening their will to fight by transforming the nationalist politics into a mystic metaphysical cult'.[15] Gandhi, in the opinion of these self-appointed men of the

---

[12] Mubarak Saghar, Oral History, NMML.

[13] Fifty-two members were elected to a Central Committee at the first Kisan Karza meeting on 3 March 1935. Home Political File 18/3/35, Fortnightly Report March 1935, NAI.

[14] 'The Anti-Imperialist People's Front in India' by Rajani Palme Dutt and Ben Bradley. Also known as 'Dutt–Bradley Thesis'. Published in *IMPRECOR*, 29 February 1936. In Basu, *Documents of the Communist Movement in India*, Vol. 3, 219–34.

[15] Home Political Report 24/1/1935, Communist Party of India Manifesto, NAI.

future, was a 'has-been' who had outlived his usefulness. At the same time, pragmatists among the communists recognised the potential of Nehru's brand of nationalism and particularly that of the Congress Socialist Party, in which swaraj and alleviating poverty were two sides of the same coin, very much the message that the communists previously had tried to convey to India's politicians.

The increasingly radical language used by Nehru made it acceptable for communists to be seen to express similar sentiments in similar terms. It also helped them appear more plausible candidates in the upcoming elections of 1937. Hence, the Punjab proved to be the seedbed of new collaborations between the Congress and communists, foreshadowing similar developments in the rest of India.

## Tickets

The Punjab Provincial Congress vociferously advocated a boycott of elected ministries after the 1937 elections. (They had no chance of winning.) Nevertheless they were determined to fight the elections. This meant that they joined in the scramble in the Punjab to obtain tickets.[16] In 1934, the tough man of the Congress High Command, Vallabhbhai Patel had tried to impose some order and control over the rank and file of the Congress. He was determined to control the nomination of all Congress candidates in the upcoming elections.[17] By strict rules on how the provinces and districts of the Congress were to be organised and disciplined, by rules on membership, the wearing of khadi and the spinning of cotton, he imposed the will of the High Command over the all-important patronage of allocating tickets to stand for election. In the Punjab at first it appeared as if these measures had achieved their purpose. Gopichand Bhargava and his faction reorganised the Punjab Congress Committee constitution under the new guidelines from above and maintained a firm grip on all of the important Congress posts in the province. However, this was not achieved without a struggle and many old Congressmen did not like the new Congress constitution. Thus began another round of complaints, accusations and wrangling. In later years, one faction was even accused of physically destroying votes cast in a local Congress

---

[16] Home Political File, 18/10/35, Fortnightly Report October 1935, NAI.
[17] Mitra, *Indian Annual Register, 1934, Volume II*, 209.

election by the novel and indigestible method of eating them.[18] It looked as if such disputes would dominate the 1937 election in the Punjab, and continue long after them. Therefore, the rules of who could be or could not be Congress candidates had to be relaxed in the Punjab. Consequently, tickets could be given to anyone the local Congress leaders believed might successfully win against Unionist candidates. With this simple strategy in the ascendant, every faction recruited individuals who were well-known communists and socialists to boost Congress's chances in rural Punjab and particularly amongst communities that hitherto had associated Congress only with urban Hindus. For instance, Master Kabul Singh, a young and enthusiastic communist, was given a ticket in rural East Jullunder, a hotbed of factional disputes.[19] Raghbir Kaur won a woman's ticket in preference to other candidates because of her socialist connections, whereas a Ghadarite communist, Swatanter Singh, was given a Sikh ticket even though he was still in jail. Overall, six radical Sikhs got Congress tickets.

Although remaining predominantly Hindu in membership in the 1937 elections, the Congress in the Punjab did put up some Muslims, such as Mian Iftikharuddin, to contest seats. Reports suggested that Iftikharuddin was more influenced by communist propaganda than that of Congress.[20] Other fellow travellers, such as Mohammad Alam, himself sometime a member of the Congress Working Committee, now set up exclusively Muslim political parties in an attempt to win the Muslim vote.[21]

---

[18] Report by Punjab Provincial Congress Committee, *Presidential election dispute*, 16 February 1939, G-58-60/1939, All India Congress Committee Papers, NMML.

[19] In late 1937, a Jullunder stalwart described him as 'a man who has spent the best portion of his life in jail and whom I have found to be very actively engaged in Congress work with his group. This group is likely to Emerge as a Workers' Party in powering the province in the real Congress elections, leaving both Dr Gopichand and Dr Satyapal high and dry. It will be for the good of this country I am sure'. Letter from G. C. Sondhi to Jawaharlal Nehru, 5 October 1937, P-17, Part 1, All India Congress Committee Papers, NMML.

[20] Home Political File 18/9/41, Fortnightly Report September 1941, NAI.

[21] Home Political File 111/1937, NAI.

The Ahrar (or Freedom) Party was another Muslim party that had its roots in the Deobandi movement of Lucknow.[22] Its following was mainly in urban Punjab and its leaders decided to cooperate with Congress, the Communists and the Congress Socialists to campaign against the 1935 constitution. Independents, such as the veteran campaigner Dr Saifudin Kitchlew and Sohan Singh Josh, also joined forces with Congress. Kitchlew had been arrested in 1919 just before the Jallianwala Bagh massacre and now stood as an independent candidate in the Amritsar Muslim urban constituency, whereas Josh stood as a Socialist Independent in the rural Sikh seat of Amritsar. Congress was not the only party to draw upon communists and socialists in this effort to garner support in the province. The Shiromani Akali Dal of the Sikhs followed suit, seeing an opportunity for the Akalis to benefit from the opportunities in the 1937 elections by making new allies among the radical Left.

## Propaganda

Following the logic of separate electorates, every candidate for election in 1937, whether Unionist, Congress, Socialist, Akali or Ahrar, had to appeal first and foremost to his or her own religious community. This blunt fact had many implications. Above all, it meant raising one's standing in the community by stressing religion. This required political ideology or a secular stance to take a back seat. However, in as far as all candidates had a similar message, Unionists included, it was the call for redistributive justice in a broadly socialist society.[23] Sikander Hyatt Khan, the leader of the Unionist party, was

---

[22] The party was founded in 1929 by ex-khilafatists and ex-Congress Muslims around a programme that combined egalitarianism and a strong religious commitment to shar'iat. See Kamran, Chapter 3.

[23] This was articulated clearly in a newspaper article written by K. B. Mian Ahmad Yar Khan Daultana, MLC, Chief Secretary of the Unionist Party, in February 1937. 'The founder of the Unionist Party, the late Mian Sir Fazl-i-Husain, was a far sighted politician. He always laid the greatest possible emphasis on his perfectly sound theory that the intellectual classes and big landlords could retain the political picture only by identifying themselves sincerely with the interests of the poor. If they want to retain their political

thus able to claim that the Unionists were the only truly secular party in the Punjab, whereas his fellow traveller, Shri Chhotu Ram, the Unionist leader of Hindu Jats in East Punjab and former President of the Punjab Legislative Council, argued that the Unionists were the 'true Congressmen' of the province. In his opinion, the Unionists alone were untainted by communalism, the central plank in their programme being the non-communal demand for a fairer deal for the Punjab peasantry.

So suddenly, the Punjab was alive with all manner and sort of politicians claiming to be the guardians of 'true' socialist and Congress ideals.

During the election campaigns, Nehru himself was one of the most frequent visitors from the High Command to the Punjab. He came not only to sort out the wrangling inside the Congress, but also to try and disseminate the Congress message. Impressed by the record of the Soviet government, Nehru also had close ties with Labour politicians in Britain and used the election campaigns to outline his vision of an independent and socialist India. Indeed, one historian has gone so far as to assert that Nehru was the first politician to make the idea of socialism popular in the Punjab.[24] Whatever the truth of such a claim, Nehru, with his high all-India profile, gave a fillip to local Congress and radical politicians alike on his whirlwind tours of the Punjab.

However limited his political influence in the Punjab, Nehru was, nevertheless, a radicalising force, delivering speech after speech on the need for independence and with independence the need to achieve a greater degree of economic equality for India's peoples. This was the heart and centre of Nehru's 'mass contact' campaign,[25] his aim being

---

leadership they must pay a price for it, the price being that they must not look to the economic interests of their own class but try to promote a socialist programme'. *Civil and Military Gazette*, 7 February 1937, Lahore, NMML.

[24] It was alleged that he introduced the concept to Punjabis in 1927 upon his return from revolutionary Russia. On describing the impact of a speech by Nehru at the annual session of the Punjab Provincial Political Conference in April 1928, Josh states, 'It was for the first time that the word socialism became familiar in the political atmosphere of Punjab'. Josh, *Communist Movement in Punjab (1926–1947)*, 80.

[25] See Hasan, 'The Muslim Mass Contact Campaign', 58–76.

to broaden the appeal of Congress among peasants and Muslims and to mobilise new and vital bases of support where the Congress message had not previously reached. This was of particular significance in the Punjab, where the social and religious background of most local Congressmen stood in the way of their making a successful appeal to the new voters, peasants and Muslims alike.

An interesting angle on Nehru comes from provincial intelligence sources, which, reluctant though they were to recommend internment of India's most prominent politicians, nevertheless kept an eagle eye on his activities and his impact upon the Punjab. One such report described Nehru's activities in the following words:

> In all his speeches he stressed economic matters and the need for a socialist order and he emphasised that the amelioration of the conditions of workers and peasants and the establishment of a socialist state could not be effected without first securing independence from British rule.[26]

Nehru also saw the elections as an important milestone in the long and hard journey towards independence, but from a rather different perspective, of course, than that of the government: 'He impressed on his hearers that the battle of freedom would not be won in the Councils, but in the fields, in the factories and in the bazaars'.[27] For the government, however, the most worrying aspect of Nehru's visits was the impact he had on rural Punjab:

> The effect of his visits to the countryside is likely to be more dangerous. The peasants are eager to hear solutions of their economic difficulties and the Pandit's visit has proved the existence among the rural class of interest in such questions as socialism and independence and has stimulated this interest.[28]

According to this report, Nehru was making socialism legitimate in the eyes of peasantry of the Punjab, which heretofore had somehow kept isolated from such a dangerous infection.[29]

---

[26] Home Political File 4/14/36, NAI.
[27] Home Political File 18/6/36, Fortnightly Report June 1936, NAI.
[28] Ibid.
[29] Ibid.

Local activists prepared for Nehru's meetings months in advance. Village and district committees set up fairs and held gatherings to ensure that the new messiah's coming was not unannounced. Nehru's visits ruptured the calm of district life, as locals took advantage of them to promote their own agendas.

> There is great activity among Socialists and communists in this district in preparation for a conference which Pandit Jawaharlal Nehru is expected to attend. Small parties are going round the villages holding meetings to advertise the conference. Much of the speaking is actionable and all of it is objectionable and dangerous when delivered to illiterate audiences. It is a crude blend of socialism, communism and hardly veiled sedition, and full vantage is being taken of any local grievance, real or imaginary to stir up discontent.[30]

The officer charged with analysing 'the Nehru effect' came to a less-generous conclusion, portraying Nehru as a glamorous would-be superstar rather than a serious politician with a cogent message. He reported Nehru as being:

> Held in great respect by the people collected in the meeting especially by the Hindu women... I believe there was no one in the meeting who understood to begin with what Jowahar [sic] Lal was driving at, and secondly no one was sufficiently interested in the subject to think out details and question him... All that they had come for was to see Pandit Jawaharlal — the man who had been educated at Harrow, had lived a luxurious life in England and in India, the man who had had his clothes washed in Paris and the man who had now forsaken all the luxuries of like and the wealth of his family and had undergone numerous imprisonments for the sake of his country.[31]

All of India — and the Punjab was no exception — loves a festival or *tamasha*, and Nehru could always be relied upon to put on a good show. After all, he was known to have renounced pelf and purse for the sake of the greater good of the people of India, something that went down well in a province steeped in traditions of martyrdom and self-sacrifice. He could, plausibly, be likened to heroes of yore

---

[30] Ibid.
[31] Home Political File 4/14/36, NAI.

in the Punjab and be presented as a model for the politically minded young men of the province.

Several aspects of Nehru's impact upon the Punjab call to be noted. First, his visits led two Hindu candidates who were opposed to Congress policy to make 'spectacular withdrawals'.[32] Moreover, in the heat of the general elections, his presence did dampen down the quarrels and rivalry in the Punjab Congress, albeit temporarily. Third and perhaps most importantly, the line he took in his speeches made it legitimate for those on the left to demand fundamental, if not quite revolutionary, changes.

By linking socialism with nationalism, Nehru helped create a context in which it was no longer out of bounds for Congressmen in the Punjab to talk about socialism and the rights of workers and peasants.

Nehru, of course, was only one of the many all-India leaders who came to the Punjab in the enterprise of attempting to dislodge the Unionists. In much the same way, Jinnah, the leader of the All India Muslim League, also realised the importance of trying to improve the League's standing in this critically important Muslim-majority province. On his famous incursion into the Punjab, Jinnah attended a number of student conferences and League meetings throughout the province, with an agenda that seemed designed to vilify the Unionist Ministry and to press for a joint League and Congress front in this anti-Unionist enterprise.[33] Interestingly, even in the election manifesto of the League, Jinnah, according to one intelligence official, included 'Congress doctrines with socialistic tendencies'.[34] The audiences he attracted consisted mainly of Muslim students and workers, who had enough of the 'reactionary'[35] Unionists. Most of these leaders, whether Congress or League, tried to raise the level of interest in the

---

[32] Home Political File 4/9/37, Extract from fortnightly report, January 1937, NAI.

[33] 'Mr M. A. Jinnah arrived in Lahore on the 10th of October and on the following day addressed a public meeting attended by about 6000 Mohammedans. The two main points from his speech were that he wanted "to break the Ministries which had already been formed here" and to hammer out a strong block to march together with the Hindus'. Home Political File 18/10/36, Fortnightly Report October 1936, NAI.

[34] Home Political File 18/6/36, Fortnightly Report June 1936, NAI.

[35] Ibid.

elections by using similar siren songs, and some of them had socialist overtones. Even though voting at the elections tended to run along tracks laid long ago, no one can doubt that the foundations had been built in the Punjab, and indeed beyond, upon which the socialist and mixed economy of independent India were to be constructed.

## Results

In vastly increasing the electorate by the 1935 Government of India Act, the British assumed that they would in these ways afforce the hands of their collaborators and friends. In almost every Hindu-majority province, the result of the elections proved to be spectacularly wrong. However, in the Punjab the elections did not upset British calculations. The Unionists achieved a landslide victory in nearly all Muslim constituencies as well as in the rural Hindu seats in the southeast of the province. In 1937, another Unionist ministry under Sir Sikander Hayat returned to office. This ministry was a coalition of the nine Hindu rural members returned by constituencies led by Chhothu Ram, three persons from the depressed classes, one European, one Anglo-Indian, two Indian Christian and all the rest Muslim, making a grand total of 95 Unionists in an Assembly of 175 members.[36]

In the Punjab, the elections of 1937 were not the victory of communal politics, but rather a triumph for the old political system that the British and their Unionist allies had set in place in the 1920s. It was a reaffirmation of the dominance of the Punjab's landlord agriculturalists and those who joined the army — in other words the traditional clients upon whom the Raj depended. In the election, the Muslim League was routed. The League was represented by only one member in the Assembly.[37]

---

[36] Chhottu Ram's group of rural Hindus will number about nine members, and will of course be staunchly Unionist. The failure of Congress in rural constituencies in the south-east, which border on the UP, is very satisfactory, and shows that, for the present at any rate, the Jats, Rajputs and Gujars of that part of the Province prefer their own tribal leaders to Congressmen'. Emerson to Linlithgow, 22 February 1937, Document 6 in Carter, *Punjab Politics, 1936–1939*, 77.

[37] Initially two League members were elected — Raja Ghazanfar Ali and Barkat Ali — but the former was tempted over to the governing party after the elections. Samad, *A Nation in Turmoil*, 31.

For its part, Congress won a mere 18 seats, only one of which was Muslim. By the make-up of the Punjab electorate and the careful drawing of constituency boundaries of the British and their Unionist allies, for the time being at least, had kept the all-India parties, whether Congress or League, out of the province.

Although Congress won only 18 seats, it was nevertheless the second largest party in the Assembly. Significantly, one in three, or six of these 18 Congress seats, were won by communists or socialists. The remainder were won from Hindu members of the Nationalist Congress Party. However meagre these victories, they were a cause for celebration in the Congress and they demonstrated just how far things had improved from the dire straits in which the party had been before the elections.

All in all, 13 persons known to have socialist and communist antecedents became MLAs (Members in the Legislative Assembly) in the Punjab Assembly. Congress had given six of them tickets to represent central rural tracts of the Punjab, including five former members of the Ghadar party. The communists Harjeet Singh and Master Kabul Singh were elected despite both of them being 'interned' in their villages under provisions of the Criminal Law Amendment Act. Indeed the government in the Punjab had to rescind these orders once they were elected as MLAs.

> Harjap Singh, the ex-State prisoner who was confined to his village, and Master Kabul Singh, another Communist worker who was ordered by Government not to make public speeches, have been released from all restrictions under the Punjab Criminal Law (Amendment) Act, 1935, to enable them to sit in the Punjab Assembly to which they were elected. Both of these members, along with other communist representatives in the Assembly, have since been very busy.[38]

Another 'radical' Congress socialist, Mian Muhammud Iftikharuddin, defeated a prominent Unionist leader at the polls. However, this triumph was attributed to Iftikharuddin being a leader of the newly enfranchised community of Arains, market gardeners, and being a scion of a prominent and wealthy Lahore family to boot, rather than a

---

[38] Home Political File 18/4/37, Fortnightly Report April 1937, NAI.

consequence of the popularity of his socialist views, of which he made much during his election campaign.[39] Sohan Singh Josh, who was returned from the Amritsar constituency, was another radical who won a seat. He described his own election campaign as being distinct and independent from both the Congress and the Muslim League, without benefit of the patronage of either party. Rather, his success was attributed to his popularity among Sikh farmers of the central Doab tracts in his constituency.[40] The 13 candidates who succeeded at the polls had taken advantage of an unprecedented opportunity to express their views in a forum from which they had previously been excluded. By gaining access to the arena of electoral politics, they now helped give the politics of the Punjab new orientations.

## Inside the Assembly

After 5 April 1937, those who had for so long dominated the Punjab Council now had to deal with a quite different breed of politicians, some of them — from their perspective — a rabble.

In the past, the Unionists, although loyal to the Raj, were wont to blame the British for all their difficulties; now the elections had changed poachers into gamekeepers. As the party in office, they had to defend what the state was doing. Before 1937, the Unionists had only one single Congress member (a woman) in opposition. Now they faced a phalanx of 35 Congress and Akali members, all of whom, on the first day the Assembly met, symbolically donned white caps and khadi clothes, as 'a visual demonstration of the new order'.[41] In the Assembly, which previously had been full of administrators and nominated members, this very visible opposition now took their seats; on the very first day, Dr Mohammad Alam asked why the members of the Assembly had to stand up to hear the Governor's speech to

---

[39] 'There is one Muslim Communist, a curious case, as he belongs to a family with very loyal traditions and was educated at the Chief's college and at Oxford. His election, however, was entirely due to his tribal influence, had no reference to communistic tendencies, and the Unionist Party ought later to be able to get hold of him'. Emerson to Linlithgow, 22 February 1937, Document 6 in Carter, *Punjab Politics, 1936–1939*, 77.

[40] Josh, *My Tryst with Secularism*, 213.

[41] Mitra, *Indian Annual Register, 1937, Volume 1*, 55.

the House.[42] In their white khadi, Congressmen brought a splash of colour to the Assembly by carrying Congress flags.

> The Congress benches in the Legislative Assembly today were gay with a profusion of miniature tricolour flags. They were placed on the desks in front of each member and showed vividly against the black plush of the seats... several members, including non-Congress members, such as Sir Mahommed Yakub, wore tricolour buttonholes on the lapels of their coats.[43]

On the second day of the session, the opposition staged a walkout over a dispute about the election of the Speaker. The tone of a much more confrontational parliamentary style had quickly been set within 48 hours. The opposition saw their role as to challenge the polite manners of high politics and the cosy closed shop of the Punjab Assembly. Many of them refused to speak in English even if they were fluent in the language;[44] and some of the newly elected members challenged each and every accepted norm of behaviour in the House. This was in line with the strategy advocated by the High Command to Congress members in provinces where they were not in a majority. These MLAs swiftly learnt the arts of becoming an effective parliamentary opposition — noisy and troublesome to boot leading a disgruntled Sikander Hyat Khan, the Chief Minister, to complain that opposition members who challenged him in the chamber were being 'disloyal'.[45]

All this was the froth and bubble rising out of deep currents in the new politics of the Punjab, and indeed of India. And it was particularly in the Punjab Legislative Assembly where radicals in opposition, whether Sikh or Congress, set themselves up as the champions of the peasantry and challenged the old Unionist claim to speak for the masses.

---

[42] Ibid., 156.

[43] *Civil and Military Gazette*, 3 April 1937, NMML.

[44] The Speaker finally made a ruling on 5 July 1938 that members could speak in the language of the province, prompting both Bhargava and, significantly, Sikander Hyat Khan to speak in Hindustani. Mitra, *Indian Annual Register, 1938, Volume 2*, 191.

[45] Zetland to Linlithgow, 27 June 1939, MSS EUR D609/11, OIOC.

On his very first appearance in the chamber, Sohan Singh Josh cut to the chase by asking how democracy should be defined. He questioned the legitimacy of an election in which 76 per cent of the population had been refused the right to vote. In his view, the Punjab could learn much from the Russian experience.[46] Thus, an Assembly in a province that had particular reason to fear the Bolshevik example now had to listen to Josh praising the Soviets and, to add insult to injury, in Urdu (a practice for which he was continually criticised since English remained the designated language of parliament in the Punjab even after permission was given for the vernacular to be used).

During the same debate, another issue was raised, which gave a hint of the wider radical agenda. It was asked whether those who collected revenue for the government, the *zaildars* and *lambardars*, and were charged with maintaining law and order and suppressing 'sedition', should, as servants and beneficiaries of the colonial state, be allowed to stand for election and represent the very people they were exploiting. A Congress Socialist colleague of Josh, Mian Iftikharuddin, was a fierce critic of things as they were in the Punjab. The system that ensured the hereditary rights of the Punjab's landed aristocracy was, in his opinion, the root of the evil.[47]

He also urged Punjabis to understand that the ways in which democracy worked in England were not relevant to India and to the Punjab. 'The position in England was that the English masses fought with their own countrymen in order to get rights for themselves. Here the situation is entirely different'.[48] Iftikharuddin, and others of his ilk, argued that Punjab's chamber was not just somewhere in which to raise the familiar themes of anticolonial rhetoric, idealising the

---

[46] *Punjab Legislative Assembly Debates*, 12 April 1937, 199.

[47] As Mian Iftikharuddin said, 'Again the problem involved here is far more important and wider than the mere question of lambardars or zaildars aspiring to represent their constituencies in this House. The question involved is as to whether the landed aristocracy is to rule us or whether the masses also are going to have a voice in the administration of the affairs of this province... It cannot be accepted as true that a post which is held on a hereditary basis makes a person who inherits it a true leader the moment the previous holder dies'. *Punjab Legislative Assembly Debates*, 12 April 1937, 200.

[48] Ibid., 79.

Soviet experience or criticising the political values of conservative Punjab. Rather, it should be a forum in which the grievances of the Punjab's underprivileged called to be addressed.

Hence, Iftikharuddin, for his part, frequently attacked the repression habitually practiced by lambardars, working in collusion with the police, of the Punjab's still mainly disenfranchised peasantry. Sohan Singh Josh and Hari Singh repeatedly tabled motions urging the government to do more for rural Punjab. When crops were destroyed by hailstorms in seven villages, it was Josh who raised the matter in the Assembly and called upon the government to step in and help. The debates of the Legislative Assembly are replete with such instances of radical intervention. When the Unionist government was persuaded to write off debt in a series of Agrarian Bills in 1938, this was seen as a victory for the Karza Committee,[49] and most Congress politicians in the Punjab had to go along with this rather more proactive line in favour of the peasantry.[50]

However, addressing the needs and concerns of the peasantry was not, of course, a new development in the Punjab. The British had seen themselves as the guardians of the Punjab peasants, their protectors against predators, moneylenders or even the vagaries of the monsoon.[51] What was new was the challenge to the old assumptions

---

[49] *National Front*, 30 October 1938, Communist Party of India Library, Ajay Bhavan, New Delhi.

[50] In the tradition of the long-standing alliance between the urban Hindu Punjabis and the Congress-led groups who had consistently campaigned against the Land Alienation Bills since 1901, Maulana Azad (the Congress Working Committee member charged with overseeing the actions of the Punjab in the Congress High Command) now ordered the Punjabi Congress MLAs to vote for the Agrarian Bills. In response, 'Dr Gopichand appears to have informed Azad that the orders will be obeyed but that he must find someone else to lead the Congress party in the Assembly, and it is said that another 14 other Congress men intend to follow Gopichand's example'. Zetland to Brabourne (Acting Viceroy), 8 August 1938, MSS EUR 609/10, OIOC.

[51] In its crudest form, 'In my time I have done what I could to serve the interests of the peoples of India, and particularly of the dumb masses who, in the tumult and the shouting of politics, are least likely to get a hearing'. O'Dwyer, *India as I Knew it*, p. x. Malcolm Darling's writings are testimony to this important aspect of the 'Punjab tradition', investigated, *inter alia*, by Clive Dewey in his *Anglo-Indian Attitudes*.

that the British were the true defenders of the Punjab peasantry. That the politicians of the Punjab had now visibly shifted their focus from the towns to the countryside was a cause for particular concern to the government.[52] Another straw in the wind that showed the changed climate was the sharp debate about the Punjab police and its relationship with the peasantry, all part and parcel of efforts to address the daily concerns of rural Punjab. Master Kabul Singh argued against a motion to increase police salaries. Indeed, Kabul Singh made unfavourable comparisons between the notoriously harsh police in Bengal and their Punjabi counterparts, and claimed that the Punjab police were if anything worse than policemen in Bengal. In the Punjab, those who tried to visit political prisoners were turned away with the simple, but deeply revealing dictum, 'This is Punjab sir'.[53] The claim that it was the police that kept the Punjab's rival communities from each others' throats was stood on its head by Kabul Singh's retort that 'I would charge the police with the responsibility for causing communal riots'.[54] These were strong words, uttered by a man who had served time; the very fact they could be openly stated in the Assembly reflects a fundamentally changed political atmosphere. In the chamber after 1937, Master Kabul Singh's words could not simply be ruled out of order as seditious. Strong language from persons who previously would simply have been thrown into jail had now to be tolerated in the state's parliamentary forum. Political Punjab, not just loyalists, lackeys and toadies, had won the right to speak out in the Assembly.

One small illustration of the radical activity in this forum is provided by a look at what actual questions they were asking in the chamber. MLAs routinely asked starred questions of ministers about the pressing issues of the day. In the Punjab Assembly, radical politicians used this procedure to repeatedly ask the same questions, about the state of political prisoners, the education of girls, the remission of taxes in areas where crops had been damaged and the corrupt practices of the Punjab police. These issues were raised in the House before 1937. However, the number of such questions

---

[52] Craik to Linlithgow, 10 May 1938, Document 46 in Carter, *Punjab Politics, 1936–1939*, 213.83 quote.
[53] *Punjab Legislative Assembly Debates*, 6 July 1937.
[54] Ibid.

increased drastically as did the time spent on them. So much so that Ministers and their opposition would conduct debates in the Punjab press over whether such questions and subsequent motions were a waste of time and tax payers' money or an integral part of democracy and giving voice to what was hitherto neglected (Figure 9.1).[55]

In short, the Punjab Assembly was a changed place, with *demos* making its tentative entry into a once strictly controlled and disciplined environment. The opposition tackled many matters previously regarded as taboo, such as the high salaries that ministers gave to themselves and all the privileges to which the old elites clung. Bit by bit, the opposition began to whittle away at the comfortably large majority the Unionists had on such issues as they voted upon. When

**Figure 9.1    Starred questions in the Punjab Assembly 1932–1940**

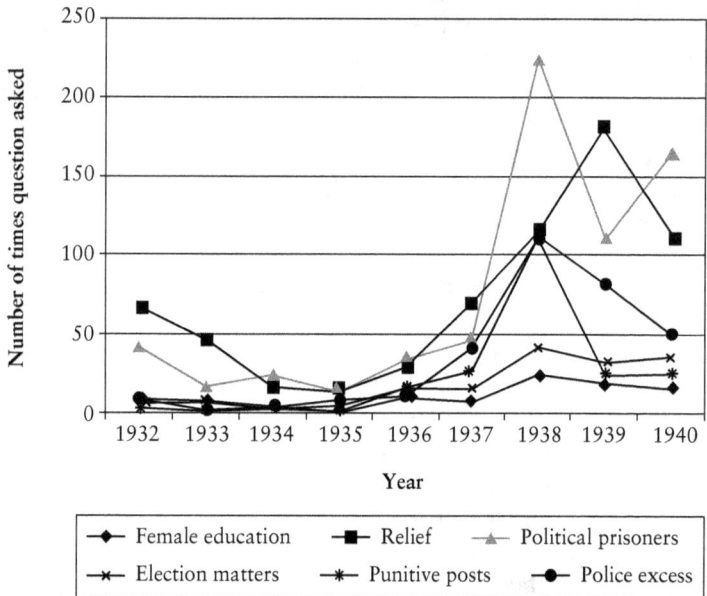

*Note:* Chart based on information supplied from the Punjab Assembly Debates, 1932–1940. One of the reasons for the rise in questions is that from 1937, the Assembly simply met for longer periods, but despite that proviso, proportionately more questions were still asked of these particular questions than the period before 1937.

---

[55] See *Civil and Military Gazette*, Lahore.

**Table 9.1 Starred questions in the Punjab Assembly, 1932–1940**

|                    | 1932 | 1933 | 1934 | 1935 | 1936 | 1937 | 1938 | 1039 | 1940 |
|--------------------|------|------|------|------|------|------|------|------|------|
| Female education   | 7    | 8    | 3    | 1    | 10   | 8    | 23   | 19   | 15   |
| Relief             | 68   | 47   | 17   | 13   | 30   | 68   | 116  | 182  | 112  |
| Political prisoners| 42   | 18   | 24   | 14   | 33   | 46   | 223  | 110  | 164  |
| Elections          | 5    | 6    | 1    | 3    | 16   | 15   | 42   | 33   | 35   |
| Punitive Posts     | 3    | 2    | 2    | 1    | 16   | 26   | 110  | 24   | 25   |
| Police Excess      | 9    | 2    | 4    | 7    | 10   | 40   | 110  | 82   | 51   |

the Assembly first met, the Unionists tended to win motions directed against their policies with majorities of between 50 and 60. However, after the defection of some key members this majority was virtually halved to around 30.

Driving these big changes was the fact that radicals, who previously had urged the Punjab to take the path of revolution outside the constitutional framework, now were making an impact inside the Assembly. This had the consequence of raising their standing in the Punjab, and also changed the ways in which people perceived the Punjab Legislative Assembly. In 1929, Bhagat Singh had thrown a bomb into the Central Legislative Assembly chamber, Delhi, in order, symbolically, to wake up those seated inside. Eight years later, the Assembly itself had become the most visible forum of dissent in the Punjab. Demonstrations and rallies often ended at its doors and this provided the politicians who sat inside the Assembly a legitimacy, which those outside now acknowledged and sought to influence. For example, 2000 students demonstrated against the government's record on civil liberties outside the Assembly in January 1938,[56] whereas thousands of peasants rallied against rising revenue and gave themselves up to be arrested in April 1939.[57]

The only way that the Punjab authorities could reassert control over the physical area around the Legislative Assembly was to put the organisers in jail and declare these meetings unlawful, a sledgehammer to break the increasingly hard radical nuts inside and outside the

---

[56] *National Front*, 13 February 1938, Communist Party of India Library, Ajay Bhavan, New Delhi.

[57] *National Front*, 2 April 1939, Communist Party of India Library, Ajay Bhavan, New Delhi.

Assembly.[58] The fact that radicals had become members of parliament provided them a legitimacy and a measure of influence that they had never previously had. Now, they were invited by trade unions to preside over their meetings; the public listened to their rhetoric with a new respect and even the authorities had to think twice before throwing them into jail. Above all, they now had licence to speak their minds.[59] The big change was that radicals used their position as elected members openly to advocate the very issues for which previously they had endured long spells in jail.

Intelligence officials were clearly worried that radical MLAs would stir up unrest among the Punjab peasants, in their eyes a once-contented 'yeomanry' now in dire danger of being infected with the virus of disaffection. Communist cadres had learnt to adapt to changing opportunities in contemporary politics and to exploit economic discontent to their political advantage.[60]

In his autobiography, Sohan Singh Josh describes how winning a seat in the 1937 election changed his own position.

> Before the election I was just a district leader. But after I was elected to the Punjab Legislative Assembly... I overnight became one of the leaders of entire Punjab. I was welcomed and honoured everywhere — a Communist getting elected to the Assembly was a big, and new, thing then in the eyes of the Punjabi people. My election not only raised my estimation in the minds of our people, but the election campaign also helped greatly the growth of the Communist movement in Punjab.[61]

Josh recognised that his victory at the polls raised his status as a leader in the Punjab and also raised the standing of communism in

---

[58] 'I have some hope that the Lahore Kisan morcha will now shortly collapse, as a considerable number of the more prominent organisers have been arrested and are being prosecuted, and the local authorities have been instructed to deal with jathas trying to enlist recruits in the districts adjoining Lahore as unlawful assemblies. During the second half of June only 124 arrests were made in Lahore on four days. On most days no people offered themselves for arrest'. Craik to Linlithgow, 7 July 1939, Document 96 in Carter, *Punjab Politics, 1936–1939*, 360.

[59] Home Political File 18/11/36, Fortnightly Report November 1936, NAI.

[60] Home Political File 18/4/37, Fortnightly Report April 1937, NAI.

[61] Josh, *My Tryst with Secularism*, 214.

the province.[62] Josh's damascene conversion to constitutionalism was not simply an obedient response to central party diktat. The process was more complex than that. However, it is undeniable that the party encouraged its followers to go down this constitutional path, as an official communist pamphlet written in 1938 suggests. Communists now began to have a different relationship with the Congress. Congress ministries were described as 'our' ministries: 'The Congress is our organisation, and therefore the Congress Ministers are people's ministers',[63] and Congress was the 'leading anti-imperialist organisation in the country'.[64] Communist pamphlets underlined the new political opportunities that came with Congress accepting office. The Legislative Assembly was now seen to be a dynamic institution, which could be deployed to transform the political scene. A new breed of politicians now had a chance to force government ministers to behave in the political arena quite differently from before.

In the Punjab, the first faltering steps towards constructing a constitutional response capable of challenging imperialism had now been taken. Finally, the constitution came to be viewed as a way of undermining the Raj. Therefore, the Left had come to accept that elections mattered and winning them was of the essence. For radicals and the colonial regime alike, the terms of political engagement had changed, and changed significantly, never to return to the unequal balance between the rulers and the ruled, which had been the essence of the Raj in the Punjab.

## Conforming to Traditional Political Mores

In these ways, during the 1930s, the colonial state and the radical Left both had to reconsider and then fundamentally transform

---

[62] Further evidence of Josh's own political acumen is perhaps indicated by the fact that he was elected General Secretary of the Punjab Provincial Congress Committee on April 16, 1939. Home Political File 18/4/39, Fortnightly Report April 1939, NAI.

[63] Home Political File 13/2/1938, C.P.I., 'The Communists and the Congress: Being the thesis on the role of the Indian Communists in the struggle for Complete Independence of India, (with a note by Krishna Swamy)' (Agra, 1938), ACI.

[64] Ibid.

their political strategies. To make the new constitution work, the Punjab administration could no longer shut out from the Assembly its political enemies, whether communists or Congress nationalists. Putting them into jail was no longer an option. For their part, the radical Left now wholeheartedly joined the electoral process, served as elected members and used their position in the Legislative Assembly to advance their cause. But, of course, these changes meant that both sides, with their very different and ultimately incompatible agendas, were bound to clash. Take, for example, the sensitive issue of recruitment in the Punjab: at all costs the British had to protect their ability to recruit soldiers from the Punjab, particularly once it was clear that war was on its way. Yet radical Punjabis had no intention of being tame collaborators, and they had the issue of recruitment very much in their sights. An essential element of the Punjab tradition was to promote the stereotypes of the martial and loyal Punjabi, the backbone of the British Indian Army. In the First World War, half the recruits of a massively increased army were recruited from the Punjab. For long, Punjabis had taken pride in their status as India's soldiers. They had done well by joining the army, both materially and in terms of social standing. To attack their role as Britain's enforcers in India and beyond was, in the Punjab, likely to be a double-edged sword. Thus, Congress and the radical Left alike had to tackle this issue differently and subtly, by lauding the martial tradition on the one hand but arguing that new channels for its expression had to be found.

The best exponent of these views, Sohan Singh Josh, proclaimed:

> They say that we Punjabis are a martial race and so we must join the British Army. I say yes we are a fighting race. We have gone to battle in the past and we shall do in the future but not for ₹18 a month, as mercenaries. We shall fight as soldiers, the battle of India's freedom.[65]

This peculiarly Punjabi stance challenged not only the Raj but also the central tenets of Gandhian nationalism, while reasserting a powerful provincial pride in martial traditions, which its people had nurtured over two centuries. Now, the radical line argued, it was important to learn the lessons of the past and deploy the martial talents of the

---

[65] *National Front*, 4 December 1938, Communist Party of India Library, Ajay Bhavan, New Delhi.

Punjab to the real enemy — colonialism. One way that politicians of all shades channelled these martial traditions was by creating militia wings of their political party. Hence, by 1939, every political party in the Punjab apart from the Unionists had set up some sort of a militia or '*fauj* hr#' of its own.[66] One example of this type of organisation was the National Militia Congress, active in both Amritsar and Lahore.[67] In these bodies, volunteers were subjected to a training as much political as physical.

Another tactic was to disrupt the steady recruitment of Punjabis to the Indian army. Gandhi took another bashing in a speech at Nowshera Punawan, in which Baba Kesar Singh 'told his audience not to repeat the mistake made by Gandhi "and people of his ilk" who, during the Great War, urged the Indians to join the Army and fight for British imperialism'.[68] The Left also used veterans from the Great War to dissuade Punjabis from yet again becoming cannon fodder for the imperial regime.[69] Punjabi women exhorted their sisters not to lose their sons on the battlefields of Europe.[70] The Naujawan Bharat Sabha developed a new line in which joining up

---

[66] 'It was decided to build up an Akali Volunteer organisation, to be known as the "Akali fauj" or "Akali Sena" at a joint meeting of the Shiromani Akali Dal and city Akali Jatha of Amritsar on the 4 of April 1939... The formation of these Volunteer organisations is the outcome of the Akali jealousy between the Akali Party and the group of rural agitators controlled by the Ghadar Conspiracy case convicts (the Babas)... The present Kisan Morcha in Lahore is further detracting from Akali influence'. CID Lahore report by W. D. Robinson, 12 April 1939. Enclosure, Craik to Linlithgow, 17 April 1939, Document 87 in Carter, *Punjab Politics, 1936–1939*, 331–32. 'So far as the Hindu groups are concerned the chief appeal to prospective members appears to be the Communal and Religious appeal. I notice for example that the Mahabir Dal, whose preferred objects are purely religious service claims 10,000 adherents in the Punjab. On the other hand, it has to be observer that in the case of other Hindu Volunteer organisations military training seems to be adopted'. Zetland to Linlithgow, 24 January 1939, MSS EUR D609/11, OIOC.

[67] Home Political File 18/5/39, Fortnightly Report May 1939, NAI.

[68] Home Political File 58/38, Director of Intelligence Report, Notes re. Anti-recruitment and Anti-war Propaganda, NAI.

[69] Home Political File 61/30, Director of Intelligence Report, Notes re. Anti-recruitment and Anti-war Propaganda, NAI.

[70] Ibid.

for the King Emperor was described as a badge of shame, not of honour. *Izzat*, or honour, of which colonial officials had previously made much to elicit loyalty, was now turned into an effective political weapon against the British by the radical Naujawan Bharat Sabha and antirecruitment agitators.

A central plank of the radical agenda was to challenge the legitimacy of colonial rule, cast doubt on its values, shame the collaborators and loyalists and break the ties between the British and their subjects by emphasising national pride over and above any material gain that joining imperial armies could bring. Even the financial benefits of being soldiers of the King were questioned by broadcasting how little an Indian sepoy was paid compared with his white counterparts.[71]

It is difficult to assess how effective this antirecruitment drive was. However, the large numbers who came to the antirecruitment meetings in the Punjab suggest that at least the message reached a wide audience, despite the undoubted and continued success of mass enlistment in the province, to which the Unionists were committed.[72] From 1937 onwards, antirecruitment meetings were held in Hoshiarpur, Jullunder, Amritsar, Ludhiana, and Lahore. Between April and August of that year, 13 meetings were convened; in September alone, there were 25 meetings.[73] In November, the League Against Fascism and War was set up in Lahore. Its members were mainly communists and Congress socialists, but some Ahrars also joined the League. The Punjab's radicals had learnt to calibrate their language to meet specific Punjabi concerns, grievances and fears and it had an impact, the hundreds of thousands recruited and the many crores raised notwithstanding.

Another aspect of the radical assault was the way it deployed religion and religious grievances to try and dissuade Punjabis from joining the army, another departure from the politics of the 1920s

---

[71] Home Political File 58/38, Director of Intelligence Report, Notes re. Anti-recruitment and Anti-war Propaganda, NAI.

[72] However, some idea of the success of Unionist recruitment methods can be gauged from the fact that Punjab recruited 800,000 combatants throughout the war and raised ₹250 million through war loans and donations. Tan and Kudaisya, *Aftermath of Partition in South Asia*, 217.

[73] Home Political File 58/38, Director of Intelligence Report, Notes re. Anti-recruitment and Antiwar Propaganda, NAI.

when the Naujawan Bharat Sabha had remained resolutely secular. Ten years later, the radicals tailored their speeches to the particular concerns of particular communities. To win over Muslims, much capital was made of the deteriorating situation in Palestine and the desecration of Mecca. For example, one worried police informer mentioned 'M. Mohammed Sharif, speaking at Hoshiarpur, remarked that as the English had opened fire on the Muslims at Mecca, no true Muslim should render them any help in times of war'.[74] Another headache for the British was the fact that radicals were linking up with the pro-Congress reformist Ahrar party.

For their part, the Ahrars tried to persuade Punjabi Muslims to ally with the Congress by taking up specifically Muslim grievances against the British. Interestingly, the Ahrars were ready to play a different game in different political arenas. A case in point was when the Amritsar Municipal Committee decided to increase the percentage of seats reserved for Muslims from 40 per cent to 49 per cent. In fact, they were entitled to 51 per cent.[75] Hence, the Ahrars condemned the Muslim members of the Committee for failing to protect the interests of their community.

All of this shows how every group in the Punjab's complex political landscape had to adapt to the new conditions created by the 1935 Act. Different constituencies demanded different agendas and, in an era when winning votes mattered, voters and their concerns were getting the whip hand over their erstwhile leaders and patrons.

The radical Left also attempted to woo Hindus. Kedar Nath 'Red Shirt' Sehgal directly appealed to the Hindu reformist sect, the Arya Samaj, urging them to defy the authorities and campaign against Punjabi participation in the war;[76] in addition, as part of the drive to boycott war recruitment, he demanded the destruction of an abattoir, bringing cow protection into play.[77]

Communists and socialists were entering zones of political expression and action they had previously left alone. They broke new ground by appealing to a range of people who had hitherto been beyond their reach, casting their appeals in terms of community and

---

[74] Ibid.

[75] Home Political File 18/5/39, Fortnightly Report May 1939, NAI.

[76] Ibid.

[77] Home Political File 58/38, Director of Intelligence Report, Notes re. Anti-recruitment and Antiwar Propaganda, NAI.

religious identities rather than class. In this enterprise, their most important success was with Sikhs. Indeed most of the antirecruitment meetings took place in the central tracts of the Punjab, where many Sikhs lived. Concerned by the fact that Sikhs were joining these radical groups, Craik told the Viceroy:

> I had a report from one of my officers a day or two ago that a Recruiting Officer, who was endeavouring to recruit 80 Jat Sikhs in the Amritsar district, was actually able to recruit only about 12. This poor response was probably due to the effects of secret anti-recruitment propaganda conducted by the local communists.[78]

Radicals were also found to be active at annual fairs and melas held up and down the province. These occasions provided communists and socialists a chance to peddle their wares, suggesting a growing synergy between radicals and the people — the political fish were now entering popular waters.[79]

In general, these festivals were an excellent opportunity for putting out the radical message because they were a central event in village life. They gave the radicals a chance to influence and woo people who would not normally have heard what they had to say.[80] The radicals also organised their own fairs, which more often than not were devoted to the celebration of past martyrs and this way began to create a popular following for their own myths and legends.

In the Fortnightly Report for the 2nd half of November, 1938, reference was made to the commemoration at Sorabah in the Ludhiana district of the death of Kartar Singh, who was executed for his part in the 1914/15 Lahore Conspiracy Case. On the 23rd of March the

---

[78] Craik to Linlithgow, 29 October 1939, Document 114 in Carter, *Punjab Politics, 1936–1939*, 395.

[79] Home Political File 18/10/36, Fortnightly Report October 1936, NAI.

[80] 'November 1937–UP. On November 17th at the District Kisan Conference held in connection with the Bhai Ghat Mela, Shahjahanpur's communists and ex-terrorist speakers were prominent. Parmanand (ex-convict in the first Lahore Conspiracy Case) in moving a resolution against participation in the next imperialist war appealed to his audience numbering between 4000 and 5000 persons to organise themselves and to bring about a revolution'. Home Political File 58/38, Director of Intelligence Report, Notes re. Anti-recruitment and Anti-war Propaganda, NAI.

notorious terrorist Bhagat Singh's death anniversary was celebrated at 6 places in the province, the most important being the Martyr Fair at his village Khatkar Kalan in the Jullunder district.[81]

Another interesting development was how the Punjab Left revived another old tradition, widely practised during the time of Ranjit Singh (and subsequently in British times too), of *'diwans'* or forums where popular grievances could be publicly aired and resolved. Similar to the British before them, the Left realised the advantages of maintaining and cultivating local political traditions and being seen to do so as the guardians of the people.[82]

## Conclusion

Because of the impending war by 22 October 1939, over 150 politicians in the Punjab were in jail,[83] and by February of the next year this had increased to 404. June 1940 saw the incarceration of another four score 'leftists' in the province, including some of those who had been elected to the Punjab Legislative Assembly. By now, the Punjab led the rest of India in having the largest number of communists and socialists in its jails,[84] statistics that highlight the anxieties of the rulers in a strategically important province rather than evidence that the Punjab was particularly radical.

In retrospect, the radical Left in the Punjab had enjoyed a relatively short-lived period when, as MLAs, they could operate openly. Like bees, they stung and then they seemed to have died. Their halcyon days in which they were able to question some of the fundamental assumptions of Punjab politics were soon cut short. Nevertheless,

---

[81] Ibid.

[82] Home Political File 18/3/37, Fortnightly Report March 1937, NAI.

[83] Mitra, *Indian Annual Register, 1939, Volume 1*, 184.

[84] A list of members of the Communist Party of Provincial and local importance who were already under trial or convicted as well as those whose movements had been restricted showed the Punjab at the forefront with 134. Bombay and Bengal followed with 91 and 82, respectively. (National leaders were omitted from this count.) Home Political File — KW to 7/1/40, NAI. The Government of India issued orders for the detention of 19 principal communist leaders under the Defence of India Rules on 23 March 1940, IOR/L/PJ/12/636, OIOC.

in this brief interlude, politicians on the left in the Punjab learnt the arts of parliamentary procedure and began to introduce their own brand of democracy into the bastions of an establishment they had first stormed in the elections of 1937.

The years 1935–1939 thus represent a period of transition both in the governance of the Punjab and in the history of communism in that province. It was also a time of transformation because for the first time these years saw communists accepting, and working within, the constitutional framework constructed by the Raj. This fact may not seem so significant today, when communists freely join the electoral process and form governments in India and elsewhere. However, for Josh and his fellows, fighting elections provided them a novel legitimacy, far removed from their past life in dingy prison cells, evidence of the unambiguous opportunism of radicals ready to deploy any weapons to rid India of the British Raj.

The 1930s began with radicals in jail and that formative decade ended with them back where they had started. However, in the interim, radicals had played a part within the constitutional frame. Men formerly dismissed as seditious jailbirds had had their moment in the Assembly and outside it and had used these new opportunities to continue their assault against their colonial masters in a new forum and to have their say without having to operate by stealth. These same people would emerge as leading politicians in independent India and Pakistan in the years after 1947. In India they would contest elections, woo voters and operate in political assemblies very similar, in terms of class make-up, to the Punjab Assembly of the 1930s. In Pakistan, they would demand elections and rights to engage on the political field. Both of these sets of activities were learnt, in this brief moment in the 1930s, when radicals viewed electoral politics as a legitimate, revolutionary endeavour.

—

# References

## Primary Sources

### Official records

Home Political Files, National Archives of India, New Delhi.

Public and Judicial Department (Separate) Files, Oriental and India Office Collection, London. Public and Judicial Department Collection, Oriental and India Office Collection, London.
War Staff Series Files, Oriental and India Office Collection, London.
Communist Party of India Collection, Archives of Contemporary History, New Delhi.

*Official Monographs and Published Government Records*

Carter, Lionel, *Punjab Politics, 1936–1939: The Start of Provincial Autonomy*, Delhi: Manohar, 2004.
*Punjab Legislative Assembly Debates*, Lahore: Government Press, 1937–1941.
Roy, Subodh, ed., *Communism in India: Unpublished Documents, 1925–1934*, Calcutta: National Book Agency, 1972.
———, *Communism in India: Unpublished Documents, 1935–1945*, Calcutta: National Book Agency, 1976.
Williamson, Horace, *India and Communism*, Calcutta: S. Ghattack, Editions India, 1976.

*Memoirs*

Josh, Sohan Singh, *My Tryst with Secularism*, New Delhi: Patriot, 1991.

*Party Records and Pamphlets*

All India Congress Committee Papers, Nehru Memorial Museum and Library.
Basu, Jyoti, Chief Editor, *Documents of the Communist Movement in India*, 26 Volumes. Calcutta: National Book Agency, 1997–1999.
Communist Party of India Collection, Archives of Contemporary History, New Delhi, Communist Party of India Archive, Ajay Bhavan, New Delhi.

*Newspapers*

*Tribune*, Lahore.
*Kirti*, Amritsar.
*Mazdoor Kisan*, Lahore.
*Civil and Military Gazette*, Lahore.

## Published books and articles

Awan, Samina, *Political Islam in Colonial Punjab: Majlis-I Ahrar, 1929–49*, Oxford: Oxford University Press, 2010.
Chand, Duni, *The Ulster of India or an Analysis of the Punjab Problems*, Lahore: Navjivan Press, 1936.

Chandavarkar, Rajnarayan, 'From Communism to "Social Democracy": The Rise and Resilience of Communist Parties in India, 1920–1995', *Science and Society* 61, no. 1 (1997): 99–106.

Chandra, Bipan, ed., *The Indian Left*, Delhi: Vikas Publishing House, 1983.

Damordaran, K., 'Memoirs of Indian Communism', *New Left Review* 1, no. 93 (1975): 35–59.

Gilmartin, David, *Empire and Islam: Punjab and the Making of Pakistan*, Berkeley: University of California Press, 1988.

———, 'A Magnificent Gift: Muslim Nationalism and the Election and the Election Process in Colonial Punjab', *Comparative Studies in Society and History* 40, no. 3 (1998): 415–36.

Guha, Ranajit, *Dominance Without Hegemony: History and Power in Colonial India*, Cambridge, MA: Harvard University Press, 1997.

Gupta, Bhabani Sen, *Communism in Indian Politics*, New York: Columbia University Press, 1972.

Hasan, Mushirual, 'The Muslim Mass Contact Campaign: An Attempt at Political Mobilisation', *South Asia: Journal of South Asian Studies* 7, no. 1 (June 1984): 58–76.

Javed, Ajeet, *Left Politics in Punjab: 1935–47*, Delhi: Durga Publications, 1988.

Jones, Gareth Stedman, *Languages of Class: Studies in English Working Class History, 1832–1932*, Cambridge: Cambridge University Press, 1983.

Josh, Bhagwan, *Communist Movement in Punjab (1926–1947)*, New Delhi: Anupama, 1979.

Juergensmeyer, Mark, *Religion as Social Vision*, Berkeley: University of California Press, 1982.

Lakhanpal, P. L., *History of the Congress Socialist Party*, Lahore: National Publishers and Stationers, 1946.

Mitra, N. N., *The Annual Indian Register*, Calcutta: Annual Register Office, 1920–1947.

Mohan, Kamlesh, *Militant Nationalism in the Punjab, 1919–1935*, New New Delhi: Manohar, 1985.

Moore, Robin James, *Churchill, Cripps, and India, 1939–1945*, Oxford: Clarendon Press, 1979.

———, *Endgames of Empire: Studies of Britain's Indian Problem*, Delhi: Oxford University Press, 1988.

Morgan, Kevin, *Against Fascism and War: Ruptures and Continuities in British Communist Politics, 1935–41*, Manchester: Manchester University Press, 1989.

Mukherjee, Mridula, 'Agrarian Change in Pre-Independence Punjab', in *Essays on the Commercialization of Indian Agriculture*, K. N. Raj, Neeladari Bhattacharya, Sumit Guha and Sakti Padhi (eds), 51–105, New Delhi: Oxford University Press, 1985.

Nugent, H. M., 'The Communal Award: The Process of Decision Making', *South Asia* 2, no. 1–2 (1979): 112–29.

O'Dwyer, Michael, *India as I Knew It*, London: Constable and Company, 1925.

Overstreet, Gene D. and Windmiller, Marshall, *Communism in India*, Los Angeles: California University Press, 1959.

Page, David, *Prelude to Partition: The Indian Muslims and the Imperial System of Control 1920–1932*, New Delhi: Oxford University Press, 1982.

Pandey, Gyanendra, *The Colonial Construction of Communalism in North India*, New Delhi: Oxford University Press, 1990.

Rai, Satya M., *Legislative Politics and Freedom Struggle on the Panjab, 1897–1947*, New Delhi: Indian Council of Historical Research, 1984.

Samad, Yunus., *A Nation in Turmoil: Nationalism and Ethnicity in Pakistan, 1937–1958*, London: Sage, 1995.

Singh, Gurharpal, *Communism in Punjab*, New Delhi: Ajanta, 1994.

Singh, Randhir, *Five Lectures in Marxist Mode*, New Delhi: Ajanta, 1998.

Singh, Ujwal Kumar, *Political Prisoners in India*, New Delhi: Oxford University Press, 1998.

Talbot, Ian, *Punjab and the Raj*, New Delhi: Manohar, 1988.

Tan, T. Y. and G. Kudaisya, *The Aftermath of Partition in South Asia*, London: Routledge, 2000.

Verma, Vandita, *From Marxism to Democratic Socialism: The Deeper Roots of Affinity*, New Delhi: Books India International, 2005.

Williamson, Horace, *India and Communism*, Calcutta: Editions Indian, 1976.

Yadav, Kripal C., *Elections in Panjab, 1920–1947*, New Delhi: Manohar, 1987.

# Index

For Product Safety Concerns and Information please contact our EU
representative GPSR@taylorandfrancis.com
Taylor & Francis Verlag GmbH, Kaufingerstraße 24, 80331 München, Germany